The Three Worlds of Social Democracy

The Three Worlds of Social Democracy

A Global View

Edited by
Ingo Schmidt

www.plutobooks.com

First published 2016 by Pluto Press
345 Archway Road, London N6 5AA

www.plutobooks.com

Copyright © Ingo Schmidt 2016

British Library Cataloguing in Publication Data
A catalogue record for this book is available from the British Library

ISBN   978 0 7453 3613 8   Hardback
ISBN   978 0 7453 3608 4   Paperback
ISBN   978 1 7837 1979 2   PDF eBook
ISBN   978 1 7837 1981 5   Kindle eBook
ISBN   978 1 7837 1980 8   EPUB eBook

Typeset by Stanford DTP Services, Northampton, England

Simultaneously printed in the European Union and United States of America

Contents

PART III   REGIONAL POWERS

Introduction: Social Democracy and Uneven Development – Theoretical Reflections on the Three Worlds of Social Democracy

Ingo Schmidt

Social democracy is a paradoxical creature. With roots going back to the Age of Revolution from 1789 to 1848, it later established itself as an independent political force aiming to replace the dictatorship of capital by a socialist order in which workers would manage their own affairs in a democratic way. This was in the second half of nineteenth-century Europe. Soon social democrats argued over strategy, the big question being whether social reforms would lead to socialism in a piecemeal process or prepare workers for the revolutionary overthrow of capitalism. They were also torn between some who thought support of imperialism would help to gain reforms in the heartlands and others who considered imperialism as capitalism's twin that had to be opposed. During and after World War I (WWI), social democracy's radical wing went its own, communist, ways, and its moderate wing settled for some kind of halfway house between capitalism and socialism (Abendroth, 1972; Eley, 2002). Somewhat unexpectedly, considering the economic and political turmoil from 1914 to 1945 that seemed to indicate capitalism's complete breakdown, social democratic goals were institutionalized in Western European welfare states during the post-WWII era (Hicks, 1999). Yet, it was in these heartlands that social democratic parties had tried to shake off commitments to the welfare state since the 1990s, a time commonly associated with neoliberal globalization and the end of the Cold War. Ironically, voters who were disappointed with the social insecurities and inequalities produced by neoliberalism repeatedly elected social democratic governments, hoping that they would offer at least some social protections. Balancing these expectations with corporate demands to lower taxes on profits and wealth and to relax all kinds of regulations is difficult enough when the economy is doing okay, but it becomes impossible in times of crises when faltering economies see government revenue plummeting and spending on unemployment benefits skyrocketing. This spectre of runaway deficits is big money's lever to push for austerity. Submitting to finance capital's demands, many social democratic governments have sacrificed the expectations of their voters and their own re-election.

Pursuing the same or even more ruthless neoliberal policies, respective successor governments often then also fall out of favour, and so we see a return of social democrats to government offices. Such electoral cycles may save the survival of social democratic parties, but that doesn't mean that social democratic policies would be pursued at any time social democrats are in office. The social democratic idea of striking a compromise between capitalism and socialism is still popular, it seems, but today's social democrats seem incapable or unwilling to deliver an update of this kind of compromise that seemingly worked so well from the 1950s to the 1970s. During this 'Golden Age' of capitalism, even conservative governments pursued social democratic policies without necessarily labelling them so. These days, social democrats pursue essentially neoliberal policies. For a while they misleadingly branded them as a Third Way, claiming equidistance to their previous commitment to the Keynesian welfare state and the neoliberalism of conservative parties (Fagerholm, 2013; Schmidt, 2012). More recently, most parties have given up any such labelling efforts. Sometimes they prescribe a lower dose of the neoliberal medicine than their conservative or other competitors, but sometimes they opt for bloodletting on a scale that their competitors preferred to avoid (Bailey et al., 2014; Escalona, Chapter 2, Kjeldstadli and Helle, Chapter 3, Crook, Chapter 4 in this volume).

Shaking off the very policies that voters are expecting from them isn't the only paradox of social democracy. Another is the social democratic turn that former communists in the East and radical movements in the South have taken since the 1990s even though, by that time, social democracy's glory days in the West were already over. After the downfall of Soviet communism, the parties that had represented it in Eastern Europe had the choice to either follow the fallen economic and political system into the dustbin of history or reinvent themselves with new politics and ideas (Gowan, 1997). Social democracy was a readily available option for them. Notwithstanding bitter infighting that followed the split between social democrats and communists during WWI and later escalated into the Cold War, which saw the mainstream of social democracy aligning themselves with US-imperialism against their erstwhile comrades, they shared the same statist and productivist principles. The fact that communist ideas and actual policies were only loosely, if at all, connected also made it easy for communist parties to drop their old label and put up a new one. Pursuing social democratic policies was a different matter though. Eastern Europe's newborn social democrats took the Third Way to neoliberalism even faster than their Western European counterparts. They left electorates behind that were fed up with old communists and disappointed by the new social democrats (De Waele et al., 2013, Part III: Central and Eastern Europe; Vachudova, 2013; Vesalon, Chapter 8 and Korsika, Chapter 9 in this volume).

In Western Europe, policies that built and expanded welfare states thrived after WWII because an exceptionally strong and long-lasting boom, along with the exploitation of the South, allowed complementary increases of profits and wages. Capitalists might have preferred to pocket these gains entirely for themselves but the very existence of Soviet communism convinced them that concessions to social democracy and their welfare state project were an advisable way to deepen the divisions between the two red flags (Childs, 2000). This turned out to be a successful move. When social democrats turned to the policies of detente in the 1960s they did this as representatives of welfare capitalism, calling it a more effective and democratic, maybe even more equal, alternative to the bureaucratic dictatorships in the East. Minorities within social democracy that sought realignment with the Soviets in order to open the way for a democratic socialism beyond both welfare capitalism and Soviet communism never gained enough ground to challenge the pro-capitalist and Atlanticist orientation of the social democratic mainstream.

When Soviet communism collapsed, capitalists saw there was no longer the need to give concessions to social democracy and massively scaled up their offensive against the welfare state, which they had already begun in the early 1980s (Schmidt, 2008). Western social democrats reacted to this offensive by developing the Third Way and made it impossible for the new social democrats in Eastern Europe to deliver anything remotely resembling Golden Age-style welfare states. After all, victorious Cold Warriors from the West were keen on downgrading their former challengers to peripheral status, good enough to allow the appropriation of surplus profits by Western capitalists but not to pay for social protections in the East. Thus, even if there had been prolonged growth after the transition to capitalism, most of the economic gains were transferred to the West and little to nothing was left for redistributive policies in the East.

These are exactly the kinds of conditions that post-colonial regimes in the South tried to escape from during the post-WWII era. These regimes, and the developmentalism they pursued, showed some resemblance to

Western welfare capitalism. Both were built around cross-class alliances trying to use the state as a countervailing power to markets shaped and controlled by capital. In the West the main goal of the Keynesian state was redistribution, in the South it was industrialization. This was considered a key step to overcome colonial or neocolonial exploitation. Resistance from Western imperialists and domestic capitalists, who were thriving on trade relations with these imperialists, along with the whirlwinds of economic crises in the 1970s, derailed the developmentalist project in ways similar to how the welfare statism in the West was derailed, just that the latter came without the imperialist interventions that the peoples in many countries in the South were facing. Many of them found themselves trapped, or pushed back, to peripheral, at best semi-peripheral, status but some, riding a wave of strong economic growth, developed into regional powers internationally and saw a social democratic turn domestically (Lanzaro, 2011; Sandbrook et al., 2007; Wang, 2012; White, 1998).

This turn may seem like a repetition of developments in Western Europe where social democracy was at its best during times of economic prosperity. But it wasn't. The emerging economies boom that had underpinned hopes to belatedly repeat social democratic successes in the South was over before much in terms of welfare state development had been accomplished. Western European social democrats had benefited from prosperity and from systemic competition with Soviet communists. In some Southern countries, communists, deprived of their Soviet allies after the latter's regime imploded, played an important role in turning to social democracy. During the struggle against apartheid the African National Congress (ANC), under significant influence from the South African Communist Party, upheld not only national liberation but even a version of anti-capitalism – the 1955 'Freedom Charter' calling for widespread nationalisation – and then after 1994 replaced them by rhetoric promoting social democracy alongside what Patrick Bond terms 'tokenistic' welfare provision (Bond, Chapter 12 in this volume; Prevost, 2006). The Chilean communists underwent a similar transformation from the time they supported Allende's Unidad Popular to their participation in post-Pinochet coalition governments (de la Barra Mac Donald, Chapter 6 in this volume). In Kerala and West Bengal, governments led by the Communist Party of India (Marxist) pursued a more Keynesian type of social democratic policies for a long time but adopted some Southern version of Third Way social democracy in the 1990s (Prashad, 2015; Sen, Chapter 11 in this volume). The Brazilian Workers Party followed a similar trajectory. Founded as a socialist party during the last years of the military dictatorship, its long-time leader Lula later ran against the social democratic candidate Cardoso, a prominent advocate of radical developmentalism in the 1970s, but also turned to Third Way policies prior to his successful bid for presidency in 2002 (Figueroa, 2015; Nowak, Chapter 10 in this volume).

Like their Western counterparts, Third Way social democrats in the South achieved some social moderation as long as capital accumulates but turn to austerity in times of crises. Not surprisingly, they also have to cope with disgruntled voters and are far from turning popular discontent into a counter-hegemonic project to neoliberalism (Féliz, Chapter 5 and Milios, Chapters 7 in this volume). The social democratic heartlands of Western Europe, new peripheries in Eastern Europe as well as old peripheries and new regional powers in the South occupy very different positions in the capitalist world economy, but on the level of politics there is a certain convergence. Neoliberalism is unpopular in all of these different worlds, social democratic alternatives are in demand, but the political formations that rally around them in election campaigns don't deliver when they are in office.

This book tries to explain why social democratic policies are in such short supply even though discontent with neoliberalism produces a persistent demand for them. It also looks at alternative ways to articulate this discontent, ranging from various populisms to right-wing fundamentalism but also to new socialist projects. To do this, this introductory chapter recaps the emergence of social democracy in the capitalist centres during the age of imperialism before analyzing the articulation between social democracy, Soviet communism and developmentalism, and then looks at the globalization of Third Way social democracy in the neoliberal age (Evans, 2009; Held, 2005). The main part of the book is made up of case studies on social democracy in its Western European heartlands, in old and new peripheries in Eastern Europe and the South and, finally, in the new regional powers, Brazil, India and South Africa. The concluding chapter discusses the possibilities and challenges of building alternatives to the left of social democracy, but also ponders the dangers of a further rise of right-wing alternatives.

NASCENT WORLDS OF SOCIAL DEMOCRACY

The family tree of what is known as the social democratic party family today (Keman, 2013) goes back to the days of the Second International. In those days, political parties became one of the two main pillars of the then emerging mass movements of workers, unions being the other. The roots of this tree go back all the way to the bourgeois and industrial revolutions that unsettled European feudalism from the seventeenth century onwards and eventually led to the rise of industrial capitalism, the very system social democracy sought to tame or, in its more radical versions, replace by an only vaguely defined socialism (Smaldone, 2014). These roots had less to do with the class struggle between workers and capitalists, notions most distinctively elaborated by Marx and Engels and translated into a 'movement language' by many of their followers in the Second International, than with the struggles of 'the people', 'commoners' or the 'Third Estate' against aristocrats and clergymen. These vague notions were picked up again by social democratic or socialist activists to rally support for the social democratic cause beyond their core constituencies in the working class. This was the case when Eduard Bernstein and his followers sought to extend social democracy's support base beyond the narrow confines of industrial working classes at the turn of the twentieth century. It was also the case when social democratic parties, though still heavily relying on industrial workers and their unions, reinvented themselves as catch-all parties during the age of Keynesian welfare states. The radical wing of social democracy tried to move from populist notions of 'the people' that had played a prominent role during the bourgeois revolutions of the early nineteenth century to more clearly defined working class politics. However, it's moderate wing, equating working class with blue-collar industrial work, thought this class will always be a minority so that winning a majority of the population for social democratic policies would require some kind of cross-class alliance. Such alliances, though relying on class power, were ideological moulded in the populist language of 'the people' rather than socialist jargon of 'the worker.'

Somewhat ironically even the communists, who started their own party family because they were so disgusted with social democratic class-collaboration, adopted the language of 'the people' or 'labouring masses', notably workers and peasants, in their claim to revive the revolutionary tradition, more precisely its Jacobin wing, against their usurping rulers. The Popular Fronts against fascism that were forged in the 1930s were another reinvention of the notion of 'the people' against privilege, power and oppression. One might even see the Popular Fronts advocated by the communists, as precursors of the social democratic catch-all parties of the post-WWII era.

If communists were the hostile brothers and sisters of the social democratic party family, developmentalist regimes were a distant relative of both. Trying to carve out their own space between the capitalist West, moderated by Keynesian welfare states, and the communist East, they identified as Third World (Prashad, 2007). This, of course, was also a reference to the struggles of the Third Estate against feudalism updated to the situation of twentieth century anti-colonialism. In other words, efforts to forge alliances amongst the popular classes and thus transcend the working class politics with which it is often identified are a recurrent part of the history of the social democratic party family. Similar efforts were made by their hostile and distant relatives, that is, communists and developmentalists, respectively. These efforts can be traced back to the Age of Revolution (Hobsbawm, 1962 [1992]), during which the pre-history of social democratic party organizing unfolded.

Another common heritage that social democrats, communists and developmentalists share goes back to the Age of Capital (Hobsbawm, 1975 [1997]), which really took off after the 'People's Spring' of 1848 was defeated. This heritage concerns the question of how the inequalities between haves and have-nots, along with economic exploitation and political suppression accompanying these inequalities, could be overcome. The basic idea, most clearly put forward by Marx and Engels, was that industrialization, pushed forward by the imperatives of capital accumulation in nineteenth-century Europe, would develop the forces of production up to a point where everybody's needs in society could be satisfied without many people suffering and enable a life of over-abundance for everybody and not only, as under capitalist rule, for a happy few. Communists and developmentalists, coming to power in countries with little or no industrial basis, adopted this idea and sought to politically drive industrialization forward and thus overcome the imperialist division of labour between industrialized centres and peripheral producers of agricultural products and natural resources. Accordingly, state-led industrialization in the Soviet Union began in the 1920s and only during the post-WWII era in the newly independent countries of the Global South (Kiely, 1998).

However, the question of industrialization and the related question about the relations between industrialized and non-industrial countries were already on the agenda of nineteenth-century social democrats in Europe (Day and Gaido, 2012). These questions about industrialization and international relations were closely related to the aforementioned issue of class relations within countries (Abendroth, 1972). True to Marxist principles, radical social democrats argued that capitalism would produce large-scale industries but, by doing so, the proletariat would become the gravedigger of capitalism. A workers' revolution would then replace the class divisions, exploitation and suppression associated with capitalism by a socialist economy, in which the means of production are collectively owned and managed. Recognizing that colonialism extended capitalist exploitation and suppression to the world scale, even though, in the nineteenth century, the colonies showed hardly any signs of industrialization let alone the formation of industrial working classes, the radical wing of social democracy denounced the actions of the great powers who were dividing up the rest of the world as colonial empires or spheres of influence amongst themselves. Reform-minded social democrats, some of them drawing on Marx's economic analysis of capitalist development but rejecting his revolutionary conclusions, and others fiercely opposing the entire Marxist tradition, thought that industrial development would create space for social reforms within capitalism and that, therefore, the question of a socialist transformation played only a minor role, if any role at all. They opposed the brutality of the imperialism they saw unfolding before their eyes but did see the capitalist penetration of still pre-capitalist parts of the world as a precondition for improving the economic and social conditions of popular classes around the world. If capitalism was necessary to produce the economic basis for socialism, or at least social reform, in the industrial and imperial centres, they argued, the colonial world might have to go through the same stage of capitalist industrialization. Eventually, this stream of social democratic thinking developed into a corporatist current in social democratic parties and affiliated unions that had no time for the entire debate about social reform or revolution. Adherents of this current were quite content to establish workers' organizations as junior partners of the capitalist system. They supported imperialism as a source for extra profits that could pay for social reform in the imperial centres without cutting into base-line profits. In other words, their goal was to reach class compromise at home on the backs of colonized peoples' abroad.

No matter how divisive or even, as it later turned out, antagonistic the positions were that revolutionaries, reformists and corporatists took on imperialism, industrialization and class relations, they had one thing in common. None of them could envision the peoples, or classes, in the colonies as agents of change whose collective action would not only alter conditions in the colonies but also effect conditions in the centre. Nineteenth-century social democrats in Western Europe had different views on the effects of imperialism on the colonial world and its economic costs or benefits for the centres. Even Marxists who understood the dialectics of exploited workers constituting themselves as a class and potential agent of change couldn't bring themselves to wonder whether exploited masses in the colonial world could constitute themselves as a collective agent in a similar way. The terms of the struggle between industrial capitalist and working classes, in which they thought about economic development and political possibilities, were simply not applicable in the colonial world and left Marxists intellectually unequipped to make sense of this world. Anti-Marxist reformists and corporatist-minded social democrats, in turn, were so focused on winning the franchise and voters that they did not take the time to develop analytical tools to understand colonial conditions, where political concepts developed by movements struggling for democracy in Europe were even less applicable than Marxist class analysis.

But in Eastern Europe, the related questions of imperialism, industrialization and class relations couldn't be avoided. The Tsarist Empire consisted of sprinkles of industrial districts in a largely agrarian country, or group of countries, whose social and political conditions had more in common with other empires' colonies than with those of Russia's industrial and financial centres. In Western Europe, even monarchies left some space for electoral policies, thereby fostering hopes for a gradual transition to democratic republics, whereas the dictatorship of Russian Tsars resembled the dictatorial regimes that colonial powers had established overseas even though some of them, notably France, had a track record of democratic developments at home. Under Eastern Europe's conditions of uneven and combined development, to borrow Trotsky's terminology (Trotsky, 1930 [2008], Chapter 1: Peculiarities of Russia's Development), social democrats first developed the idea that Russia, like any other non-industrialized country, eventually would move from feudalism, based on agriculture, to industrial capitalism and later socialism. During the transition from feudalism to capitalism, social democrats would support the emergent industrial bourgeoisie in its struggle against the Tsarist regime. Yet, it was all too obvious that industrial capitalism had already taken root in, and then co-existed with, feudal agriculture. Without support from the peasantry, miniscule working classes had no hope of making any political advances. Consequently, the radical wing of Eastern European social democracy around Lenin dealt with the question of agency of non-industrial classes but eventually decided to subordinate it to the leadership of the industrial working class. Another resemblance between the Tsarist Empire and colonial empires was the suppression of various nationalities, leading Lenin and his comrades to advocate for the right of nations to self-determination. This strategy of forging cross-class alliances and propagating national independence was developed as a pathway to revolution in Russia, and was seen as the opening shot of revolution in the West. As it turned out, though, the inspiring effect of this strategy on anti-colonial revolutions in the South was much more significant than its trigger effect on workers' revolution in the West.

In fact, once Western Europe was on the road to fascism rather than socialism, the Soviet Union and the Comintern (Communist International) actually urged their Western allies to adopt policies that had much in common with the social democratic visions of Organized

Capitalism that had been decried as an expression of class betrayal a few years earlier. The Popular Front, which became the rallying cry of communist politics in the 1930s, shared with Organized Capitalism (Hilferding, 1924; Smaldone, 1998, Chapter 4: The Republican Theorist) the idea of forging a cross-class alliance against monopoly capital, which was seen as the main force promoting fascism. Whereas Organized Capitalism already bore all the technocratic signs that would characterize Keynesian welfare states in the post-WWII era, Popular Frontism tried to reinvoke the revolutionary spirit of the Age of Revolution. The difference this time, though, was that the labouring masses weren't up against the parasitic class of feudal landowners and absolutist monarchy, but against monopoly-capitalists, bankers and their fascist henchmen. At the same time that a bureaucratic counter-revolution consolidated its power in the Soviet Union through a reign of terror reminiscent of the Thermidor of the French revolution, its communist allies in the West were glowing fighters for democracy. Not surprisingly, Popular Frontism resonated strongly in France where a series of revolutions and counter-revolutions from the storming of the Bastille in 1789 to the Paris Commune in 1871 had produced the language in which every progressive strategy from republicanism to Jacobin vanguardism and council communism was expressed. Popular Front agitation against monopoly capitalists also echoed the struggle against corporate tycoons that had been fought during the Progressive Era in the USA and was reinvigorated by Roosevelt's New Deal. Moreover, agitation against the power of bankers or finance capital resembled the vision of the 'euthanasia of the rentier' that Keynes (1936 [1967], Chapter 24: Concluding Notes on the Social Philosophy towards which the General Theory might Lead) put forward in Britain.

Organized Capitalism was a blend of reformist Marxism, drawing theoretically on Hilferding's Finance Capital and strategically on Bernstein's anti-Marxist revisionism. It saw the democratic republic as a venue for turning class conflict into corporatist management of the economy so that the anarchy of markets, the main reason for recurrent crises in some versions of Marxist thought, could be overcome by political means. Polanyi (1944 [2001]) expressed this idea most clearly by saying that the unleashing of market forces would lead to economic crisis, but also trigger a counter-movement in order to control the destructive aspects of market rule while retaining their efficiency-enhancing role. The 1920s, when social democrats, notably in Germany, tried to rally support for Organized Capitalism, were a bad time for a political strategy arguing that capitalism was well on its way from a crisis-ridden past to future prosperity. Communists, including their dissident currents, were certainly closer to the truth by warning that finance capital, supported by the petty bourgeoisie that was facing ever stiffer competition from large corporations and had lost its financial wealth during the great inflations following WWI, was organizing to roll back social reforms that workers had won during the revolutionary upheavals in the immediate aftermath of the war.

Yet, in the midst of the Great Depression and in the face of the rise of fascism, when Organized Capitalism seemed at least, if not more, utopian than socialist revolution, ideas very similar to it were coming from different political corners and different places. The Popular Front, designed in Moscow and exported to communist party activists around the world, British Keynesianism and the American New Deal can all be understood as variations on the theme of Organized Capitalism. The stage was set for the making of Keynesian welfare states in the post-WWII West but also for developmentalism, the post-colonial variety of Organized Capitalism. As it turned out, these two actually existing forms of Organized Capitalism even bore similarities with Soviet communism, similarities that neither social democrats nor communists were ready to admit during the Cold War.

SOCIAL DEMOCRACY IN THE AGE OF THE THREE WORLDS

Social democratic parties played important but differing roles in the making of Western welfare states. In some countries, notably Scandinavia, they became quasi naturally ruling parties who could use government position to take a leading role in welfare state development (Sejersted, 2011). In others, such as Germany, conservative and liberal parties adopted the social democratic commitment to welfare state expansion in order to keep the latter out of government offices (Schmidt, 2009). Britain, where social democrats were in and out of office a few times during the post-war period, showed clearly that the prospect of social democrats winning elections was real even outside their Scandinavian heartlands (Miliband, 1961). Things in Italy and France were even worse as left governments there would also have included communist parties with their deep roots in unions and working class neighbour-hoods (Ross, 1982). However, whatever the electoral fortunes of social democratic parties were and in whichever way they did their part in welfare state expansion, in all Western countries welfare states rested on the formation of a historical bloc centred on a compromise between industrial capital and organized labour. Social democratic revisionists offered the brokering of such a compromise, as they had since the late nineteenth century.

Back then, Western European ruling classes didn't take much notice of such offers. Until WWI, they might have felt uncomfortable in the face of the emergence of unions and mass parties of workers but were far from recognizing labour as junior partner to secure their dominant position in society. It was the social democratic left that responded to revisionist ideas of class compromise. The left insisted that there wasn't much room for social reform under capitalism and warned that abandoning the goal of socialist revolution in the hope this would lure ruling classes into a compromise would disarm workers' movements and diminish even further the room for reformist manoeuvre. Moreover, crises, seen as an indispensible ingredient of capitalism by the social democratic left, would undo whatever reforms were won during boom times anyway and put socialist revolution back on the agenda (Luxemburg, 1899 [2011]). And this is exactly how the Age of Catastrophe, 1914 to 1945, with its wars, economic crises, revolutions and counter-revolutions (Hobsbawm, 1995, Part I) unfolded. In an ironic twist of history, though, the same string of events produced the conditions for class compromise and welfare state expansion during capitalism's Golden Age from the 1950s to the 1970s (Hobsbawm, 1995, Part II).

Whereas talk about socialist revolution could be easily dismissed as verbal radicalism in the nineteenth century, the Russian revolution produced an actual challenge to capitalist rule. Although revolutions in the West either failed or never developed beyond the very first steps, ruling classes were now much more on the alert than they had been before. Moreover, economic crises in the aftermath of WWI and the revolutionary wave from 1917 to 1923, and even more during the depression of the 1930s, showed very clearly that liberal principles of sound finance and waiting for the next boom to come automatically no longer worked. At the same time, mass organizing by workers' movements and, probably even more importantly, mass mobilization for the war effort put an end to the old ways of doing politics in exclusive clubs and boardrooms. One way or the other, the masses had to be reckoned with. Fascism was one form of mass integration. It also allowed the turn from the failed liberal policies to the then new Keynesianism without having to deal with demands coming from independent workers' movements (Kalecki, 1943). However, the capitalist embrace of fascist rule produced not only unprecedented suffering and death for millions of people but also turned into a disaster for capitalist rulers. While they had succeeded in warding off the challenge of revolutions from below that had been ignited by the Russian revolution in 1917, they helplessly watched while the Soviets expanded their sphere of influence with every mile the Red Army pushed the Nazi invaders back from Moscow and Stalingrad to Berlin.

In view of the emergence of the Soviet Union as a superpower, Western European ruling classes overcame the rivalries that had driven them into two world wars, and lined up behind the new superpower on the other side of the Atlantic to form the US-led bloc against the Soviet Union (Silver, 2003: 149–61). This international bloc was reinforced by domestic class compromises that included the recognition of unions as legitimate bargaining partners of capital and the acceptance, however grudgingly, of social democrats as part of the new political realities of mass electoral parties. The tripartite arrangements between capital, organized labour and the state produced the sharing of productivity gains and thus softened the economic and political class struggles that brought capitalism close to collapse between the two world wars (Marglin and Schor, 1991).

Workers who, as soldiers but also at the home fronts of arms factories and hospitals, made so many sacrifices during the war expected some kind of material gratification once the Axis powers had surrendered. At the same time, capitalists feared that economies would fall back into depression once arms production, which had played a crucial role in dragging them out of the 1930s depression, was reduced to peacetime levels. A clash between workers who expected rising wages and social securities and a depression economy with mass unemployment and downward pressure on wages was a real possibility. This was all the more alarming in countries, like France and Italy, where communists were widely respected for their lead role in anti-fascist resistance movements. Social democrats jumped at the opportunity of presenting themselves as a lesser evil to capitalists and could quite legitimately claim to represent a democratic alternative to Soviet communism (Filippelli, 1989; Weiler, 1988). After all, while communists fought heroically against the Nazis in the ranks of the Red Army and underground resistance movements, Stalinist terror continued to discredit socialist or communist ideas.

However, the class compromise that was offered meant different things to different currents within social democracy. For corporatists it was an end in itself, whereas democratic socialists saw it as an intermediate step on the worker's march from capitalism to socialism. Not surprisingly, capitalists watched such tendencies with suspicion. The world available for capitalist trade and investments had already been gravely curtailed by the expansion of Soviet communism in Eastern Europe and parts of Asia. Now they worried that government regulations and welfare state expansion in the heartlands might put additional pressures on sales and profit rates. Such worries were further aggravated with the coming to power of developmentalist regimes in the South. Seeking an escape route from their role as subordinate providers of natural resources and agricultural products, some of these regimes drew inspiration from the fast-tracked industrialization of the Soviet Union, and even the more moderate ones began building Keynesian state apparatuses as a means to foster industrialization.

Developmental states had a dual character. On the one hand, they did limit the scope of Western investments in resource extraction and agriculture, and thus challenged the old imperialist division of labour between industrialized centres and non-industrial peripheries. On the other hand, they did open new markets for machinery and equipment. Though always happy to exploit new business opportunities, Western capitalists worried that sales to, and investments in, the post-colonial South could lead to a loss of control of the technological development that played an important role in generating rents to feed class compromises in the West. Even worse, a radicalization of developmentalism from state-led industrialization to non-capitalist development might have led to outright nationalizations. If in doubt, Western capitalists preferred neocolonial rule to developmentalism even if this implied the continuation of the development of underdevelopment and thus foregone sales for their industries.

Capitalists weren't the only ones, though, who had mixed feelings about Southern developmentalism. The theoretical debates that divided social democrats in the late nineteenth century assumed a much more practical meaning in the second half of the twentieth century. In line with Western capitalists, corporatist-minded social democrats were anxious about the emergence of industrial competitors that might cost jobs in the West. They were also aware that cheap resources and agricultural imports from the South boosted the purchasing power of pay cheques in the West. From this angle, developmentalism was seen as a threat to social reforms in the West. Accordingly, corporatist-minded social democrats were either ignorant of, or even complicit with, imperialist interventions in the post-colonial countries whose rulers were deemed to be deviating from the 'acceptable' path of capitalist development. Democratic socialists, though, understood developmentalism to be complementary to welfare state building in the West. Both types of social democrats tried to balance the imperatives of capital accumulation with the development of the forces of production enforced by the accumulation process, but left-leaning social democrats also tried to replace the reign of capital with collective forms of ownership one step at a time. This strategy culminated in quests for a New International Economic Order (NIEO) (Cox, 1979) that were put forward by the Non-Aligned Movement in the 1970s and also supported by social democratic leaders Brandt, Kreisky and Palme (Holbraad, 2003). Designs for such an order were fraught with ambiguities though (Amin, 1979). They aimed at channelling a massively increased share of revenues from resource exports into the industrialization of the South and, by doing so, sought to overcome economic dependencies that were still weighing heavily on post-colonial regimes. At the same time, they tried to soothe Western capitalists' concerns about a loss of influence in the South by pointing at the business opportunities arising from a NIEO, to no avail.

In the context of efforts to travel to socialism on the parliamentary road, most prominently in Chile, or by revolutionary warfare, as in Vietnam, capitalists saw quests for a NIEO as just another left front infringing on businesses in the South. They found support from Western social democrats for these quests was even more alarming as it connected anti-imperialist mobilizations in the South to the new social movements and militant workers' struggles in the West. Complementary demands for higher resource prices to pay for Southern industrialization, higher taxes so that marginalized groups could be included in Western welfare states and higher wages fuelled inflationary pressures that had been created by the USA paying for the war in Vietnam by printing money. These pressures transpired to other countries through the Bretton Woods system of fixed exchange rates, but also contributed to the breakdown of the Bretton Woods system. Export successes of German and Japanese industries during the post-WWII boom pushed the American trade balance into the red and caused concerns as to whether the USA would be able to pay concurrent debts. In 1973, the US government decided that fixed exchange rates were an impediment rather than promoter of US business interests and allowed the Greenback to float vis-à-vis other currencies. Yet, the result was not a rebalancing of the world economy but financial turbulences, dealing a further blow to capitalists' propensity to invest. A global crisis of overproduction in 1974/75 had already shaken the post-WWII belief that endless prosperity had succeeded capitalist crises once and for all (Brenner, 2006, Part 3: From Boom to Downturn).

In the face of these challenges, capitalists expected social democrats to discipline labour in order to contain the spectre of a profit squeeze and put the burden of actual economic crises on workers' shoulders. However, social democrats weren't up to that task. Rank-and-file militancy, operating independently from union bureaucracies affiliated with social democratic parties, and new social movements were a clear indication that the scope of social control exerted by welfare states and the organizations supporting it was limited. Moreover, left wingers within social democratic parties, some of them coming out of labour and new social movement activism, sought to use the momentum of these movements to push social democratic policies from class compromise to socialist transformation (Schmidt, 2011). Such efforts met considerable opposition from social democratic right wingers who were in fear of losing their role as capitalists' junior partners. Growing tensions inside social democracy played a crucial role in convincing capitalists that it might be time to move away from class compromise in the opposite direction. Neoliberalism became the capitalists' alternative to the challenges that Keynesian states had produced in the West and in the South. Under the banner of Hayek, capitalists began rolling back the reforms that workers and other subordinated classes had won during the post-WWII boom and had been able to, partially at least, institutionalize in welfare and developmental states, respectively (Schmidt, 2008).

The turn from Keynes to Hayek within countries came with a turn from the policies of detente to a Second Cold War (Halliday, 1986). Following the fears of imminent nuclear Armageddon that had stifled social movements of any kind through the 1950s and into the early 1960s, the adoption of the policies of detente helped overcome these fears and thus contributed to the rise of more assertive movements from the mid 1960s onwards (Suri, 2003). They also played a part in loosening the ties between the Soviets and their comrades in Western Europe. Eurocommunism, then, encouraged the social democratic left to push for an end of the Atlanticism that had been so inscribed in the post-WWII bloc, with its blend of anti-communism and Keynesian welfare states (Boggs and Plotke, 1980). Anti-communism had been an effective constraint on social reform. With the former being alleviated, the possibility that the latter would go beyond capitalists' tolerance levels was significantly enhanced. It thus made perfect sense for them to complement their domestic quest to restore class power with the adoption of hawkish foreign policies.

As it transpired, the turn to neoliberalism and the Second Cold War, respectively, marked the beginning of the end of the three worlds. While the neoliberal counteroffensive proceeded at very different speeds across countries in the West and in the South through the 1980s, it was the collapse of the Soviet Union and the capitalist turn in China that led to neoliberal globalization. With this came a massive scaling up of neoliberal counter-reforms that put the social democratic hopes that neoliberalism might have just been an interlude to rest. The 1990s saw social democrats of all currents struggling to find their place in the new world of global capitalism (Evans and Schmidt, 2012).

THREE WORLDS OF SOCIAL DEMOCRACY

Social democrats were suspicious that capital mobility was undermining state capacities to manage aggregate demand and employment levels since the late 1970s (Scharpf, 1991). The massive increase of cross-border flows of capital that followed the end of the Bretton Woods system, along with a whirlwind of stagflation, found social democrats torn between demands for capital controls, coming from its left wing, and a push to downgrade reformist ambitions, coming from its right. Difficulties adjusting to increasingly open economies and, compared to the post-WWII boom, slower growth had taken the steam out of the welfare state project but not derailed it. That didn't happen until Soviet communism disappeared. The integration of formerly communist countries into the capitalist world market saw a further increase in international capital flows but, more significantly, also a massive increase in the global supply of labour, significant parts of it highly skilled. Arguably, pro-market reforms since the 1980s wouldn't have turned China into the workshop of the world if the Soviet regime in Moscow hadn't collapsed. Whatever the conjecturing in Moscow and Beijing during the tumultuous years from the late 1980s to the early 1990s, capitalists and their ideologues in the West didn't waste the chance to announce the victory of capitalism over socialism, which, to them, meant not only Soviet communism but also the Keynesian state intervention in the West and in the South. Greatly enhanced possibilities to bypass legal standards and union contracts, they conjectured, would economically dry out the remaining bastions of welfare and developmental states. The race-to-the-bottom, creating a level but low playing field for private firms and states that were competing for scarce finances, and for workers from around the world, who were competing for jobs, was imminent.

In response to neoliberal globalization, social democracy moved further to the political centre. Left wingers put commitments to socialist transformation on hold and fully concentrated on defending what was left of Keynesian welfare states after the Reagan and Thatcher offensives against it during the 1980s. Their claim was that globalization was just a myth and that capitalists trumpeted the race-to-the-bottom-thesis as part of a scare campaign to score points in their quest to boost profits at the expense of wages and public sectors in the West. Busting these myths, they hoped, would encourage party activists and voters, but also unionists, to stand firm in their defence of reform gains made in the past. At the same time, the social democratic right accepted the neoliberal claim that the collapse of Soviet communism had changed the world fundamentally, and also offered the same interpretation as was offered by the advocates of neoliberalism, though sometimes in a more ornate language (Giddens, 1999). Consequently, they saw long-standing commitments to the Keynesian welfare state as a liability that had to be abandoned to ensure social democracy's survival in the electoral market.

To drastically downsize the welfare state, the social democratic right fought left wingers, charging them with nostalgia and denial of current realities, and suggested a Third Way future beyond the Keynesian past and the neoliberal present.

The Keynesian welfare state and the neoliberal project of rolling back the welfare state came out of long intellectual and political struggles (Dowd, 2004; White, 2012). One such struggle dating back to the days of the Second International and proto-Keynesians like John Hobson, the other representing the anti-socialist traditions from Ludwig von Mises and Hayek onwards. In comparison to these two projects, the Third Way was an intellectual lightweight devoid of any tradition. Yet its intellectual vagueness and lack of tradition might have been a good fit for the zeitgeist during the years following the end of the Cold War. After all, this was the time when the history of all hitherto existing societies with their class struggles had allegedly come to an end (Fukuyama, 1992). Moreover, the obscurity of the Third Way might have been a reflection of, and thus appealed to, the discontent that many people felt at the time without having a clear idea of what they wanted instead. Be this as it may, neoliberal hopes that social democracy would follow Soviet communism into the dustbin of history were disappointed. By the end of the 1990s, social democratic parties were in office in most Western European countries. Even more surprisingly, some of the previously ruling communist parties in Eastern Europe reinvented themselves as social democrats and managed to win elections too. Likewise, left-wing organizations, ranging from Brazil's Workers Party to South Africa's ANC, which played important roles in fighting military dictatorships or apartheid, either got elected on social democratic platforms or turned to social democratic policies after being elected on more radical platforms. In Kerala and West Bengal, where communists have been part of coalition governments for a long time, they transformed themselves from developmentalists into Third Way social democrats.

What this suggests is that the 1990s, rather than seeing the disappearance of social democracy, witnessed its globalization. Despite the similarities it shared with developmentalism in the South and Soviet communism in the East, social democracy had a distinct Western European flavour until the end of the Cold War. The neoliberal globalization that succeeded the Cold War produced a string of economic crises beginning with the Mexican peso crisis in 1994, widening into financial crises in Asia, Latin America and Russia from 1997 to 2002 and culminating in the global economic crisis in 2008/9. It also produced social insecurities and inequalities on an unprecedented scale. Arguably, capitalism since the 1990s is closer to Marx's depictions in *Capital* than at the time of its writing. Yet, the end of the Cold War did mark the end of the various left projects that had, more or less successfully, tamed or overcome capitalism since Marx's own days. More succinctly, the end of the Cold War didn't signal the end of history but it does mark the end of left histories as they were known from 1789 to 1989. If anything was left on the left, it was a very sceptical socialism, unsure of itself and far from mobilizing masses to build a new world (Miliband, 1994). Soviet communism was discredited by Stalinism and proved to be unable to overcome its bureaucratic ossification during its post-Stalinist period. Welfare states and developmentalist regimes were sandwiched between expectations of the popular classes and neoliberal counter-reform during a period of slow growth even before the collapse of the Soviet Union tipped the global balance of power in neoliberalism's favour. The vacuum that was left behind was filled, to some degree at least, by Third Way social democracy. Yet, its globalization occurred in a highly uneven world.

Contrary to speculations about a race to the bottom eroding West-South divisions after the disappearance of the East, global capitalism is marked by old and new geographical divisions. To different degrees, post-communist regimes in Eastern Europe were downgraded to peripheral status (Bohle and Greskovits, 2012). They joined the ranks of the majority of the world's countries who have little say in world politics, and who are exploited by coalitions of foreign capital and domestic compradors. Russia, despite its sheer size, resource supplies and the world's second largest nuclear arsenal, moved from superpower status to empire of the periphery (Kagarlitsky, 2008). China, where communists tightened their grip on political power while embarking on full-blown world market integration, became global capitalism's economic powerhouse with an increasing clout in politics as well (Li, 2008). On a smaller scale, Brazil, India and South Africa established themselves as regional powers (Bond and Garcia, 2015).

In the 1990s, social democracy scored successes in its old Western European heartlands, in some of the new Eastern European peripheries and also in some of the old peripheries and emerging regional powers in the South. In Western Europe, the old social democratic parties went through painful internal battles before turning from the Keynesian welfare state to the Third Way. In the absence of institutions of, or personnel committed to, the Keynesian welfare state, some of the old communist parties in Eastern Europe found it much easier to adopt Third Way policies as they reinvented themselves as social democrats. The Brazilian Workers' Party, the South African ANC and the Indian CPI(M) stuck to their original names and had little interest in Third Way rhetoric while they moved from their original blend of socialism and national liberation to social democracy. Organizational and programmatic trajectories of social democracies in the capitalist centres, peripheries and regional powers were quite different and also varied from country to country within each of these groupings. What they had in common, though, were efforts to balance the imperatives of capital accumulation with measures that limit the polarizations and devastations produced by it. As a matter of fact, striking such a balance has lain at the heart of social democracy ever since revolutionary socialists split from the Second International during WWI. Since that time, reformist socialists and capitalist reformers negotiated internal balances that then shaped the policies pursued by social democratic parties. This core of social democracy has survived the dramatic goodbyes that Third Wayers said to the Keynesian welfare state.

What has changed after the Cold War, and what was reflected in the victory of Third Way advocates and stalwarts of Keynesianism, is the economic and political conditions under which social democrats act. These changes led to a dramatic internal shift from reformist socialists, whose defence of the Keynesian welfare state appeared both defensive and backward, to capitalist reformers, whose Third Way message sounded fresh and open to the future. However, the weakening of the social democratic left made it next to impossible for social democracy as a whole to resist capitalist quests for concessions. The social democratic right had always been reliant on its internal counterweight on the left in its dealings with capital. After the left had lost the internal battle, the right was no longer in a position to negotiate with the capitalists. The threat that failure to strike a deal with the right would strengthen the left and make life for capitalists more difficult was gone. As a consequence, social democrats turned from struggling for social reforms to minimizing concessions made to capitalists. This turn came at a time when voters expected more, not less, social protections.

For a while, the contradiction between voters' increased expectations and social democracy's reduced ability to deliver was concealed by the economic boom of the 1990s. Yet, while capitalists, politicians of all stripes and economists in the West still nurtured the dream of a New Economy, in which prosperity might overcome social conflict, the downgrading of Eastern European countries revealed the impotence of the newly minted social democrats there to build welfare states remotely similar to those still existing in the West. Not surprisingly, then, social democratic successes in Eastern Europe were even more short-lived then they were in the West. In Hungary, Poland and Slovenia, social democracy was reduced to electoral insignificance. In the Czech Republic and Romania, social democrats maintained not only a significant electoral presence but were also able to win elections. Yet, in order to do so, they felt that adding a solid dose of nationalism to their programme was required.

Advancing left alternatives to neoliberal capitalism is difficult in a part of the world where Stalinist rule has discredited all kinds of left politics, including those who have been consistently critical of Stalinism and post-Stalinist communism. It is much easier, then, to articulate discontent in nationalist terms. This nationalism amalgamates incantations of national greatness with nostalgia for the social protections that people enjoyed before the transition from capitalism to communism. The fact that these protections were provided by the same communist regimes that are mostly remembered for their bureaucratic and, at times, terrorist, rule is conveniently forgotten in these new nationalist narratives that are permeating all across Eastern Europe. Adapting to the nationalism propagated by the political right may help social democrats in winning some votes, occasionally even winning elections, but doesn't change the capitalist dynamics that are producing discontent and a desire for change in the first place. Nationalism, whether pursued as a matter of conviction by the right or for opportunistic reasons by the left, does not offer economic alternatives. Thus, governments elected on nationalist platforms are destined to disappoint electorates behind whose ballots lay the desire to escape dire social conditions.

Things looked slightly better in new regional powers of the South where high growth resumed quickly after the Great Recession of 2008/9. This was largely driven by continuously high investments in China, propped up by the government after the Great Recession, a commodity boom maintained by Chinese demand for resources and further fuelled by capital inflows from the stagnation-plagued West. On this basis, governments in Brazil, South Africa, Kerala and West Bengal were able to finance some poverty alleviating measures. Yet, to pay for these measures, they backed the accumulation by dispossession that, with its enclosures and privatizations, destroyed domestic and subsistence economies. Consequently, the ranks of the dispossessed and destitute are swelling, some of them finding paid work under the most deplorable conditions while many are struggling in burgeoning informal sectors (Bieler et al., 2008; Ness, 2015). In short, governments in these states supply some social protections but at the same time contribute to an ever-increasing demand for them. Balancing these opposing trends was difficult enough as long as growth was strong but has become all but impossible since the growth in these emerging economies has slowed. Hopes that at least parts of the South could belatedly follow the post-WWII model of combining prosperity and class compromise are fading, while the new social democratic governments in the South are facing an explosive mix of rising discontent amongst different layers of the population, increasing fiscal pressures and the dangers of foreign debt and currency crises. This mix is pretty similar to the one that derailed the social democratic project in the West during the 1970s. But, in fact, it represents an even greater challenge for today's social democrats in the South than it did to their Western predecessors in the 1970s. The latter had to deal with a whole pile of economic problems but at least sovereign debt wasn't one of them. Moreover, the social bloc that had pursued welfare state expansion during the preceding prosperity was much stronger in the West than the support base of social democratic governments in the South. It had established considerable institutional power whose undoing took time. Not much of this exists in the emerging economies of the South. As in other parts of the world, Southern social democrats will find it impossible to uphold their political principles. They will disappoint their actual and potential voters and party activists at a time when the desire for social protections is further increasing. However, the limits to social democracy may open ways beyond social democracy. To be sure, such left alternatives have to grapple with the same problems that social democrats are facing these days, notably a weakening of the social basis able to give any kind of left politics some clout. But at least alternatives to the left of social democracy may not be hung up in the illusion that economic prosperity might deliver social reforms that can only be won through struggles against capital.

BIBLIOGRAPHY

Abendroth, W. (1972). *A Short History of the European Working Class*. New York: Monthly Review Press.

Amin, S. (1979). 'NIEO: How to Put Third World Surpluses to Effective Use'. *Third World Quarterly*, 1 (1): 65–72.

Bailey, D., De Waelle, J.-M., Escalona, F. and Vieira, M. (eds) (2014). *European Social Democracy During the Global Economic Crisis: Renovation of Resignation?* Manchester: Manchester University Press.

Bieler, A., Lindberg, I. and Pillay, D. (eds) (2008). *Labour and the Challenges of Globalization*. London and Ann Arbor: Pluto Press.

Boggs, C. and Plotke, D. (eds) (1980). *The Politics of Eurocommunism*. Boston: South End Press.

Bohle, D. and Greskovits, B. (2012). *Capitalist Diversity on Europe's Periphery*. Ithaca and London: Cornell University Press.

Bond, P. and Garcia, A. (eds) (2015). *BRICS – An Anti-capitalist Critique*. Chicago: Haymarket.

Brenner, R. (2006). *The Economics of Global Turbulence*. London and New York: Verso.

Childs, D. (2000). *The Two Red Flags – European Social Democracy and Soviet Communism Since 1945*. London and New York: Routledge.

Cox, R.W. (1979). 'Ideologies and the New International Economic Order: Reflections on Some Recent Literature'. *International Organization*, 33 (2): 257–302.

Day, R.B. and Gaido, D.F. (eds) (2012). *Discovering Imperialism: Social Democracy to World War I*. Chicago: Haymarket.

De Waele, J.-M., Escalona, F. and Vieira, M. (eds) (2013). *The Palgrave Handbook of Social Democracy in the European Union*. Houndmills, Basingstoke: Palgrave Macmillan.

Dowd, D. (2004). *Capitalism and its Economics*. London and Ann Arbor: Pluto Press.

Eley, G. (2002). *Forging Democracy: The History of the Left in Europe, 1850–2000*. Oxford: Oxford University Press.

Evans, B. and Schmidt, I. (eds) (2012). *Social Democracy After the Cold War*. Athabasca: Athabasca University Press.

Evans, P. (2009). 'From Situation of Dependency to Globalized Social Democracy'. *Studies in Comparative International Development*, 44 (3): 318–36.

Fagerholm, A. (2013). 'Towards a Lighter Shade of Red? Social Democratic Parties and the Rise of Neoliberalism in Western Europe, 1970–1999'. *Perspectives on European Politics and Society*, 14 (4): 1–24.

Figueroa, M. (2015). 'The Workers Party's Contradictions and the Contours of Crisis in Brazil'. *New Politics*, 15 (2): 61–6.

Fillipelli, R.L. (1989). *American Labor and Postwar Italy, 1943–1953 – A Study in Cold War Politics*. Stanford: Stanford University Press.

Fukuyama, F. (1992). *The End of History*. New York: Free Press.

Giddens, A. (1999). *The Third Way: The Renewal of Social Democracy*. Malden: Polity.

Gowan, P. (1997). 'The Post-communist Socialists in Eastern and Central Europe'. In D. Sasson (ed.), *Looking Left: Socialism in Europe After the Cold War*. New York: The New Press: 143–76.

Halliday, F. (1986). *The Making of the Second Cold War*. London and New York: Verso.

Held, D. (2005). 'At the Global Crossroads: The End of the Washington Consensus and the Rise of Global Social Democracy?'. *Globalizations*, 2 (1): 95–113.

Hicks, A. (1999). *Social Democracy and Welfare Capitalism*. Ithaca: Cornell University Press.

Hilferding, R. (1924). 'Probleme der Zeit'. *Die Gesellschaft*, 1: 1–17.

Hobsbawm, E. (1962). *The Age of Revolution, 1789–1848*. London: Abacus 1992.

——(1975). *The Age of Capital, 1848–1875*. London: Abacus 1997.

——(1995). *The Age of Extremes, 1914–1991*. London: Abacus.

Holbraad. C. (2003). *Internationalism and Nationalism in European Political Thought*. Houndmills, Basingstoke: Palgrave Macmillan.

Kagarlitsky, B. (2008). *Empire of the Periphery – Russia and the World System*. London and Ann Arbor: Pluto Press.

Kalecki, M. (1943). 'Political Aspects of Full Employment'. *Political Quarterly*, 14 (4): 322–30.

Keman, H. (2013). 'Democratisation and Social Democracy – The Emergence of a Complex Party Family'. In K. Armingeon (ed.), *Staatstätigkeiten, Parteien und Demokratie*. Wiesbaden: Springer: 219–40.

Keynes, J. M. (1936). *The General Theory of Employment, Interest and Money*. London: Macmillan 1967.

Kiely, R. (1998). *Industrialization and Development*. London: University College Press.

Lanzaro, J. (2011). 'Social Democracy in the Global South: Brazil, Chile and Uruguay in a Comparative Perspective'. *Social Europe Journal*, 6 (1): 33–43.

Li, M. (2008). *The Rise of China and the Demise of the Capitalist World System*. New York: Monthly Review Press.

Luxemburg, R. (1899). 'Reform or Revolution'. In *Rosa Luxemburg Speaks*. New York: Pathfinder Press 2011: 50–124.

Marglin, S. and Schor, J.B. (eds) (1991). *The Golden Age of Capitalism: Reinterpreting the Postwar Experience*. Oxford: Clarendon Press.

Miliband, R. (1961). *Parliamentary Socialism: A Study in the Politics of Labour*. Pontypool: Merlin.

—— (1994). *Socialism for a Sceptical Age*. London and New York: Verso.

Ness, I. (2015). *Southern Insurgency: The Coming of the Global Working Class*. London: Pluto Press.

Polanyi, K. (1944). *The Great Transformation*. Boston: Beacon Press 2001.

Prashad, V. (2007). *The Darker Nations*. New York: The New Press.

—— (2015). *No Free Left: The Futures of Indian Communism*. New Delhi: Left Word Books.

Prevost, G. (2006). 'The Evolution of the African National Congress in Power: From Revolutionaries to Social Democrats?'. *Politikon: South African Journal of Political Studies*, 33 (2): 163–81.

Ross, G. (1982). *Workers and Communists in France: From Popular Front to Eurocommunism*. Berkeley: University of California Press.

Sandbrook, R., Edelman, M., Heller, P. and Teichman, J. (2007). *Social Democracy in the Global Periphery*. Cambridge: Cambridge University Press.

Scharpf, F. (1991). *Crisis and Choice in European Social Democracy*. Ithaca: Cornell University Press.

Schmidt, I. (ed.) (2008). *Spielarten des Neoliberalismus*. Hamburg: VSA Verlag.

—— (2009). 'German Labour Experiences Since World War Two: A Suggested Interpretation'. *Labour/Le Travail*, 63 (Spring): 157–79.

—— (2011). 'There Were Alternatives: Lessons From Efforts to Advance Beyond Keynesian and Neoliberal Economic Policies in the 1970s'. *WorkingUSA*, 14 (4): 473–98.

—— (2012). 'It's the Economy, Stupid! Theoretical Reflections on Third Way Social Democracy'. In B. Evans and I. Schmidt (eds), *Social Democracy After the Cold War*. Athabasca: Athabasca University Press: 13–44.

Sejersted, F. (2011). *The Age of Social Democracy: Norway and Sweden in the Twentieth Century*. Princeton: Princeton University Press.

Silver, B. (2003). *Forces of Labor: Workers' Movements and Globalization Since 1870*. Cambridge: Cambridge University Press.

Smaldone, W. (1998). *Rudolf Hilferding – The Tragedy of a German Social Democrat*. DeKlab: Northern Illinois University Press.

——(2014). *European Socialism*. Lanham: Rowman & Littlefield.

Suri, J. (2003). *Power and Protest: Global Revolution and the Rise of Détente*. Cambridge, MA: Harvard University Press.

Trotsky, L. (1930). *History of the Russian Revolution*. Chicago: Haymarket 2008.

Vachudova, M. (2013). 'The Positions and Fortunes of Social Democratic Parties in East and Central Europe'. In M. Keating and D. McCrone (eds), *The Crisis of Social Democracy in Europe*. Edinburgh: Edinburgh University Press: 47–67.

Wang, X. (2012). 'Social Democracy or Neoliberal Freedom? Globalization and Contemporary Chinese Intellectual Politics'. *Critique: Journal of Socialist Theory*, 40 (4): 511–31.

Weiler, P. (1988). *British Labour and the Cold War*. Stanford: Stanford University Press.

White, G. (1998). 'Building a Democratic Developmental State: Social Democracy in the Developing World'. *Democratization*, 5 (3): 1–32.

White, L.H. (2012). *The Clash of Economic Ideas: The Great Policy Debates and Experiments of the Last Hundred Years*. Cambridge: Cambridge University Press.

Part I
Heartlands

2

France: Who Wants to be a Social Democrat?

Fabien Escalona

The French Parti socialiste (PS) has always stood apart in the social democratic family. Having evolved in a country that irrefutably belongs to the centre of European capitalism, it has developed characteristics closer to those of the socialist parties in its southern periphery than to those of the social democratic parties found in Nordic and Central Europe (Bartolini, 2000: 498–9).

In fact, the PS has never been a mass party with links to powerful unions. Its internal workings have been marked by significant doctrinal divisions, while its sociological base has always remained fairly heterogeneous, with only a minority of the working class electorate. Starting in 1920, its communist challenger, the Parti communiste français (PCF), turned out to be both strong and durable, going so far as to beat the socialist party in the legislative elections of 1945 and 1973. During the so-called 'golden age of social democracy', French socialists barely had the opportunity to weigh in on the country's political economy. This was done mainly during the Liberation after expanding the public sector and implementing social security, and again in 1956–57 after securing new rights for employees along with a more expansive economic policy. For everything else, the party would have to settle for a junior partnership with centrist coalitions or a seat on the opposition benches for a number of years during the Fourth Republic (1946–58). From the arrival of the Fifth Republic to 1981 the party was excluded from power until François Mitterrand finally won the presidential elections following two fruitless attempts (in 1965 and 1974). His victory coincided with the rise to power of other socialist leaders in the recently democratized countries of Southern Europe. Both they and Mitterrand shared a number of traits, including charismatic leadership and autonomy from their enfeebled party structures. They also used a similar strategy by initially opting for a far left stance to reinforce their control over that specific camp before re-centring themselves once in power (Grunberg, 1996).

The PS did, of course, develop its own characteristics at the same time. The intellectual professions enjoyed a privileged place in the party, while its most well-known leaders – Jaurès and Blum – were respected for both their doctrinal and political work. An adherence to the republican regime and its ideals stood at the heart of their socialist ideas, as France is one of the rare countries where a number of leftist forces built regimes that excluded monarchs at the end of the nineteenth century. In this sense, the socialists have long been stuck between their exteriority and their integration within the republican camp (Fontaine, 2013). On the one hand, they represented a subversive force proclaiming the existence of opposing social classes and the imperative of collectivizing the means of production. On the other hand, they were willing to join those who defended the Republic against its reactionary enemies. To ensure the effectiveness of this defence in dangerous times, the party had to avoid compromising its unity by too eagerly supporting the policies of the bourgeois camp. For this reason, they were slow to grant parliamentary support to the *Radicaux* (centre-left) during the Third Republic and were only able to assume government responsibilities in the framework of a *Front Populaire* (1936–38) designed to confront the 'fascist threat'. Finally, the longevity of French socialism cannot be understood without acknowledging the means by which it has implanted itself into society. Firstly, its link to the working class was very real, even if those links were never institutionalized following the classical social democratic model. Socialist and unionist militants often fought side-by-side and this dual socialist/unionist partisan identity was regularly encouraged. Secondly, the number of locally elected representatives, along with their considerable territorial implantation, represents a significant factor in the resilience of French socialism beyond the twists and turns it endured on the national stage. Thirdly, their control on these authorities helped them to cultivate their links to various social networks and spheres, providing them with many socially influential intermediaries: teachers, Masonic lodges, human rights organizations etc. (Morin, 2007).

Newly founded under the leadership of François Mitterrand at Epinay in 1971, the strength of the PS rested on its renewal of these faded networks. New connections were being established with the feminist movement, leftist Christians, student unions and the interprofessional Confédération Française Démocratique du Travail (CFDT) union, along with associations dedicated to the improvement of democracy at the local level. During this time, the PS benefited from weakened opponents when attracting the country's elite. Former radical Pierre Mendès France, once very popular with the progressive intelligentsia, destroyed his political future after a bitter defeat in the 1969 presidential elections; Gaullism in power had undertaken a move towards economic deregulation and thus lost the support from many high-ranking senior officials in power; and the communist party was on its way to becoming increasingly sectarian towards intellectuals. Thanks to the PS, the politically orphaned managers were promised a leading and mediation role within a 'class front' that would bring together the new middle and working classes. In programmatic terms, France's socialists were claiming to forge a compromise between the old capitalism supersession project and new aspirations founded by the movements of May 1968. The PS sought to 'change life' and rejected any reference to social democracy, now seen as too timid to manage the current order. The 110 propositions that were put forth by François Mitterrand in 1981 were part of a modernization and democratization agenda, despite being more moderate than the programmes that were actually adopted by his party (Kesselman, 1984).

THE 'AUSTERITY TURN' (1982–83), OR THE NORMALIZATION OF THE PS ECONOMIC POLICY

The first two years under a socialist government were marked by societal reforms (abolishing the death penalty, decriminalizing homosexuality) and the implementation of a Marxist-Keynesian economic programme. On the one hand, the socialists fought unemployment by creating public jobs and relaunching aggregated demand with redistribution methods that would reduce inequalities and benefit low-income workers. On the other hand, their interventionist policy would transform the country's productive capacity by nationalizing a number of lending institutions and industrial groups.

Yet, faced with growing commercial and financial difficulties, this economic policy was progressively abandoned between 1982 and 1983. Through the implementation of several austerity measures, along with the decision to keep the franc in the European Monetary System (EMS), President Mitterrand effectively altered the objectives and methods surrounding his economic policy (Lordon, 1998). Reductions in the inflation rate and external imbalances became a priority that called for a compression of domestic demand and the restoration of corporate profitability, which led to salary restrictions, economic austerity and financial deregulation. In addition, management criteria for state-owned companies were aligned with those of the private sector. One year later, socialism once again retreated from its ideals by abandoning any attempt to bridge the private and public education systems. Social mobilization surrounding the principle of 'freedom of choice' defeated reforms built on the principles of republican equality and secularism. The President replaced Pierre Mauroy with Laurent Fabius as prime minister to 'ratify' this political U-turn. From that moment on, the emphasis shifted to the 'corporate spirit' and the country's inclusion within international economic competitiveness. Mitterrand embraced the building of Europe as his new 'big project' (Ross, 1995).

There were many causes behind this reversal. For one, it clearly rested on discrepancies between his desired economic strategy and the international environment at the start of the 1980s (Hall, 1987). Contrary to certain forecasts, worldwide growth had not recovered in the months following the socialists' arrival to power. France's isolated recovery profited its commercial partners, who were applying domestic austerity measures but refused any attempt to coordinate expansion during the 1982 G7 Summit in Versailles. A degraded national supply could not adequately respond to an increase in domestic demand, especially because the effects of the industrial policy would only appear in the long term. That said, additional factors should be considered to understand why this political turn went in a neoliberal way rather than in a socialist one.

Indeed, no internal or external incentives existed that could have encouraged an executive's move in this second direction. Within the PS, as in the government, proponents of an alternative policy were divided. For some, leaving the EMS would have made French products more competitive, but this was not construed as a genuine alternative to austerity. In addition, the social movement remained hopelessly sluggish. Ironically, this situation had been anticipated by the socialist party's left flank. Jean-Pierre Chevènement (1974), then leader of the Centre d'études, de recherches et d'éducation socialiste (CERES) faction, feared that any pursuit of the state apparatus would only lead to the responsible management of capitalism should 'mass movement' fail to stimulate government. The communist party also had a role to play in this framework. Its ultimate electoral weakening in 1981 was double-edged; the PCF had diffused the fears of many voters when the time came to vote for a second-round socialist candidate, but it was also relegated to a subordinate role in the leftist alliance in power. This decline, along with strategic mistakes of the communist leaders, explains the PCF's thorough failure to become a mobilizing factor for alternative policies, much like the unions, whose influence and combativeness had already begun to erode (Jenson and Ross, 1988). France was also under pressure to implement an orthodox policy from significant centres of power, including the senior public treasury service, the French central bank and the institutions of the European Community. These stakeholders were aligned with German leaders, who found a favourable response in François Mitterrand (Quatrepoint, 2013). Indeed, Mitterrand had been marked by the events of the Second World War and believed that the political preservation of the Franco-German partnership at the heart of the European project mattered more than any economic consideration at the time.

The consequences of the socialist policy shift were significant in French society. The years 1981 and 1982 saw an increase in household purchasing power and the share of wages in value added, while income inequalities continued to drop. These trends reversed in 1983, in large part due to the pressures of mass unemployment on real wages (Husson, 2012; Piketty, 2001). While the PS and its allies were supposed to defend employee interests against the right during the last years of the Giscard d'Estaing presidency, they adopted an economic paradigm that fuelled these threats and favoured the employers, along with a strong currency at the expense of full employment. In the aftermath, the entire French economic model was overturned. The first socialist governments of the Fifth Republic began dismantling the public's ability to intervene in the production sphere, while simultaneously implementing social measures to help those who had lost under modernization. The PS therefore became instrumental in the state's transformation from '*dirigiste* to anaesthetist', i.e. a shift characterized by top-down market deregulation and support for large-scale public expenditures intended to cushion the impact (Levy, 2008).

THE UNTRACEABLE FRENCH SOCIAL DEMOCRACY

Following the 1983 turning point, references to social democracy were no longer seen as slanderous for most of the factions within the PS. The party even espoused social democratic ideals at the 1985 Toulouse Conference, while simultaneously affirming its support for the Laurent Fabius government. This was paradoxical in that all the key markers of social democracy – considered a typical political practice during the Fordist era – were absent. Economic cycles were no longer being controlled by Keynesian techniques to ensure full employment and moderate inflation, organized interests were not committed to any neo-corporatist agreement under the auspices of the state, the latter had ceased to expand its role, and the contradictions between working class interests and those of the national economy had deepened. While the pre-1981 socialist project had intended to go beyond social democracy, François Mitterrand's public policies cemented its failure. Rather than forming an alliance between managers and the working class that would impose economic democratization on capital owners, the latter secured the subordination of managers with regard to their objectives and became the winners in this newly emerging phase of capitalism.

Jean Poperen, the party's second in command between 1981 and 1986 and leader of a left-wing internal faction, pleaded for an authentic social democratic compromise. Without rejecting the choices made in 1983, he deplored the government's pro-business policy as having been implemented without any exchange of consideration from managers. According to Poperen, renouncing the rupture from capitalism should not have to result in the normalization of the PS on the French and European political landscapes. His proposal for 'contractual policies' had assumed that the party would recognize the conflict between social forces and provide support for the organized voices of labour. But the conditions for a French-style neo-corporatism had never been in place. In addition to a Jacobin tradition that includes the pre-eminence of law over contracts, union and management organizations remained insufficiently representative, fragmented and ideologically polarized. As of 1970, like elsewhere in Europe, the declining growth rate also had the effect of reducing the potential for compromise regarding any sharing of the social surplus (Lavelle, 2008).

The turning point of 1982–83 was therefore not a 'socially democratic' one. Rather, it indicated that the PS political economy had been integrated to a neoliberal paradigm, *both reluctantly and actively*. The reluctance of socialists could be seen in their decision to avoid any attack on the public service (which includes a number of socialist voters), as well as their avoidance of any large-scale deregulation of the labour market. They did not succeed in preventing its dualization, or in challenging right-wing reforms, but they did adopt a number of social policies against poverty and insecurity. But the integration to the neoliberal paradigm was also an active one through their significant contributions to the liberalization of commercial trade and financial systems (Amable et al., 2012). Mitterrand's first term deregulated and developed the exchange markets, stock markets and bond markets. His second term (1988–95) negotiated and implemented the free flow of capital both inside and outside the European Union (EU). Many French socialists working in international organizations were instrumental in achieving this liberalization. The head of the European Commission, Jacques Delors, argued for this transformation, and so did his chief of staff Pascal Lamy, along with senior official Henri Chavranski from the Organisation of Economic Co-operation and Development (OECD) (Abdelal, 2007). Prior to this, the choice of the European Single Market implied the acceptance of free-trade expansion, which was reinforced by an expansion of the EU into Central and Eastern Europe in the 2000s. Under the Lionel

Jospin government (1997–2002), the *gauche plurielle* (pluralist left) went further by adopting a law for new economic regulations that encouraged entrepreneurial governance based on Anglo-Saxon standards, that is, regulations that favour market finance over other stakeholders in the firms involved.

Thus, the political economy of the French social democratic family *sustainably* lost its originality *before* the end of the Cold War. European integration superseded socialist ideals while simultaneously being presented as their necessary precondition. At the Toulouse Conference mentioned above, First Secretary Lionel Jospin clearly stated that left-wing policies had lost all flexibility on the national stage. According to him, they could only be recovered on the European stage. French socialists were therefore among the first to support the European 'Faustian pact' that would reinforce the neoliberal paradigm that social democrats had sought to prevent by overcoming the national level of government (Escalona and Vieira, 2014).

The end of the Cold War did, in fact, significantly help consolidate the normalization of the PS, insofar as it paved the way to German reunification. This geopolitical event led François Mitterrand to offer Germans a single currency that would definitively bind it to its European partners. In exchange, the currency would be managed by institutions and regulations that complied with Germany's ordoliberal approach, which involves budgetary discipline, financial stability and a lack of political primacy in currency management. Governance in the Eurozone thus remained fragmented between its member states, the European Commission and the European Council. Its monetary policy was assigned to a single stakeholder, the European Central Bank (ECB), which, compared to other central banks, holds unprecedented independence (Théret, 2013). The loss of monetary autonomy and the significant constraints of France's budgetary policies thus became insti-tutionalized. The country would now become linked to a kind of new gold standard defined by the same deflationary bias found in the gold standard that had so crippled social democrats at the turn of the century (Notermans, 2000).

The experience of the *gauche plurielle* illustrates the strength of the factors that prevented any social democratic revival. When Lionel Jospin became prime minister following early legislative elections, convened by the right-wing president Jacques Chirac, he claimed he would reconcile budget and price stability with an interventionist policy geared towards the reduction of unemployment and greater social justice. He succeeded partially using heterodox means (a reduction in working hours, for example), along with a favourable climate characterized by significant worldwide growth and the easing of interest rates by the ECB. Starting in 2000, this climate deteriorated due to increasing oil prices and the bursting of the Internet bubble in the United States, along with a more restrictive economic policy. Unemployment once again rose, fuelling social insecurity and a deterioration in working conditions, which had been neglected by the government. Concurrently, the socialists failed to significantly alter the neoliberal EU and Eurozone framework maintained under the Amsterdam Treaty (1997) and Barcelona Accord (2002), both of which had been signed by the Jospin government. For socialists in France, this episode confirms that the more growth rates slide downwards, the less likely they are to escape the neoliberal framework they both accepted *and* shaped. It is therefore not surprising that the socialist president François Hollande adopted a very orthodox policy in 2012 under a full-blown capitalist and Eurozone structural crisis.

THE PS' ORGANIZATION AND ELECTORATE AFTER NORMALIZATION

Before addressing more recent times, attention must be drawn to the fact that normalization of the economic policies of the PS came while the party continued to position itself as the main alternative against the right. The apparent paradox can be explained by the structures of the political competition.

Firstly, like the left, the right had failed to reduce mass unemployment while creating unpopular policies, nor was it spared from popular sanctions. It also had to contend with the irruption of the Front National (FN), a radical right-wing party whose main themes of mobilization are immigration and insecurity. Contrary to misconceptions, the FN obtained more voters by challenging the right than it did by challenging the socialists and communists. Secondly, the centrality of the presidential elections and the legislative voting methods involved (single member, two-round system) tends to close and bipolarize the French political competition. The enrolment cost for new and/or radical political forces at decisive national elections is very high. Coalitions tend to form around the two most credible candidates in an effort to obtain a majority of second-round votes. When the PS became one of these two forces after Mitterrand's victory and the PCF's marginalization, the ensuing disappointments did not prevent the party from recovering repeatedly during its years in opposition. Thirdly, the PS remained attractive for important fringes of the electorate with regard to non-economic issues. It consistently defended the rights of women, along with sexual and ethno-racial minorities. It is largely thanks to socialist governments that same-sex couples are able to obtain status and marriage rights. Faced with a soaring FN, the PS stood as the guardian of democratic and universal values by triggering memories of anti-fascism and using these against the entirety of the right (Table 2.1).

Table 2.1 Socialists and Executive Power in France since 1981

	Power	Opposition
Presidency of the Republic	1981–88 (François Mitterrand I) 1988–95 (François Mitterrand II) 2012– (François Hollande)	1995–2002 (Jacques Chirac I) 2002–07 (Jacques Chirac II) 2007–12 (Nicolas Sarkozy)
Government	1981–86 1988–93 1997–2002 2012–	1986–88 1993–97 2002–07 2007–12

Note: Since 2002, presidential terms have lasted five years instead of seven, and the electoral calendar has been inverted to allow for legislative elections a few weeks after presidential elections.

The electoral fate of the PS has undergone many variations, none of which have threatened its privileged status in the party system that stabilized after 1981. The sociological composition of its electorate has always been inter-classist, and the same is true today. Similarly, the overrepresentation of the PS among non-believers and civil servants is permanent. By contrast, its overrepresentation among the upper (and no longer strictly middle) salaried strata began to develop in the 1990s. Along with intermediary professions (technicians and socio-cultural professionals, for example), management and higher intellectual professions share an anti-authoritarian value system that places them at the *avant garde* of cultural liberalism and provides increasing motivation for the socialist vote (Tiberj, 2012). These observations are consistent with the evolution of the party's electoral geography. The strongest socialist areas can now be found in the west and southwest of the country, where the service sector continues to thrive. By contrast, their influence has decreased substantially in the declining industrial basins of the eastern and Mediterranean departments (these latter tending to attract pensioners with a good standard of living). Also telling is the growing success of the PS in the larger metropolitan areas that are more integrated by globalization (Escalona and Vieira, 2012). These areas are home to a high concentration of the educated fringes, made up of an urban labour force working in centres of public and private decision-making. The consolidation of the PS in poor metropolitan neighbourhoods reflects its massive over-representation of citizens stemming from extra-European immigration. It is also worth noting that the socialists have shown greater resilience than the PCF among the popular classes, having demonstrated more adaptability to their sociological renewal (Gougou and Martin, 2014) (Table 2.2).

Table 2.2 Electoral Results of the PS in France, 1981–2012 (percentage of total votes)

	Presidential Elections	*Legislative Elections*
1981	25.8	36.3
1986	–	31.6
1988	34.1	34.9
1993	–	17.5
1995	23.3	–
1997	–	23.8
2002	16.2	24.1
2007	25.9	25.0
2012	28.6	29.2

Note: Presidential election results apply to all of France and legislative results apply to metropolitan France.

The pursuit of electoral trophies at the local and national levels has become increasingly prevalent in the internal life of the PS. This feature is of primary importance to its structure and allows for the cohabitation of different sensibilities that might otherwise belong to different parties in a proportional system. Since its victories in the 1977 municipal elections and its rise to government in 1981, the newly founded Epinay PS has lost its militant strength and melded with public institutions (Juhem, 2006; Lefebvre and Sawicki, 2006). The party, in short, has become state-controlled and professional. Its declining membership, factional infighting and inability to settle leadership issues paved the way to organizational reforms at the start of the 1990s. The currents were circumvented with additional powers for individual members along with the introduction of primaries for the nomination of presidential candidates. Between 1995 and 2012, this process became increasingly open to all socialist sympathizers. Such innovations have made the party's classical pyramid structure more complex and reinforced its presidentialization (Escalona and Vieira, 2013). They did not, however, help the party define its own identity, despite a series of declarations of principles that only solidified its acceptance of a capitalist economy and its responsiveness to emerging issues like environmentalism (Parti socialiste, 2008). Overall, the party has become de-ideologized, having never put forward a coherent doctrine. Electoral strategy and practice of power now trump any other concern. As the 1982–83 political turning point was decided at the government level, the party initially remained estranged from redefining its own identity. The various mergers and alliances that followed in an effort to control the party did little to clarify this identity.

THE PS IN POWER AFTER THE GREAT RECESSION

Among several other factors, the post-2008 economic crisis helped defeat the outgoing candidate Nicolas Sarkozy in 2012. François Hollande, who acted as first secretary of the PS between 1997 and 2008, won the presidential election on a very moderate platform. The institutional factors mentioned above, along with austerity measures that remained modest under the right, help to explain the country's choice of a prudent, centre-left response to the crisis. Even for those observers who were not expecting anything revolutionary under a new socialist government, the orthodoxy of Hollande's economic decisions was striking nonetheless, as was the abandonment of his most emblematic electoral promises (Bouillaud, 2014).

Several measures were thrown out or stripped of their substance, like his 'fiscal revolution' for a simplified and far more progressive income tax code, or the separation of banking activities. An unprecedented budgetary consolidation under the Fifth Republic took place, initially through an increase in the overall tax burden, then by focusing on reductions in public spending. This pro-cyclical approach reflected a desire for 'credibility' in the socialist executive with regard to financial markets and European authorities. With the sovereign debt crisis, the budgetary constraints of member states were legally strengthened with treaties that the new socialist powers had otherwise intended to renegotiate. Under this new framework, recommendations from Brussels incited the French government to implement 'structural reforms' that would increase the competitiveness of private firms while reducing public involvement. As a result, a number of important measures, never mentioned during the electoral campaign, were imposed on socialist party members and voters. The 'responsibility pact', consisting of a transfer of household income to private companies (approximately €50 billion), became a symbol of the government's supply-side policy. The latter also accumulated a number of deregulations on the labour market, like the deregulation of working on Sundays or a reduction in the cost of layoffs (including those considered unjustified). These measures, coupled with the efforts of the employers' representatives to pay fewer and fewer taxes while complying with fewer and fewer social obligations, have destroyed Hollande's dream of introducing a culture of social compromise in France.

Rarely has the welfare state been eroded in such a systematic fashion under a socialist government. The modest decisions that were made in favour of households have done little to conceal the deteriorating situation of employees and the unemployed. While the budgetary policy has helped to depress economic activity in France and in Europe, the measures that were implemented were poorly targeted and rendered ineffective in a deflationary environment (OFCE, 2014). No significant decommodification measures have been attempted, nor has any reconsideration of neoliberalism. On the contrary, the socialist government has used the rhetoric attached to this economic paradigm to justify its policy. Private initiatives are the only avenues considered appropriate when revitalizing economic growth and employment. During a press conference, Hollande went against all the previous teachings of Keynes and his successors by referencing the classical economist Say and declaring that 'supply creates its own demand'. This has made France's current debate on Hollande's supposed 'social democratic turn' all the more surrealistic. One could, however, state that his actual policies resemble those of other contemporary social democratic governments, but nothing would lead one to believe that these policies are *substantially* social democratic unless considered through the prism of a 'market social democracy', as conceived during the Blair-Schröder years (Nachtwey, 2013). The government has, in fact, based its actions on financial orthodoxy and microeconomic interventions designed to improve the performance of the private sector, along with notions of social justice that tend to promote equal opportunity over equal outcome.

Once again, this orthodox policy can be explained through a mixture of personal convictions, European constraints and economic crises. François Hollande won the 2011 primaries against Martine Aubry, then first secretary of the PS. She had initiated a programmatic renewal that was incomplete but less orthodox than Hollande's economic intentions. The new president distanced himself from the party's 2012 manifesto while stating his plan to impose a policy of growth across Europe. However, he quickly renounced any confrontation with Germany, whose domestic decisions and ordoliberal ideas have been reproduced throughout the Eurozone while undermining theories of continental recovery (Clift and Ryner, 2014). The fear of breaking up the Franco-German marriage – though imbalanced – has contributed to an alignment with Berlin. This alignment indicates an acceptance of France's geo-economic subordination on the part of socialist leaders and reveals the party's unwillingness to engage in a conflict that would result from an alternative to neoliberalism. In order to achieve full employment with a true environmental transition, a left-wing government should, in fact, reduce working hours, radically modify income distribution and apply drastic management measures on private financing while granting the state the role of investor and employer of last resort (Husson, 2014). Insofar as the space for social compromise has withered, no middle ground will be found between this radical path and the European orthodoxy currently in place.

Like several analysts had predicted, François Hollande's policy did not produce any positive results in terms of reducing unemployment, despite having imposed this as a condition for his upcoming candidacy in 2017. The policy has been contested in the country as well as the party. The intermediary elections (municipal and European in 2014, departmental in 2015) were bitter failures for the PS, while a minority of its members, called 'rebels' (between 20 and 50), have refused to vote for the government's legislations on several occasions. During the last party congress, held in 2015, the left factions failed to reverse the intrapartisan imbalance within the PS. A number of their partisans failed to renew their membership and this internal opposition was unable to rely on Martine Aubry's friends, who wound up rallying for the pro-government majority. Unity of the PS is currently not under threat, the party remains dominant on the left while the right, and especially the FN, continues to rise. The party executive intends to use this threat to discipline the PS, along with the entirety of the left. With this in mind, it also hopes to place its status as guardians of both the Republic and its values in the foreground. This rhetoric has been increasingly used by socialist leaders since the January 2015 terrorist attacks on French soil.

THE FRONT DE GAUCHE:
THE NEED TO GO BEYOND SOCIAL DEMOCRACY

The trajectory of the PS in France can be added to the list of case studies conducted by Ashley Lavelle to gauge the demise of social democracy – but only as a *project*, not as a *party family*. Several organizations to the left of the PS have indeed attempted to fill the political gap left by this transformation, but they have done so without resurrecting the social democratic ideal of a capital/labour compromise under the framework of a mixed economy. This has never been the goal of the Trotskyist parties, whose electoral upswing between 1995 and 2002 eventually faded. Following its 'mutation' under Robert Hue's management (1994–2003), the PCF was able to create the impression of becoming a kind of neo-social democratic organization. This process required a democratization of the organization and some ideological revisions, including its integration in the system of PS alliances in order to preserve its position of power and 'weigh in' on socialist policies. The process also involved lessening communist opposition towards European integration. At the end of the 2000s, the PCF however managed to redirect its strategy by building the Front de Gauche with socialist and Trotskyist dissidents.

The Front de Gauche is still a cartel of parties threatened by internal divisions, but it has monopolized the radical left space at the expense of its extreme-left opponents, who have now been marginalized (Escalona and Vieira, 2016). At the national level, the organization has chosen independence from the socialists. But the situation is more complex at the local level. In no way is it structured like a mass labour movement; rather, it seeks to build a radical pole open to various social movements and categories of citizens who are dissatisfied with the institutional and socioeconomic order. Certain aspects of the Front de Gauche programme (2012) (entitled *L'humain d'abord*, or 'Humans First') could be interpreted as Keynesian, insofar as they seek to respond to the crisis by boosting salaries and public spending. But it also contains elements that point beyond the classical social democratic project. For example, 'ecological planning' and the 'green rule' (do not take or throw away more resources than the ecosystem is able to renew or absorb over an equal period of time) display a genuine doctrinal effort to unite anti-capitalism with anti-productivism. Likewise, an upheaval of ownership structures and a new set of goals for the production apparatus go hand in hand with any modification of the institutional order; the Front de Gauche therefore promotes the election of a constituent assembly tasked with designing the Sixth Republic. It should be noted that this programme also includes a call for 'disobedience' to the European treaties. Such innovations were largely inspired by presidential candidate Jean-Luc Mélenchon, whose dissidence and defection from the PS were accompanied by a radical critique of the social democratic project, which he considers obsolete due to the mutations of capitalism and the challenges posed by the ecological crisis.

Three main reasons explain the electoral stagnation of the Front de Gauche after showing strong results at the last presidential elections (11 per cent). Firstly, austerity measures have not produced devastation on the scale found in Southern European countries. The social movement remains subdued and a significant portion of the middle class is still protected from mass unemployment. Secondly, as mentioned above, the structures of the political competition are hostile to any new participant who is not allied with one of the two major political alternatives. Thirdly, this radical left coalition has been undermined by strategic disagreements, paving the way for a heterogeneous political supply at local elections. This lack of clarity is damaging with regard to the electorate.

CONCLUSION

As a representative of the French social democratic family, the PS has been effective in that it has preserved its status as the main alternative to government, which it (re)conquered in 1981. In exchange, the party has had to normalize its economic ideas and policies that, currently, can barely be qualified as social democratic, particularly since François Hollande took power. The 'competitive disinflation' strategy used between 1980 and 1990, along with the so-called 'supply-side socialism' that has emerged since 2012, have clearly come at an electoral cost. The consequences were partially remedied through PS cultural progressivism, adapted for a French society in transformation, and by the self-protections provided through the institutional architecture of the Fifth Republic. Since the end of the 2000s, the radical left has undertaken an unprecedented process of regrouping, but the foundation of its programme functions less as a revival of social democratic ideas than as a fragile eco-socialist approach that includes an opposition to European treaties.

As a result, France is no longer home to any party that, having emerged from class divisions, currently represents an authentic social democratic project. The socializing rhetoric of the FN is nowhere near it, insofar as it is entirely shaped by xenophobia, nationalism and authoritarianism. This rhetoric has seduced more than one third of workers who still vote, but those who have migrated from the left remain in the minority. The working class has not distanced itself from the PS any more than the overall electorate. In fact, since the 1980s, the whole citizenry has been affected by the crumbling of right-wing political cultures (Gaullism, Christian democracy) as well as left-wing political cultures (democratic socialism, communism). The PS is among those who have crafted this landscape of disenchantment, all the while continuing to monopolize the elected offices of the French political system.

BIBLIOGRAPHY

Abdelal, R. (2007). *Capital Rules. The Construction of Global Finance*. Cambridge, MA: Harvard University Press.

Amable, B., Guillaud, E. and Palombarini, S. (2012). 'Changing French Capitalism: Political and Systemic Crises in France'. *Journal of European Public Policy*, 19 (8): 168–87.

Bartolini, S. (2000). *The Political Mobilization of the European Left, 1860–1980. The Class Cleavage*. Cambridge: Cambridge University Press.

Bouillaud, C. (2014). 'The French Socialist Party (2008–13): Not Revolutionaries, Not Luminaries, Just Normal Guys Amidst the Tempest'. In D. Bailey, J.-M. De Waele, F. Escalona and M. Vieira (eds), *European Social Democracy During the Global Economic Crisis*. Manchester: Manchester University Press: 153–75.

Chevènement, J.-P. (1974). *Le vieux, la crise, le neuf*. Paris: Flammarion.

Clift, B. and Ryner, M. (2014). 'Joined at the Hip, but Pulling Apart? Franco-German Relations, the Eurozone Crisis and the Politics of Austerity'. *French Politics*, 12 (2): 136–63.

Escalona, F. and Vieira, M. (2012). 'La social-démocratie des idépôles'. In J.-M. De Waele and M. Vieira (eds), *Une droitisation de la classe ouvrière en Europe?* Paris: Economica: 121–41.

Escalona, F. and Vieira, M. (2013). 'France'. In J.-M. De Waele, F. Escalona and M. Vieira (eds), *The Palgrave Handbook of Social Democracy in the European Union*. Houndmills, Basingstoke: Palgrave Macmillan: 127–62.

—— (2014). 'It Didn't Happen Here Either: Why Social Democrats Fail in the Context of the Great Economic Crisis'. In D. Bailey, J.-M. De Waele, F. Escalona and M. Vieira (eds), *European Social Democracy During the Global Economic Crisis*. Manchester: Manchester University Press: 19–41.

—— (2016, forthcoming). 'The French Radical Left: Business as Usual Rather than *le Grand Soir*?'. In D. Keith and L. March (eds), *Europe's Radical Left: From Marginality to the Mainstream?* Lanham: Rowman & Littlefield.

Fontaine, M. (2013). 'La République est ouverte à toutes les classes sociales'. In M. Fontaine, F. Monerand and C. Prochasson (eds), *Une contre-histoire de la IIIe République*. Paris: Editions La Découverte: 150–62.

Front de gauche (2012). *L'humain d'abord. Le programme du Front de Gauche et de son candidat commun Jean-Luc Mélenchon*.

Gougou, F. and Martin, P. (2014). 'Gauche, droite et vote populaire'. *Commentaire*, 145: 45–54.

Grunberg, G. (1996). 'Existe-t-il un socialisme de l'Europe du Sud ?'. In M. Lazar (ed.), *La Gauche en Europe après 1945*. Paris: PUF: 477–512.

Hall, P. (1987). 'The Evolution of Economic Policy under Mitterrand'. In G. Ross, S. Hoffmann and S. Malzacher (eds), *The Mitterrand Experiment: Continuity and Change in Modern France*. Cambridge: Polity Press: 54–72.

Husson, M. (2012). 'France: baisse de régime. Les salaires sur longue période'. *La revue de l'IRES*, 73 (2): 237–69.

—— (2014). 'Ce que pourrait être une politique économique de gauche'. *L'économie politique*, 63: 77–85.

Jenson, J. and Ross, G. (1988). 'The Tragedy of the French Left'. *New Left Review*, I/171: 5–44.

Juhem, P. (2006). 'La production notabiliaire du militantisme au Parti socialiste'. *Revue française de science politique*, 56 (6): 909–41.

Kesselman, M. (1984). 'Dilemmas of Socialist Transition in France: Modernizing the Republic versus Democratic Socialist Transition'. *Insurgent Sociologist*, 12 (1/2): 71–82.

Lavelle, A. (2008). *The Death of Social Democracy*. Aldershot: Ashgate.

Lefebvre, R. and Sawicki, F. (2006). *La société des socialistes*. Bellecombe: Editions du Croquant.

Levy, J. (2008). 'From the Dirigiste State to the Social Anaesthesia State: French Economic Policy in the Longue Durée'. *Modern & Contemporary France*, 16 (4): 417–35.

Lordon, F. (1998). 'The Logic and Limits of désinflation compétitive'. *Oxford Review of Economic Policy*, 14 (1): 96–113.

Morin, G. (2007). 'Les socialistes et la société française. Réseaux et milieux (1905–1981)'. *Vingtième siècle*, 96: 47–62.

Nachtwey, O. (2013). 'Market Social Democracy: The Transformation of the SPD up to 2007'. *German Politics*, 22 (3): 235–52.

Notermans, T. (2000). *Money, Markets, and the State: Social Democratic Economic Policies since 1918*. Cambridge: Cambridge University Press.

OFCE (2014). *L'économie française 2015*. Paris: Editions La Découverte.

Parti socialiste (2008). *Déclaration de principes*.

Piketty, T. (2001). *Les hauts revenus en France au XXème siècle*. Paris: Editions Grasset et Fasquelle.

Quatrepoint, J.-M. (2013). 'Comment la France a perdu la guerre monétaire'. *Le Débat*, 174: 10–25.

Ross, G. (1995). 'The Two Bankruptcies of French Socialism and the End of Social Democracy'. In J.-P. Beaud and J.-G. Prévost (eds), *La social-démocratie en cette fin de siècle*. Sainte-Foy: Presses de l'Université du Québec: 9–42.

Théret, B. (2013). 'Dettes et crise de confiance dans l'euro: analyse et voies possibles de sortie par le haut'. *Revue française de socio-économie*, 12 (2): 91–124.

Tiberj, V. (2012). 'La politique des deux axes'. *Revue française de science politique*, 62 (1): 71–106.

3

Social Democracy in Norway

Knut Kjeldstadli and Idar Helle

Founded in 1887, Arbeiderpartiet (AP), the Norwegian labour party, followed a winding road.[1] Six distinct turns can be discerned: (1) classical social democracy in its formative years (1887 to 1910); (2) radicalization (1910 to the early 1930s); (3) new reformism (1930s to 1949); (4) social democratic capitalism with a humane face (1950 to the 1980s); (5) a trend towards neoliberalism (1980s to 2001); and (6) consolidation and a red-green project (2002 to 2013).

EARLY YEARS: REFORM, REVOLUTION AND NEW REFORMISM

Let us make some introductory remarks on the three periods until 1949, the remaining three are the subject matter of this chapter.

Arbeiderpartiet was established in 1887 as a political force *within* the existing society. After getting its three first representatives elected in 1903, the party had a breakthrough in 1906 winning 16 per cent of the votes. The party was closely linked to the unions, so the development of industrial relations also illuminates the political character of the party. In a collective agreement in the mechanical industry in 1907, the unions swapped the owners' right to lead the firm for the recognition of the right to unionize and union representation.

From approximately 1910, a process of radicalization took place. The movement looked forward to creating a 'new world', not just carving out a piece of the existing bourgeois society. In 1920, in the union movement, a radical faction reached the majority within the National Trade Union Congress, the Arbeidernes Faglige Landsorganisasjon (AFL, the workers' national trade union organization, abbreviated to LO, Landsorganisasjonen i Norge, in 1957). These radicals demanded a much more militant practice. Industrial action was also seen as an essential part of the 'semi-syndicalist' strategy for power favoured by the radical faction in the party, who had gained the majority in 1918. For a short while (1919 to 1923) the Arbeiderpartiet was a member of the Communist International (Comintern). This was due to a mix of admiration for the

Russian revolution and a misunderstanding. Arbeiderpartiet was a mass party built to a large extent on the unions, but was never a Leninist elite party. The classical social democrats seceded in 1921, and then joined the ranks again in 1927. The communist party Norges Kommunistiske Parti (NKP) was founded in 1923 at the time Arbeiderpartiet left the Comintern. From 1915 until 1930 Arbeiderpartiet and these two splinter groups pulled well above 30 per cent in parliamentary elections.

The economic crises of the 1920s and early 1930s undermined Arbeiderpartiet's strategy for gaining power through industrial action, strikes were no longer effective during times of mass unemployment. At the same time, crisis-stricken small peasants threatened by debt flocked around Arbeiderpartiet, increasing its parliamentarian strength. A deep-felt need for immediate solutions induced a Keynesian crisis policy bent on 'getting the wheels rolling' here and now. In addition to ameliorating the situation for the popular classes, the purpose was to keep fascist groups from finding fertile ground among unemployed youth (Maurseth, 1987).

In 1935 the labour movement entered into a double class compromise: *Hovedavtalen*, a general agreement later nicknamed the 'constitution of working life', was signed by the employers' union and AFL, the Norwegian union federation. The agreement institutionalized class cooperation and 'regulated' class struggle. Secondly, a 'crisis agreement' with the agrarian party opened the way for Arbeiderpartiet to gain governmental power under Prime Minister Johan Nygaardsvold, a former saw mill, agriculture and railway worker. In the 1930s Arbeiderpartiet pulled roughly 40 per cent of the voters, in the 1950s this increased to close to 50 per cent. The party remained in power from 1935 to 1965, including while in exile in London during the war, except for a short interlude in 1963. Union density rose accordingly. The initial political programme of the period from 1933 to 1949 was reminiscent of some aspects of classical social democracy, with reformism and legalism as the means, and socialism and public ownership of key economic institutions as the goal – in the future. Then in 1949 the goal shifted from socialism as a specific kind of society, to socialism conceived as a set of more abstract values that might be realized within 'a capitalism with a humane face'. More attention was paid to increasing production, and unions should not primarily ask for a bigger share of the cake, but contribute to 'bake a bigger cake' (Bergh, 1990).

THE SOCIAL DEMOCRATIC VARIETY OF CAPITALISM

When social democracy came to power in Scandinavia in the 1930s, the aim was to abolish unemployment, poverty and unbearable social inequalities. The means to do so was the Scandinavian model of society (Moene, 2015: 225). The model built upon institutionalized class collaboration, and had obvious positive effects. In Norwegian terms, this concept of an authentic 'social democratic order' of society, coined by the socialist politician and historian Berge Furre, characterized Norway from the time of restoration after World War II (WWII) until 1977. He outlines the following characteristics (Furre, 1991: 248, our translation):

- a strong state with ambitions and means to plan and direct the development of society
- extensive economic transfers between social groups through the public authorities in order to further political goals such as greater social equality and regional development
- economic growth and full employment as the unifying aim for the economic life
- priority to the industrial sector, the engine of growth
- a mixed economy with an element of state-owned industry in a primarily privately owned business life
- a corporative system of negotiations with the state and organized interests as participants' 'governing' society along with the parliamentary system.

In 'the social democratic order', Furre also included extensive market regulation in fields such as agriculture, fisheries, reindeer nomadism and public land transport, and furthermore a welfare state with free and universal access to health care and education, and state responsibility for cultural institutions, such as broadcasting. Summing up, he said, '[t]he social democratic order was both a visionary political project, a hegemonic societal ideology, the "grand narrative" of the post-war period about itself' (Furre, 1991: 248–53). This idea of a social democratic order is related to, but not identical to, theoretical concepts such as Fordism (Aglietta), 'organized capitalism' (Scott and Ury), 'managed capitalism' (Fulcher) and 'social corporatism' (Schmitter).

The fact that governments led by Arbeiderpartiet and a stable social democratic order lasted for a generation beg the question: 'What were the causes of this long-lasting period of social democratic order?' Several factors are relevant.

'The hard thirties' and a fairly effective crisis policy during the 1930s had left a legacy in people's collective memory. Arbeiderpartiet was seen as the trustworthy alternative when it came to jobs and social security. After WWII, the population enjoyed a welfare state, including the introduction of a general pension system (*Folketrygden*) in 1967. Arbeiderpartiet managed to take the credit for this, and a positive attitude to social benefits was fairly common amongst various political parties including in other Western European countries. Underneath was a production regime with a 'Fordist' character: serial and batch production and corresponding mass consumption. As a curiosity, 'Standard' was the name of a well-known Norwegian shoe factory. Internationally, the Bretton Woods system gave a certain stability. The 'standard worker' in Fordism – usually a male industrial or manual worker, working full time and enjoying a high degree of job security – associated his good position with the unions and the labour movement in general. Labour also managed to keep the support, developed between the wars, of small peasants and agricultural and forest workers. And the party also made inroads into some groups of the salaried middle class, in particular those in public employment. Finally, the competitors presented no real challenge. The efforts to form a 'bourgeois cooperation' were feeble. And the social democrats' handling of the challenge from groups to the left was heavy-handed and effective. Their methods included cooperation with police surveillance, harsh organizational methods and a branding of communists and other leftists as more or less illegitimate (the Lund Commission report, 1996).

REGIONAL POLITICAL CULTURES

There are also other reasons why Arbeiderpartiet could remain strong: Norwegian politics have been characterized by very strong regional variations (Hagtvet, 1987; Øidne, 1957). This is also the case with Arbeiderpartiet. It has to some extent shown an ability to adapt to various regional cultures, and has thereby gained political and electoral access in all parts of the country. This has brought great strength to social democracy in Norway, and generally in all of Scandinavia.[2] Still, there are large regional differences in the strength of support for Arbeiderpartiet and the labour movement, showing a pattern that has remained remarkably stable for almost a full century.

When the social democrats broke through, first as a local and then as a national political force, in the first decades of the twentieth century, they were already based upon two clearly separate social segments of the population. As in most Northern European countries, the social democratic party profited from the disciplined building-up of an army of organized labour. This 'army' was concentrated in the bigger cities of Oslo (eastern region), Drammen (eastern region), Bergen (western region) and Trondheim (mid region).

At the same time, the party experienced surprisingly strong support from certain rural areas in the far north. Here fishermen and small farmers lived under suppressed conditions set by local economic big men who wielded an almost feudal power. In 1903, the first parliamentary representatives of Arbeiderpartiet came from this area.

These early regional successes were followed by others. Through the work of travelling agitators and party newspapers such as *Social-Demokraten*, Arbeiderpartiet was able to build local organizations and strong support amongst the road and railroad construction workers, and amongst the new industrial workers in the smelters and factories along the coast from ca. 1905 onwards. After WWI the rural proletariat of forest workers and marginalized small farmers in the inland regions of Østlandet and Trøndelag also joined the party in large numbers. By 1930, Arbeiderpartiet had established itself as the number one party on a national basis, backed by four out of ten voters.

Two neighbouring regions, however, remained apart from the social democratic hegemony. The southern and the western regions continued to express strong support for the smaller parties in the political centre – Venstre (the social liberal party), Senterpartiet (the agrarian party) and Kristelig Folkeparti (the Christian Protestant party). In the 1980s, the southern and western parts turned significantly to the right in the political landscape, favouring Høyre (the conservative party) and Fremskrittspartet (the populist right party).

The reasons for this southwestern exceptionalism in Norwegian political history are a matter of controversy. But two points may be made. (1) The two southern and western regions were, even by Norwegian standards, less marked by economic and social inequality than the capital city, the rural inlands and the high north. (2) When the breakthrough for the labour movement came after 1900, these two regions, and especially the more populated western region, were already strongly influenced by the strong counter cultures against the establishment in the capital of Oslo. These counter cultures had different bases: Christian Protestant lay-religion, the question of what should be considered as the genuine Norwegian language, and teetotallers working for legislation against alcohol. To some extent, the lower classes had already been won over by these counter cultures when unions and socialists arrived on the scene. So, in these districts the labour movement remained a pure workers' movement, it never succeeded in reaching out to small independent peasants and fishermen.

WOMEN AND THE UNIVERSAL WELFARE STATE

From the 1970s, the strengths of Norwegian social democracy gained another vital source. Norway is often portrayed as one of the most generous and universal welfare state regimes in the Organisation for Economic Co-operation and Development (OECD) area (Sørvoll, 2015). The broad and universal character of public services and social security has been considered a common good by most of the population. However, there is somewhat of a consensus, also among left-wing feminists, that the Norwegian welfare state has been especially successful in improving the conditions of women in paid work. The reasons for this are that public services, such as as child care, the school system, health care and homes for the elderly, have made it more convenient and attractive for women to seek full-time work and at the same time be able to take care of family life and the prospects of children. Thousands of women have found paid work exactly in these sectors. For decades this has contributed to a favourable labour market for many women, a labour market also characterized by a relatively high level of salary compression compared to most countries in the OECD area (Moene, 2015).

Most political parties, perhaps with the exception of the populist right and traditionally male-biased Fremskrittspartiet, have vigorously tried to appeal to female voters on these social policy issues. In the electorate, however, it is Arbeiderpartiet and to a lesser degree the socialist left party, Sosialistisk Venstreparti (SV), that are perceived as the drivers and architects of this universal welfare system that has brought social progress to large groups of women in Norway. Two political highlights in this development were the Act on gender equality (1978) and some years later the 'women government' (1986) of Gro Harlem Brundtland and Arbeiderpartiet, in which 8 out 18 ministers of government were women. In this respect, the efforts of social democracy and the left have been rewarded. Among female voters, the support of Arbeiderpartiet and SV is between 10 to 20 percentage points higher than among men (Aardal et al., 2014: 21). The social democrats are often portrayed not primarily as a workers' party anymore but as a party of the middle classes or the public sector. This may be so, but more significant is probably the success of the social democrats among working women.

POPULAR MOVEMENT AND GOVERNMENTAL APPARATUS

A process of 'institutionalization' had already occurred in Arbeiderpartiet before WWII (Heidar, 1977). Monetary contributions from the unions secured a more spacious financial position for the party. The number of party and trade union officials grew. More people from the unions were recruited to party posts or as congress delegates. A lifelong career employed in the labour movement was within reach. Increased political clout opened the way for Arbeiderpartiet's politicians to municipal and other public posts. It might have been dubbed an apparatus for governance. As Bertolt Brecht once asked about another apparatus: 'What is the party? A house with many telephones?'

Yet, the party was more. Its most striking characteristic was its duality – an apparatus *and* a popular movement (Keul and Kjeldstadli, 1973). This double heritage was visible into the 1970s. On the one hand, its apparatus character became more evident. Participants at party conventions were recruited to a large extent from the apparatus. Young activists in the youth organization spoke about their future political engagement as 'becoming politicians'. Many were recruited as 'political broilers'. They had no ordinary job, but were groomed to make a career solely within politics. To some extent, societal elites joined the party or, more often, the movement functioned as a career ladder. Having been a junior minister in a government of Arbeiderpartiet was definitely not a drawback in job applications. In fact, a labour market developed where party and union officials and representatives circulated into the government staff or the ministries, going on to relatively important jobs in private corporations, and then sometimes coming back as top politicians.

Norway has been marked by a societal corporatism, a tripartite system, uniting state, capital and unions (Furre, 1991). In a way, the system is replicated within the labour movement itself. All of the first five prime ministers of Arbeiderpartiet had been manual workers. The last of them was Trygve Bratteli, who resigned as prime minister in 1976 at a time when the classic industrial working class base had begun to shrink after its peak in 1974. Labour, and other, politicians were increasingly recruited from the ranks of professionals, 'broilers' and academics, in particular economists.

On the other hand, Norwegian social democracy has shown a remarkable resilience and is still popular. Over and over the 'crisis' or even 'death' of social democracy has been proclaimed. From the top level of 48.5 per cent of the votes in 1957, the share has decreased to an average of between 30 and 35 per cent after 2000. Still, Arbeiderpartiet is by far the largest party in Norway. Thousands of members contribute in the election campaigns. Union density reached a peak with 57 per cent in 1995. Even though there has been a considerable decrease in the private sector, LO and the other confederations have been able to keep the union density rate slightly above 50 per cent of the workforce.

FOREIGN POLICY AND THE EUROPEAN UNION QUESTION

One key to understanding Arbeiderpartiet's approach to foreign policy is the link to the USA. All the way back to the tough debate on North

Atlantic Treaty Organization (NATO) membership in 1949, there exists a premise that the USA shall come to the rescue in any case of conflict or war. In order to secure this support, Norway has to prove its loyalty, time and again. For example, in 1975 it was revealed that the navigation systems Omega and Loran C were not for civil purposes but designed for serving American nuclear submarines. Arbeiderpartiet rallied in defence of the instalment of these systems, and even threatened two socialist left MPs with impeachment. Also, in 1979, strife developed over the NATO double-track decision to deploy middle range missiles in Europe while at the same time saying that this deployment might be reversed if the Soviet Union withdrew its SS20 missiles from Eastern Europe. Broad criticism of NATO manifested itself over this issue, not only on the socialist left but also within Arbeiderpartiet. Many had qualms. Yet, when it came to a vote within NATO in December 1979 the Arbeiderpartiet government followed the USA (Rasmussen, 2015). In later years Norway followed the US military into Yugoslavia, Afghanistan and, as army councillors, Iraq. In Libya 2011, Norwegian bombers were in the front in an operation under European leadership. These close ties to the USA and European Union (EU) have led the Arbeiderpartiet government to take positions that were decided outside Norway. If Norway were outside these alliances, it might perhaps have chosen differently with respect to the boycott against Russia during the conflict in Ukraine (2014–15). Some deviances may be traced, however. In 2003, Norway under the centre-right Bondevik government, backed by Arbeiderpartiet, chose not to join the US-British invasion forces in Iraq. In 2005, the red-green government acknowledged the Hamas authorities in parts of Palestinian territory (Gaza).

While Norway and its dominant party are super-normal, so to speak, with respect to NATO, there is a deviation when it comes to EU membership. In his works of political sociology, Stein Rokkan underlined a set of political cleavages that in his view had dominated the societies in Western Europe up until the mid twentieth century: political centre versus periphery; religion; urban versus rural interests; and finally, from the industrial age, the question of social class (Rokkan, 1987). Several of these cleavages play an important role in the broad social mobilization and coalition building around the referendum on the membership in the European Community (EC) (1972) and then on the EU (1994).

For a contemporary observer of Cold War politics in Europe, the Norwegian no-vote in 1972 must have been regarded as against all odds. In the original six EC countries, there were political forces both on the left and the right that were against the Treaty of Rome (1957) and the foundation of the Common Market. However, they were not able to connect and build sustainable alliances with social groups and economic interests that could turn the tables against the elite project of European economic integration. If we look at the labour movement for benchmarking, up until the mid 1970s, mighty union confederations like the Confédération Générale du Travail (CGT) in France, the Confederazione Generale Italiana del Lavoro (CGIL) in Italy and the Trades Union Congress (TUC) in the UK were more critical of the EC politics than the top level of LO and the Norwegian labour movement. However, the labour unions in those countries were not part of any broad centre to left alliances that were strong enough to challenge the supporters of further economic integration. In Norway the situation was quite different. The 'No to EC' movement could mobilize along several of the axes mentioned by Rokkan. Especially important were the alliances between the parties and youth parties on the left, important trade unions and farmers' organizations, and the economically important agricultural-industrial complex (Seierstad, 2014).

How was the EU membership question conceived inside Arbeiderpartiet and Norwegian social democracy? Both in 1972 and 1994 the party leadership followed the general line of the social democratic parties in the Socialist International, recommending Norwegian membership in the EU. But, among the labour unions and the working class voters of the party there existed a strong resistance against membership. In 1972, left-wing members of Arbeiderpartiet set up an information committee against membership. Many people from this internal opposition group left the party after the national referendum on this issue. A majority of the anti-EU committee activists joined a leftist socialist electoral alliance (SV).

Leading up to the second referendum of 1994 there was, quite surprisingly, a very narrow 'no' vote by the membership at an extraordinary LO congress called to deal with this question. However, this time the opposition against EU membership was not used as a tool to break away from Arbeiderpartiet as had happened in 1972. The union apparatus and the organizers behind the ad hoc organization, 'Social Democrats Against EU' were very careful to keep the EU membership battle within boundaries that wouldn't break the unity of the party and the social democratic movement (Kallset, 2009).

As the majority of Norwegian voters said no to EC membership in the 1972 referendum, a gale of radicalization swept the political landscape. In the ensuing parliamentary election, Arbeiderpartiet was the big loser. The left-wing electoral alliance constructed by the socialist people's party, the Moscow communists, the radical anti-EU activists among the social democrats and independent socialists did well, with 11.2 per cent of the votes. Many former labour voters punished the Arbeiderpartiet for its pro-EC stance and for a political campaign that had been tough and authoritarian by Norwegian standards. In the 1973 election, Arbeiderpartiet drew only 35 per cent of the votes, its worst result since 1930.

In order to regain terrain, the remaining 1970s were the days of fairly progressive and sometimes even radical policies. Arbeiderpartiet deliberately tried to reconquer the electors lost to the socialist left party through a tactical swing to the left. Among other measures the government secured a progressive Work Protection Act in 1977. The law demanded a sound work environment and had paragraphs on reduced work hours, on strengthened protection against getting unconditionally sacked and on the right to be off if ill or giving birth (Bergh, 2009).

Another issue that could have continued the trend towards progressive positions was the question about industrial democracy in 1980. Instead, the fate of this question can be seen as a definite turn away from the progressive 1970s. A joint committee of Arbeiderpartiet and LO, led by metal workers' union chairman Lars Skytøen, proposed that workers should have half of the seats on the executive boards and company assemblies *(bedriftsforsamlinger)* in all share-owned companies with more than 150 employees. In case of parity of votes on a certain decision, the chairman elected by the shareholders should have a double vote (Bergh, 2009: 239).

The proposal from the Skytøen committee was considered a radical shift towards increased strategic power to workers and organized labour. The proposal had its roots in traditional socialist claims by the labour movement, particularly with backing from the metal workers, a union that remained the strongest of the federations in the LO (Bergh, 2009: 239). The proposal was seen as a continuation of the progressive reforms of the decade after 1968 that were already accomplished, i.e. the law on workers' representation on company boards (1971), the Work Protection Act (1977) and favourable wage raise agreements throughout the 1970s.

As time went by, the proposal on industrial democracy turned out to be a dead end. The new Arbeiderpartiet government with Gro Harlem Brundtland as prime minister took the proposals off the table for good. The idea of extended power to workers was contrary to the new line of Harlem Brundtland, which sought a more business friendly balance of power in industrial relations. The Skytøen proposal was a last battle cry of the progressive decade after 1968, but it came too late. In Norwegian social democracy there was no longer the common will to pick up the fight for extended industrial democracy and a society where capitalism met clear and immediate political and democratic boundaries.

ON THE ROAD TOWARDS NEOLIBERALISM (1981 TO 2001)

The left swing of social democracy in Norway was abandoned from 1981 and onwards. 'The fight against mass unemployment was in many ways a fight against Gro and her inner circle' (Bergh, 2009: 332). This quote from the LO leader Yngve Haagensen on three times prime minister and party leader Gro Harlem Brundtland goes to the core of the change in relations between Norwegian social democracy and the trade union movement in the 1980s and 1990s.

When Arbeiderpartiet in 1986 returned to power after five years in opposition, it soon became apparent that when it came to economic policy the party leadership was willing to leave the commitments to full employment and workers' interests behind. The following Brundtland governments (1986–89 and 1990–96) had economic austerity as their main focus. The point of departure was the economic havoc created by the conservative government (1981–86), leaving in its wake massive trade deficits and crisis-prone financial markets. Prime Minister Gro Harlem Brundtland and the Arbeiderpartiet government pushed through drastic means to stabilize the economy and regain competitive performance. Brundtland, educated as a medical doctor, and her inner circle, did not share union concerns about the austerity effects on the labour market.

The new austerity politics had four steps, all of them with social consequences for the working classes: (1) a 12 per cent devaluation of the Norwegian *krone* (crown); (2) a steep rise in interest rates, 5 to 7 percentage points on the population's mortgages and credit loans; (3) substantial cuts in public budgets; and (4) a tripartite pact with unions and employers to avoid wage growth (Eilertsen, 1997). One or maybe two of these four harsh austerity measures could arguably have worked out well. However, four such measures simultaneously ended in an economic cool-down comparable to that of Euro member states after 2008. For the first time since 1945 Norway had a negative growth rate several years in a row. To the organized working classes and the electoral base of the Arbeiderpartiet, the most critical point was the immense growth in unemployment. From 1986 to 1993 the number of unemployed workers increased from 40,000 to 160,000. In the worst year, 1993, there were nearly 7 per cent unemployed in Norway (just 2 per cent below the EU and OECD level at the same time). What had not been considered possible had happened: mass unemployment was back in the Norwegian labour market, and it had amazingly been brought back due to the politics of Prime Minister Brundtland and with the social democrats in government.

As one can easily see, there have been reasons for alienation between the party and its base. Efforts have been made from time to time to engage broader strata in the party and to encourage unions to send in proposals for the programme, or participate in ideological issues, such as a staged debate on 'freedom' in 1985 to 1989, stressing individual choices more than security through collective arrangements, in a somewhat liberalist fashion. The aim being to rid the party of its image as a state-based regulation and control party. How much impact such organized debates have on the party is an open question. This sending of papers for a hearing, this 'hearocracy', does not amount to real democracy, critics have said. The leadership may pick out some ideas from among the suggestions, but the process does not lead to any decisive conclusion. Conclusions are drawn from within an oligarchy, by a kind of professional aristocracy.

Yet, despite the obvious mistakes of too harsh austerity politics during the Brundtland years 1986 to 1996, these years forged the political legacy that is associated with the social democratic labour movement today, 20 years later. A steady economic policy and responsiveness to financial markets have more and more become the trademark of Arbeiderpartiet. The party leaders after Gro Harlem Brundtland also followed this line. Together with LO and the strong trade union movement, the social democratic party has worked to avoid inflation and too high wage raises during the long boom period in the petroleum sector from the end of the 1990s until 2014. In this quite long prosperous conjuncture there was economic stability. The Norwegian state built up the world's largest financial fund based on petroleum income. This fund has lubricated the economy. Norway has so far (2016) not had to resort to real austerity measures. This constitutes a large part of the explanation of why Arbeiderpartiet has maintained much of its political capital in the same period as social democratic parties all over Europe have lost the grip on their own core principles as well as losing many of their voters.

Nonetheless, from the mid 1990s a protracted silent civil war was taking place in the central circle of the party. There was a sharp competition for the party leadership between Thorbjørn Jagland, the present general secretary in the Council of Europe, and Jens Stoltenberg, the present general secretary of NATO. Jagland is the son of a local party secretary and close to the LO leadership. Stoltenberg is the heir of a previous foreign minister. He finally won the battle and ousted Jagland as prime minister in 2000 and chairman of the party in 2002. Jagland had some unfortunate last years as party leader and prime minister (1996 to 1997). His defeat can partly be explained by his unpopularity in the media and among elite groups in the capital. They strongly favoured the aristocratic style and neoliberal politics of Stoltenberg. The first Arbeiderpartiet government of Jens Stoltenberg in 2000–01 was staffed with four corporation managers as ministers.

Among trade unionists and party members there was a rising feeling that the party had left them. Many voters left the party. The 2001 parliamentary election was catastrophic with only 24.4 per cent going to the social democrats. The old ambition of controlling capital had become weak. The 2001 convention went for a partial privatization of mainstays in the Norwegian economy, the publicly owned oil company, Statoil and Telenor, a publicly owned telecommunications giant.

Why did this swing to the right occur? There were obviously structural limitations; the problems of 'socialism in one country' are not only a Trotskyite worry. The frames for a more progressive policy were not wide. One very important limitation on Norwegian policies today is the treaty on the European Economic Area (EEA) with the EU.[3] Through this treaty Norway is bound to comply with the fundamental principles of the EU, the rigorously understood free movement of products, services, capital and labour combined with the non-discriminatory right of establishment and economic policies leading to the fiercest possible competition through deregulation and privatization. The leadership of Arbeiderpartiet has since the days of Gro Harlem Brundtland been the main architect of the EEA as a hegemonic political arrangement in Norwegian politics. It has somewhat gloomily been said – and exaggerated – that in 1994 the opponents of the EU won the referendum, but lost every day since.

Yet, there are also other answers to why the Arbeiderpartiet has chosen a capital-affirmative policy. Some factors may be noted. The swing to the right is partly due to general global ideological conjunctures. Some critics on the left see Arbeiderpartiet as being permeated by neoliberalism (Nilsen and Østerberg, 1998). This is not untrue, but maybe a somewhat unbalanced evaluation. Even Jens Stoltenberg's policies differed from the road of Tony Blair and Gerhard Schröder. Also, Norway's class structure has changed. Labour strategists have offered different solutions, one being the tactic of steering for the centre of politics, trying to capture voters from the conservatives and liberals.

Probably the structural changes in society, an emerging new class structure, are most important. Middle strata have risen. Arbeiderpartiet and the LO first noted this rise of these categories with trepidation (Messel, 2009). On the left wing of the party, it was stressed that at least those who were publicly employed did not show a less solidaristic attitude. In fact, they were the main supporters of the welfare state as ideal principles and self-interest joined hands. However, the new service proletariat has not been reached by the unions, these people think that their place in 'the burger proletariat' is only temporary. In depth, the unions have not acknowledged that these groups are vital parts of the new working class.

There has also been a transformation within social democracy itself. The party came to contain a faction that might be called a new bourgeoisie or aristocracy connected to state capitalist and semi-privatized enterprises. There is a clear element of self-interest for this new bourgeoisie. After privatizations, managers of these enterprises have reaped substantially bigger salaries, bonuses and fringe benefits etc. These milieus were particularly open to influences from general global ideological conjunctures.

Another possible explanation for the swing to the right stresses changes in the party organization. It has been weakened, and it has been bureaucratized. The Arbeiderpartiet was once dubbed the 'eagle among Norwegian parties', now 'the eagle has landed', according to a book title by a previous party chairman (Steen, 2003). The labour party has become more similar to the other main parties, like one big crow among others.

THE RISE AND FALL OF THE RED-GREEN ALLIANCE (2001 TO 2015)

The electoral catastrophe in 2001, with only 24.3 per cent of the vote for Arbeiderpartiet, provoked a certain reorientation within the social democratic party. One lesson learned was the need to avoid the alienation of the unions. The party's ties to the unions had not been severed, but were somewhat worn out. There are closer connections between party and unions in Norway than, for instance, in Denmark or during the Blair years in Britain. At the convention in 2005 the party secretary, Martin Kolberg, hammered home the message on allies: 'The Unions! The Unions! The Unions!' He could draw on a long party tradition, going back to the origins of the party and the union confederation late in the nineteenth century. Despite its neoliberal tendencies at this point, the party kept formal connections to the unions. After the defeat in 2001 Arbeiderpartiet did not go down the 'third way' of Tony Blair and Gerhard Schröder. Party chairman Jens Stoltenberg seemed to have picked up the message, and kept a different course during his two next administrations.

Old habits die hard. The self-image of the labour party as the 'natural' party of the state blocked the option of government coalition with other parties for years. Yet, the election results from the 1980s onwards demonstrated clearly that the era of the one dominant party was over. The option of a minority government backed either by the centrist parties (liberals, agrarians or the Christian people's party) and/or by the socialist left party, or of a coalition, had been voiced from time to time, including by party leaders, since 1973. But after the electoral defeat in 2001, this solution gained additional weight as the LO leader Gerd-Liv Valla actively worked for it (Bergh, 2009).

A kind a red-green alliance was active in the two EU referendum campaigns in 1972 and 1994. Left-leaning unions and agricultural organizations joined hands on both occasions. Although the social democratic leadership opposed this alliance, it may have left a legacy, making grass-roots members positively inclined to this cross-class coalition. In 2005 a new red-green cooperation developed, and now it also involved the social democrats. A three-party governmental alliance was forged. This included Arbeiderpartiet, the socialist left party and the primarily agrarian and rural Senterpartiet. And it carried the day; the election was a victory. Arbeiderpartiet won 61 of 169 seats, socialist left party 15 and Senterpartiet 11. Together, they drew 48 per cent of the votes. The government issued a declaration on policy that was probably the most progressive, left social democratic platform of any government in contemporary Europe. However, this progressive spirit was most apparent in the beginning. Amongst the genuine victories – from a left perspective – were the repeal of privatization of public postal services and of the permission to start a large number of private schools that had been on the brink of being pushed through by the previous centre-right government Also, changes to the Work Protection Act detrimental to wage earners were stopped. Furthermore, the government delivered legislation demanded by the unions against social dumping in the labour market. Added to this, at the international level the Minister of Foreign Affairs, Jonas Gahr Støre, recognized Hamas as the legal territorial authority in Gaza after being elected by a majority of Palestinian voters.

This first four-year period, 2005–09, witnessed a certain will and ability for this coalition to make policy changes. However, signs of wear started to appear. The progressive platform was only one condition for pushing Norwegian social democracy to the left. Another condition was not met; a fairly strong electoral base for the left; 8.8 per cent for the socialist left party in the election in September 2005 was disappointing compared to spring opinion polls that had shown around 20 per cent. A third basis for radical strength also crumbled: in 2005, unions and solidarity organizations declared their support for the red-greens. After the victory a feeling of 'having done the job' spread, the movements became passive and hesitant. Well installed in the corridors of power, the Stoltenberg government was neither willing nor able to work closely with the unions and other popular organizations.

Come the 2009 parliamentary election, the drive in the government to make progressive change seemed exhausted. Although the coalition won once more, this was due to representation rules, not to a numerical majority among the electors. The movements were no longer invited in as part of a 'team' for societal change. The successes that did come did not form a part of a more ambitious strategy. There was social policy, but no progressive societal policy. There were reforms, but no structural reforms, that is, measures changing the power relations between labour and capital, or between democratically elected bodies and market forces. There was in fact no debate about such changes in governmental circles at all. The social democratic vision may reach to the defence of a (maybe privately contracted) welfare state, but not to a vision for another kind of society.

In particular, the socialist left party was hit by this situation. The percentage of voters fell to 6.2 in 2009 and to 4.1 in 2013. This was just above the election threshold securing extra mandates.[4] Such a decline may, of course, be the result of several contingent factors. However, it is most probably caused by the one lasting structural condition – the socialist left party being a junior partner in a government ruled by a much bigger party that was not without the arrogance of power. The socialist left party never found a workable formula for tackling this problem – if such a formula actually does exist. The electoral and political fate of the French communist party in the Mitterand government, of the previous radical ambitions of the German greens in coalition with the German social democratic party, SPD, and of the Danish socialist people's party in government with the social democrats testify to this difficulty.

As the support for the socialist left party dwindled, after two periods in government, Jens Stoltenberg was offered the job as NATO general secretary. His successor as Arbeiderpartiet leader, Jonas Gahr Støre, has clearly looked for support in other camps. Keeping parliamentary elections in 2017 in mind he has approached the centre party, the greens and the Christian people's party. Støre has even wooed the liberals, which in issues of working life have positioned themselves in an aggressive neoliberal stance to the right of even the present right-wing government, that is, the conservatives and the right-wing populists.

POSSIBLE FUTURES

The organization of Arbeiderpartiet has become more open. The social democratic tradition of internal control had a kind of proletarian discipline as a starting point. It was then forged in bitter party fights in the 1920s that left militants with a deep resistance to factions, and was strengthened during the Cold War to the point that disagreement and debate was frowned upon. The long-time Prime Minister Einar

Gerhardsen, who was party chairman from 1945 to 1965 and head of government most of the time, personified this system. His dictum, while presenting his conclusion at the start of meetings, was famous: 'Some of us have talked together.' This meant, of course, that the case had already been decided. The general radicalization of the 1970s, a new middle class and a stronger female base made this style old-fashioned. And the successors of Gerhardsen simply had to appear, and maybe really were, more open. The present party leader, Jonas Gahr Støre (2014–), had no childhood and youth years in the movement. He lacked an extensive network of his own and was in no position to resort to organizational disciplinary means.

The political profile of Jonas Gahr Støre as party leader has so far been ambiguous. He comes from a very wealthy family and attended French elite schools – at the same time he has reached out to milieus in the trade union movement. He expresses counter arguments and doubts, which can be understood as a high level of reflection, but is also portrayed as indecision. This duality is shown in both of the political fields that may become dominant – environment and climate, and in the classic class axis – between labour and capital.

The Norwegian labour movement has been heavily oriented towards industry. Smoking factory chimneys have been read as signs of increased production and welfare. After WWII industrialism supplanted socialism as Arbeiderpartiet's ideology, it has been claimed (Slagstad, 1998). From the 1970s the Norwegian social formation may be called petro-industrial. The discovery of oil in the North Sea, the development of policy where operators of oil fields had to transfer technology to Norway and the establishment of the state-owned company Statoil, were all linked to the social democrats. Directors of Statoil and oil lobbyists came from the Arbeiderpartiet, and Statoil leaders have served as ministers.

The increasing dilemma has of course been how one may reconcile oil, income, jobs and welfare, on the one side, and environmental concerns, on the other. The social democratic answers have been technical. The Stoltenberg government after 2005 promised a 'new moon landing' – an effort to purify gas. In the end it was deemed as insufficiently effective and much too costly and was closed down. Another 'solution' was much favoured by Stoltenberg (who actually wrote his economics Master's thesis on this theme) – international trade with carbon dioxide quotas. The problem is of course that the total sum is not set low enough to push down total emissions.

This technological and technocratic approach has led the greens to speak of Arbeiderpartiet as one of the 'grey' parties, no better than the two right-wing parties Høyre and Fremskrittspartiet, in government since 2013. How Arbeiderpartiet might position itself on the 'climate axis', in addition to the positions of the party on issues of social class and also migration, could determine its future.

Then there is the labour and capital axis. One important fact is that Norwegian trade unions have been able to withstand the weakening of trade union power better than unions in most other European countries. Many see a deep exceptionalism in this and hail 'the Norwegian model'. Now this rests on a premise – a strong trade union movement. A critical evaluation indicates that in the long run it will be difficult to defend trade union power in Norway and other Nordic countries without an efficient common trade union strategy confronting the neoliberal forces at the European level. There are few signs of a common trade union strategy at the European level counteracting these neoliberal forces. So, Norway may find itself exposed to the storms in the global economy. Whether the social democrats then ally themselves with popular forces or align themselves with capital, as several of their brethren in Europe have done, remains to be seen.

At the 2015 party congress, Arbeiderpartiet did put social reforms into its programme: free school lunch, and a nationwide norm for teacher density in the schools. This moderate left turn helped the social democrats look more like a clear political alternative to the present right-wing government. Arbeiderpartiet has also committed itself to a pro-union line and said that in government it will reverse the liberalization of the law on work environment.

A critique of Arbeiderpartiet from the left would be that what is missing are the structural reforms to decrease inequalities and limit the power of capital. This was also a critical point under the red-green alliance in power (2005–13). Instead, the social democratic government then continued neoliberal policies, such as turning social housing – municipal and cooperative – into commodities. Also, there has been no signs to reverse the unfortunate growth of temporary works agencies, allowed by law in 2002, which have been detrimental to the standing of the 'standard worker'. Furthermore, amongst the social democratic leadership, privatization of public services is considered only a pragmatic issue, not as a question of what is the common good and what kind of society to aspire to.

A third axis concerns immigration and its results – a multicultural society. On these matters too, Arbeiderpartiet displays a duality. On the one side, the party has hailed a moderate version of multiculturalism – wanting immigrants to integrate, not to assimilate. This relative openness has also been demonstrated in the party's links to the immigrant population. At elections, Arbeiderpartiet has been the number one choice for most immigrants (Bjørklund and Bergh, 2013). Its youth organization, Arbeiderpartiets Ungdomsfylking (AUF), is probably one of the youth organizations with the greatest success in recruiting people of minority backgrounds. The present (2016) deputy party chairman Hadia Tajik was raised in Norway by parents from Pakistan, and the present youth organization chairman Mani Hussaini has Syrian roots. This aspect of the party has triggered veritable hate from the radical right. It was no accident that the ultra right-wing, solo terrorist Anders Behring Breivik gunned down 69 participants at the social democratic youth summer camp at Utøya in 2011. He held the social democrats responsible for what he saw as an internal destruction of Norwegian society through immigration.

On the other hand, the party has advocated a quite restrictive migration policy. In 2008 the red-green government pushed through measures intended to slow down immigration. The socialist left party objected to most of them, but remained in government. In the wake of the huge migratory movements of refugees in 2015, the right-wing government imposed draconic measures in 2016. One measure is the confiscation of all valuables and money above a rather low level in order to make refugees pay for themselves. This led to sharp criticism from the left, but the leadership in Arbeiderpartiet said they agreed to such measures.

The concept of a social democratic order (Furre, 1991) aligns well with the idea of a Norwegian model. As mentioned earlier, a key dimension in this model is that industrial relations are marked by cooperative ties between labour and capital. Two other vital parts are a production system that promotes efficiency and a welfare state that maintains social security. In addition to these core elements, a long list has been suggested as typically Norwegian – such as a stable political system and high level of female participation in the formal economy. What are the chances of maintaining these social democratic core elements of the Norwegian model in the years ahead?

It is obvious that the social democratic backbone of the Norwegian model is under pressure (Dølvik et al., 2015). The research institute FAFO has calculated possible outcomes with respect to employment rates, union density and income inequality – taking the best and the worst national results and developments as alternate scenarios: 'In the worst case scenario, with income inequality continuing to increase as in Sweden and employment falling to the Finnish level, the Nordic countries as a whole in 2030 would find their levels quite close to the Europe averages of today except in relation to union density' (Dølvik et al., 2015: 147, our translation). The growing economic inequality in Norwegian society is also pointed out by the economist Kalle Moene, who brings up hard data to show that Scandinavian social democracy no longer constitutes a limit to the political and economic power of the upper classes, and, in fact, that the Scandinavian countries contain a larger upper economic class as part of the society than in the USA (Moene, 2015: 239).

When pundits comment on the future of the social democratic model, general tendencies are often mentioned – such as globalization, climate changes etc. If we try to be more specific, we may go back to the three constitutive elements of the model. Firstly, productive efficiency has been most easily obtained in commodity producing industries. Will this work also with services – or is there a limit? Secondly, large-scale migration allowing employers access to reservoirs of cheap labour invites a technological 'primitivization' process. This development has already been documented in the building and construction sector (Fri Fagbevegelse no. 09.10.2015. Internet magazine provided by LO Media). Thirdly, as to the welfare state there are signs of an upper class revolt. Interest in private schools has grown. As long as these tempted only the really rich this was in a way not a big problem. The problem comes when broader middle class strata choose the same solution. In this case, their willingness to contribute through taxes to the public schools is going to shrink.

Underlying these challenges to the social democratic model is a new phase of capitalism, a new set of industrial relations. There has been a shift from industrial capitalism to information and service capitalism and a shift from Fordism to post-Fordism with its flexible accumulation. The result is the fragmentation and dissolution of the old working classes and the subsequent rise of part-time work, temporary wage agencies and outsourcing. One victim of these changes may be union organizing. The disappearance of wage earners' power *would* pervert the positive dimensions of the Norwegian model. Trust, feelings of security and mutuality rest on power, not only on normative ties. So the big question for social democrats – and others on the left – is whether income differences, new class cleavages and the weakening of collective action put at risk the social fabric, the necessary social cohesion in society. In these decisive years ahead for Norway and the global community, is it still possible to imagine social democracy as an empowered alternative to capitalism without a human face?

NOTES

1. Founded in the southern town of Arendal in 1887 as Det Forenede norske Arbeiderparti (the United Norwegian Labour Party), the name was changed to Det norske Arbeiderparti (DNA, the Norwegian Labour Party) four years later, in 1891. That name was kept for 120 years, and through several party secessions, until the party convention in 2011, when Arbeiderpartiet (AP, the

Labour Party) became the official name of the party. Here the contemporary name Arbeiderpartiet (abbreviated AP) is used throughout the chapter.

2. There are five main regions comprising 19 counties in Norway. The eastern region Østlandet (eight counties), the southern region Sørlandet (two counties), the western region Vestlandet (four counties), the mid region Trøndelag (two counties) and the northern region Nord-Norge (three counties). The eastern region, including the capital of Oslo, has by far the highest population. More than half the Norwegian population of 5.3 million people is located in the eastern region.

3. EEA comprises the EU countries – and Norway, Iceland and Liechtenstein.

4. Most MP seats are distributed by winning seats directly in a county. To avoid skewed results a party may also get some additional and compensating seats securing that the distribution mirrors the election results. To gain such extra seats a party has to get 4.0 per cent or more of the votes.

BIBLIOGRAPHY

Aardal, B., Bergh, J. and Hennum Haugsgjerd, A. (2014). *Velgervandringer og valgdeltakelse ved stortingsvalget 2013*. Oslo: Institutt for samfunnsforskning.

Aglietti, M. (1979). *A Theory of Capitalist Regulations: The US Experience*. London: Verso.

Bergh, T. (1990). *Storhetstid (1945–1965)*. Arbeiderbevegelsens historie i Norge Volume 5. Oslo: Tiden norsk forlag.

——(2009). *Kollektiv fornuft. Volume 3 LOs historie 1969–2009*. Oslo: Pax forlag.

Bjørklund, T. and Bergh, J. (2013). *Minoritetsbefolkningens møte med det politiske Norge, Patrivalg. Valgdeltakelse. Representasjon*. Oslo: Cappelen.

Bjørnson, Ø. (1990). *Arbeiderbevegelsens historie i Norge. Volume 2. På klassekampens grunn*. Osloo: Tiden norsk forlag.

Bull, E. (1985). *Arbeiderbevegelsens historie i Norge. Volume 1. Arbeiderklassen blir til (1850–1900)*. Oslo: Tiden norsk forlag.

Dølvik, J.E., Fløtten, T., Hippe, J.M. and Jordfald, B. (2015). *The Nordic Model Towards 2030. A New Chapter*. Oslo: FAFO.

Eilertsen, R. (1997). *Moderasjonslinja – suksess for hvem?* Oslo: De Facto.

Fulcher, J. (2015). *Capitalism. A Very Short Introduction*. Oxford: Oxford University Press.

Furre, B. (1991). *Vårt hundreår. Norsk historie 1905–1990*. Oslo: Samlaget.

Hagvet, B. (ed.) (1987). *Stat, nasjon, klasse*. Oslo: Universitetsforlaget.

Heidar, K. (1977). 'The Norwegian Labour Party. Social Democracy in a Periphery of Europe'. In W.E. Paterson and A.H. Thomas (eds), *Social Democratic Parties in Western Europe*. London: Croom Helm: 299–315.

Kallset, K.-E.N. (2009). *Makta midt i mot. Kampen om EU og Arbeiderpartiets sjel*. Oslo: Forlaget Manifest.

Keul, V. and Kjeldstadli, K. (1973). 'DNA- fra folkelig bevegelse til herskerapparat'. In V. Keul and K. Kjeldstadli (eds), *DNA- fra folkebevegelse til statsstøtte*. Oslo: Pax forlag: 95–126.

Kjeldstadli, K. (2009). 'Rom for venstrepolitikk? Et Historisk perspektiv'. *Vardøger* no. 31.

Lash, S. and Urry, J. (1988). *The End of Organized Capitalism*. Madison: University of Wisconsin Press.

Lund Commission report (1996). Dokument nr. 15 (1995–96) – Rapport til Stortinget fra kommisjonen som ble nedsatt for å granske påstander om ulovlig overvåking av norske borgere. Document no. 15 (1995–96) – Report to the Storting from the commission which was appointed in order to investigate allegations of illegal surveillance of Norwegian citizens.

Maurseth, P. (1987). *Arbeiderbevegelsens historie i Norge. Volume 3. Gjennom kriser til makt (1920–1935)*. Oslo: Tiden norsk forlag.

Messel, J. (2009). *LO og 'de nye gruppene'. Konseptualisering av arbeidstakerne 1975–1989*. Oslo: University of Oslo.

Moene, K. (2015). 'Overklassen og sosialdemokratiets suksess'. In A. Holt-Jensen and S. Dyrvik (eds), *Likeverd. Grunnlaget for demokrati*. Oslo: Res Publica: 225–241.

Nilsen, H. and Østerberg, D. (1998). *Statskvinnen. Gro Harlem Brundtland og nyliberalismen*. Oslo: Aschehoug.

Nordby, T. (1994). *Korporatisme på norsk 1920–1990*. Oslo: Universitetsforlaget.

Nyhamar, J. (1990). *Nye utfordringer (1965–1990). Arbeiderbevegelsens historie i Norge*. Volume 6. Oslo: Tiden norsk forlag.

Øidne, G. (1957). 'Litt om motsetninga mellom Austlandet og Vestlandet', in Syn og Segn 3/1957.

Pryser, T. (1988). *Arbeiderbevegelsens historie i Norge, Volume 4. Klassen og nasjonen*. Oslo: Tiden norsk forlag.

Rasmussen, T. (2015). *Offentlig parlamentarisme. Politisk strid og offentlig mening*. Oslo: Pax forlag.

Rokkan, S. (1987). 'Geografi, religion og samfunnsklasse. Kryssende konfliktlinjer i norsk politikk'. In B. Hagvet (ed.), *Stat, nasjon, klasse*. Oslo: Universitetsforlaget: 111–205.

Schmitter, P.C. and Lembruch, G. (1979). *Trends Toward Corporatist Intervention*. Beverley Hills, CA: Sage.

Seierstad, D. (2014). *Folket sa nei. Norsk EU-motstand frå 1961 til i dag*. Oslo: Samlaget.

Slagstad, R. (2008). *De nasjonale strateger*. Oslo: Pax forlag.

Sørvoll, J. (2015). *The Norwegian Welfare State 2005–2015: Public Attitudes, Political Debates and Future Challenges*. Kent: University of Kent.

Steen, R. (2003). *Ørnen har landet: Om Arbeiderpartiets strateger*. Oslo: Tiden forlag.

Stokke, T.A. (2000). 'Norway'. In B. Ebbinghaus and J. Visser (eds), *Trade Unions in Western Europe since 1945*. Houndmills, Basingstoke: Palgrave Macmillan: 503–44.

Thomas, A.H. (1986). 'Social Democracy in Scandinavia: Can Dominance be Regained?'. In W.E. Paterson and A.H. Thomas (eds), *The Future of Social Democracy. Problems and Prospects of Social Democratic Parties in Western Europe*. Oxford: Clarendon Press: 172–222.

van der Linden, M. (2003). 'Metamorphoses of European Social Democracy (1870–2000)'. In *Transnational Labour History*. Aldershot: Ashgate: 95–116.

4

British Social Democracy Without the Labour Movement, 1997–2015

Max Crook

THE BASIS OF BRITISH SOCIAL DEMOCRACY

British left politics and British social democracy unlike in many other European states has been centred almost entirely on one political party, the Labour Party. All rival political parties of the left and Labour Party splinters have been quickly marginalized. The Communist Party of Great Britain (founded in 1920), the New Party (1930), the Independent Labour Party (disaffiliated in 1932), the Common Wealth Party (1942), the Socialist Labour Party (1996) and Respect (2004) have all failed to challenge the dominance of the Labour Party. Even the Social Democratic Party (1981) founded by some of the leading members of the Wilson and Callaghan governments failed to gain a permanent presence during the 1980s. This seems unlikely to change at the UK level in the near future, with the Green Party maintaining one Member of Parliament in the 2015 general election, and attracting a higher percentage of middle class former LibDem voters than working class Labour supporters in the process (GQRR, 2015; Lord Ashcroft Polls, 2015). Labour's historic dominance over the left has been driven by the First Past the Post Electoral system and the fact that the Labour Party was founded by and remained firmly connected to the labour movement. In the infamous words of interwar trade union leader Ernest Bevin, the Labour Party emerged from the 'bowels of the Trades Union Congress' (Worley, 2005: 4). Without this connection to the labour movement, Labour would, as Harold Wilson claimed, be 'uneasily poised between the Liberals and the Bow Group' (a pressure group within the Conservative Party) (Wilson, quoted in Panitch, 1979: 55). The union connection has essentially rooted Labour in the working class movement, automatically placing competitors outside it and therefore at a major disadvantage.

The British labour movement not only played a prominent role in the historic dominance of the Labour Party, it was also the key driver of the social democratic post-war consensus. During World War II the rising political and economic influence of the trade unions, and the 'changing balance of class forces' this entailed, combined with the need to maintain working class morale drove the governing parties to establish a social democratic consensus (Panitch, 1977: 76, 79). Essentially, both governing parties came to realize that political and economic success was dependent on the granting and maintaining of substantial concessions to organized labour and the working class, namely, a commitment to full employment, and an expanded welfare state. Full employment was by far the most important objective for the organized working class (Trades Union Congress, 1944: 7), and was the essential basis of the social democratic state. This is because the commitment to very low levels of unemployment created distortions in the workings of what would be (without full employment) a still relatively liberal mixed economy and eventually forced on the British state various forms of corporatism, incomes policies and state intervention designed to contain the economic consequences (in terms of inflation and economic com-petitiveness) of full employment in a society with strong trade unions. The commitment to full employment was arguably the core pillar upon which the social democratic state was established. Throughout the social democratic golden age the abandonment of full employment and ever increasing social expenditure was regarded as too risky, liable to lead to electoral losses and class conflict (Dell, 1996: 238; O'Hara, 2007: 12). Political parties that wished to remain in power would therefore in this era seek to place a high priority on maintaining full employment and high levels of state spending. Thus, social democracy was in the post-war 'golden age' based on political pragmatism in a society with a strong labour movement.

THE FALL OF THE BRITISH LABOUR MOVEMENT

Because of the centrality of the labour movement to the Labour Party and the rise of the social democratic state, it was the surprisingly rapid collapse of the trade unions that was by far the most important 'achievement' of 18 years of Conservative rule. In 1979, '13.3 million people belonged to a trade union, giving the unions a density of 55.4 per cent, the highest level ever both in terms of numbers and density achieved in Britain' (Howell, 2005: 131). The year 1979 had also seen the most working days lost in strike action since 1926, the year of the General Strike. These strikes strongly contributed to the electoral defeat of the Labour government, just over five years after the unions had played a defining role in the collapse of the Edward Heath-led Conservative government (1970-74). Therefore, in 1979 there seemed to be no doubting the strength and influence of the trade unions. But the unions, in part because of the substantial political dislocation caused by the 'Winter of Discontent' and the role this played in the collapse of the Labour government's incomes policy (and the legitimizing of a Thatcherite solution to inflation and industrial relations), were unable to resist the Thatcher government's anti-trade union laws and monetarist economic policy in the same way they had Heath's earlier attempts to pursue a more liberal economic strategy (Upchurch et al., 2009: 94). With the unions unable to force a U-turn on the Conservatives, and the electorate abandoning the Labour Party in 1983 (a defeat so substantial that any return to power in the 1980s was effectively ruled out), the organized working class was left to be decimated by unemployment and the government's anti-trade union laws. Unemployment disproportionately hit those industries where trade unions were traditionally strong. Employment in mining dropped from 235,000 to under 18,000 and in steelworks from 150,000 to 36,000 during the 18 years of Conservative rule (Dell, 1999: 547). Therefore, industries that had previously been the centre of trade union strength and trade union membership had been severely weakened if not totally destroyed during the Conservative era. These jobs were on the whole replaced by jobs in a highly polarized service sector, an area 'where unions were traditionally weakest' (Hyman, 2001: 104). By the mid 1990s there was little left of the powerful labour movement of the 1970s. This is reflected in the fact that strike levels were by then 'the lowest since records began being kept in 1891' (Howell, 2005: 131). Britain, which used to be strike prone, was now much less militant than European countries whose industrial relations were historically much more 'cooperative' and moderate (McIlroy, 2000: 14). Membership had also fallen drastically, from over 13 million in 1979 to under 8 million by 1997, and would continue to fall albeit at a slower pace under New Labour (Lindley and Machin, 2013: 174). The decline in trade unionism in terms of membership, if anything, understates the collapse in the private sector. Trade unionism in the UK has now become an increasingly professional and 'predominantly public sector phenomenon' (Daniels and McIlroy, 2009: 98). This collapse has left the British labour movement a vastly reduced but also increasingly sectional force, making it difficult for the unions to maintain the claim of being representative of the working class.

As the above shows, the decline in the collective power of the working class was dramatic and it has had an absolutely fundamental effect on British governance and British social democracy. Their declining economic and political power, and the total failure of the Labour Party to provide an effective opposition, allowed the Thatcher governments to successfully demonstrate that the abandonment of the post-war consensus and a confrontational relationship with the organized working class was in reality 'much less risky than the old Toryism had supposed' (Hobsbawm, 1983: 9). A 'return to high unemployment, regressive use of the taxation system, drastic cuts in the public services and the marginalization of the trade union movement' all proved 'no barrier to Conservative electoral success' (Bogdanor, 2007: 171). The Conservative government essentially showed that it was no longer politically necessary to maintain full employment (or indeed anything close to it) and have a close working relationship with the trade unions. Because of this, concessions to the trade unions ceased to be a vital element of the 'national interest'. Issues such as inflation and industrial competitiveness could now be dealt with through unemployment and confrontational anti-trade union laws. The destruction of the labour movement essentially made economic management and the appearance of economic competence simpler for governments, and much more in favour of capital, as the need to maintain a successful economy had ceased to be shaped and constrained by the need to maintain legitimacy with the trade unions and the working class as a class for itself. This change in power relations has inevitably reduced the influence the trade union movement or the working class can have over any government. The fact that what increasingly weak unions did or did not do was now of limited importance for the achievement of political legitimacy and successful economic management represents the most fundamental social and economy change shaping the contemporary prospects of British social democracy. Social democratic polices, such as full employment and incomes policies, had essentially been turned from the 'national interest' in the 1970s into a radical challenge to the neo-liberal economic order and prevailing class relations by the late 1990s (due to the economic and political power such policies granted labour).

NEW LABOUR IN POWER

New Labour had after 18 years of opposition completely broken with the traditional social democratic policies of 'old' Labour governments, and had generally accepted the Conservative's neo-liberal economic model. This choice was not particularly surprising for a party that had been out of power for 18 years. During this time Labour had suffered four general election defeats, the second of which was absolutely crushing and allowed blame to be apportioned on Labour's post-1979 move to the left; therefore, those that wished to move further towards the perceived centre ground had the political advantage (an advantage that was strengthened by every defeat). This was reflected in the fact that the party as a whole and the trade unions generally acquiesced to the New Labour project (McIlroy, 2009: 174), with Tony Blair gaining by far the most trade union support in the 1994 leadership election. Although this does not mean that the Labour Party had no political room for a slightly more leftist approach, particularly as it is widely believed that a John Smith-led (the Labour Party leader from 1992 until his unexpected death in 1994) Labour Party would have won in 1997, if not with a similar landslide (Stuart, 2014). Nevertheless, what Labour was offering in 1992 and 1994 was already a long way from the social democracy of the 1970s – 18 years of Conservative rule had changed British society, transforming political expectations and economic management. In this new environment any attempted return to the social democracy of the 1970s would have been regarded as almost politically unthinkable (for a Smith or Blair-led Labour Party), particularly as many policies of the era, such as incomes policies, extensive price controls and an 83 per cent top rate of tax (Smith like Ed Miliband was hoping to bring it up to 50 per cent), already appeared as scarcely believable relics of an apparently bleak and collectivist age (despite the general economic and social success of the era). It would also represent a radical crusade against the prevailing order, rather than the consensual governance that all past Labour governments had pursued. It would have represented a radical crusade due to the fact that it was now simply unnecessary. The government no longer needed to grant major concessions to win over the trade unions because what the unions did or did not do was very unlikely to fundamentally effect the economy or the government's electoral prospects. Governing parties as a whole generally seek to govern within the prevailing consensus, they do not seek to break radically from the prevailing order, unless the alternative is very clearly more politically viable (which neo-liberalism arguably was in 1979, for a Conservative Party that would have found it politically suicidal to impose a statutory incomes policy). Changes in British society, particularly the collapse of the labour movement and the change in the balance of class power this entailed, had without a doubt made a return to the social democratic policies of the 1970s a highly radical choice, rather than a set of policies deemed politically necessary to demonstrate economic competence and maintain political legitimacy. New Labour, like all governing parties who tend to place a priority on winning election/re-election, now had every political incentive to accept the prevailing neo-liberal consensus and seek relatively consensual social reform without shattering its fundamentals. New Labour had therefore arguably not adapted to the new consensus due to incontestable structural changes in the global economy, but largely for reasons of political expedience. Just as the Conservatives had so seamlessly adapted to the new social democratic order in 1951 (and were also rewarded with 13 years of government).

Since the New Labour government was seeking to govern within the prevailing economic consensus, it was determined to immediately gain the confidence of the markets and therefore be freed from the constant crises that 'old' Labour governments faced. To achieve this, New Labour sought to clearly demonstrate its commitment to long-term fiscal and monetary stability. This was based on a strategy of 'constrained discretion', and involved the party using 'targets and rules to voluntarily constrain its own room for manoeuvre' (Weldon, 2013: 22). To attain this 'constrained discretion', the government immediately granted independence to the Bank of England with a mission to set interest rates in line with a target of 2.5 per cent inflation. As well as this, Gordon Brown, then Chancellor of the Exchequer, laid out two 'golden rules' for borrowing, which were to keep debt below 40 per cent of gross domestic product (GDP) and only borrow to finance public investment, not to fund current spending. Alongside the commitment to macroeconomic stability, the government also sought to make it clear that they would maintain the Conservative's reforms with regards to trade unions and the labour market. Essentially New Labour was determined to do as little as possible to disturb the fundamentals of the successful economy they inherited from the Conservatives. In this objective New Labour was highly successful, gaining the confidence of the markets and presiding over a decade of consistent growth and low inflation. To put New Labour's economic success in context, they governed during the longest period of sustained economic growth since 1945, surpassing that experienced in any G7 nation (Lee, 2008: 70). This growth remained so strong and consistent because of very strong consumer demand (driven by house price inflation and easily available credit) and a booming financial sector, which saw its share of GDP almost double under New Labour (Kitson and Wilkinson, 2007: 811; Tomlinson, 2010: 71).

This liberal economic model, while incredibly successful in the key economic indicators (growth, inflation and unemployment), contained major downsides. British manufacturing continued to decline throughout the New Labour years, as the economy became ever more geared towards financial services. The manufacturing share of GDP fell from 20 per cent in 1997 to 11.3 per cent in 2008 (Daddow, 2015: 113). This decline was driven by the appreciation of sterling, which was in part the product of New Labour's determination to maintain price stability. This continued deindustrialization substantially contributed to the widening of 'the regional prosperity divide' (Kitson and Wilkinson, 2007: 812), and made the North and West increasingly dependent on a growing public sector (Coutts et al., 2007: 860). Most importantly, the neo-liberal economic model contributed to the continuation of the polarized and unequal society created by 18 years of Conservative rule. This was in part because New Labour sought to maintain a highly flexible labour market. This flexibility provided Britain with a superior unemployment record when compared to that of other large European states, but it also meant that the UK continued to maintain more insecurity and inequality. Not to mention that hiding outside the official unemployment figures was the fact that those on out-of-work benefits never fell below 4.5 million (Goodhart, 2015: 276). This is not to say that New Labour did nothing about inequality in the labour market, they did seek to establish minimum individual rights, accepting the European Social Chapter and introducing the National Minimum Wage. Nevertheless, their strong commitment to price stability and their wish to maintain competitive and flexible labour markets meant that the strengthening of the trade unions and the shifting of power relations in favour of workers was out of the question. There would also for the above reasons be no return to full employment as understood in the social democratic era (with all its positive effects on equality and trade union strength). They aimed only to keep employment at levels compatible with what they considered to be the NAIRU (the non-accelerating inflation rate of unemployment). New Labour would only seek to reduce unemployment if it could be done without generating inflation, and this demanded further flexibility, structural reforms and even higher levels of labour migration (Goodhart, 2015: 271). These factors would increase the supply of labour (and therefore competition), and make it increasingly cheap to employ, allowing more of the population to be employed without driving up wages and inflation. Essentially, to 'lower the NAIRU, collective labour power has to be restrained' (Whyman, 2006: 67). To Hay, this makes any commitment by New Labour to full employment 'frankly, disingenuous' (Hay, 2004: 46).

As the above shows, New Labour had almost totally accepted the neo-liberal economic model. This allowed them to oversee a period of unprecedented economic success (albeit followed by a substantial economic crisis), but it also meant that they presided over an economy that continued to produce massive inequality, a declining manufacturing sector and where full employment remained a distant memory. Nevertheless, New Labour was not the same as the preceding Tory government. New Labour unlike the Conservatives used the growth generated by the neo-liberal economy to reduce poverty and revive public services. They therefore differed not primarily in how they ran the economy but how they spent the revenues raised. This is summed up by Heffernan, who states that New Labour 'raised its money in, to put it at its crudest, a "Thatcherite" way, but it spent some of that money in a non-"Thatcherite" way' (Heffernan, 2011: 167).

With regards to poverty reduction, the New Labour government placed particular attention on child poverty and pensioner poverty. Blair famously pledged to remove child poverty within a generation, and while the government missed its own ambitious targets, increased child benefits and working family tax credits meant that there was still very substantial improvements in the living conditions of families with children, with relative poverty amongst children falling 'from 27 percent in 1996–7 to 17.5 percent in 2010/11' (Lupton et al., 2013: 49). Pensioners had similar good fortune, with relative poverty amongst this group falling substantially, 'from 25 percent in 1997/8 to 17 percent in 2010/11' (Joyce and Sibieta, 2013: 192). Thus, poor families with children and pensioners did particularly well due to changes in the tax and benefits system designed specifically to reduce poverty amongst these groups, but relative poverty amongst low-income workers without children actually increased because they did not receive these benefits (Joyce and Sibieta, 2013: 192, 200). Nevertheless, the government's reforms managed to help the poor as a whole, with the two poorest quintiles seeing their incomes 'rise marginally faster' than 'the richer groups during the Blair era' (Stewart, 2007: 430), while relative poverty (less than 60 per cent of median income) fell 'from about 20 percent in 1997/8 to about 16 percent in 2010/11' (Joyce and Sibieta, 2013: 191). This poverty reduction record looks highly impressive when it is made clear that relative 'poverty more than doubled between 1979 and 1991' (Stewart, 2007: 408). Thus, there remained a very clear social democratic commitment to helping the poor and reducing poverty through redistributive taxation and spending, even though some of their success in terms of reducing poverty would start to go into reverse after 2005 (Gregg, 2010: s28; Lee, 2008: 215).

It was though in terms of public spending rather than poverty reduction where New Labour's most prominent claim to be upholding the social democratic tradition lay. New Labour used the continued growth of the economy and the confidence they gained from the financial markets to oversee a 3.2 per cent average annual rise in real total public expenditures in the period 1997–98 to 2007–08, this is compared with just 1.5 per cent under the Conservatives (Grimshaw and Rubery, 2012: 118). This represented a real terms increase in public spending larger than that experienced under any previous Labour or Conservative government (Smith, 2014: 602). This spending was so substantial that between 1997 and 2007 Britain experienced the second highest increase in public spending as a percentage of national income in the Organisation for Economic Co-operation and Development (OECD) (Chote et al., 2010: 7), with public spending rising from 40.6 per cent in 1997 to 44.1 per cent of GDP in 2007 (Chote et al., 2010: 7). This spending was felt most strongly in health and education. Spending on health rose from 5.3 per cent of GDP in 1997 to 7.5 per cent in 2010, while spending on education rose from 4.6 per cent to 6.2 per cent (Cobham et al., 2013: 14). The above makes it very difficult to simply characterize New Labour as Thatcherite or Tory-light, as there remained a very strong commitment to reviving the welfare state. As Smith states, 'Labour's policy, particularly after 2000, was different from previous Labour Governments not in its rejection of tax and spend but in the degree to which it increased public spending' (Smith, 2014: 601).

SOCIAL DEMOCRACY CONTINUED?

The answer to this is both yes and no. The 'yes' is due to the fact that New Labour clearly placed a very high priority on the thoroughly social democratic goals of reviving the public sector and reducing poverty. Labour remained like past Labour governments a progressive force within the prevailing capitalist consensus. There was therefore clearly continuity with the social democratic tradition, and indeed substantial success. Yearly real terms increases in public spending larger than that experienced under any previous post-war government and the second largest increase in public expenditure as a percentage of national income in the OECD (before the economic crisis) are social democratic achievements if ever there were ones. The 'no' though is more fundamental; Labour did not in any fundamental way alter the prevailing economic model. The British economy remained neo-liberal, and became increasingly dependent on financial services, to the benefit of the Southeast, rather than Labour's heartlands (although of course the revenues raised by the City were playing an important role in Labour's revival of the public services). This economic model contributed to severely limiting social democratic results. A deregulated, flexible and competitive labour market, an absence of full employment, heavily weakened trade unions, a booming City and ever rising house prices all produced inequality and poverty within some groups (workers without children) that New Labour's redistributive tax and spend policies simply could not fully avert. Essentially, the continuation of a neo-liberal market, and the maintenance of the unequal power relations between capital and labour this entailed, greatly limited Labour's achievements and made it difficult for them to attain the results of past Labour governments in terms of inequality and poverty reduction, both of which remain well above their 1979 levels (Lupton et al., 2013: 13, 51; Machin and Van Reenan, 2010: 108). These results required more than 'social democratic levels' of public spending. What was needed was a working class with strong bargaining power. Bargaining power that in the social democratic era contributed to ever increasing levels of equality, with the final two years of this era (1977 and 1978) seeing modern Britain at its most equal as measured by the Gini Coefficient (Institute for Fiscal Studies). This leads to the conclusion that the upholding of a neo-liberal economy and highly unequal power relations is not compatible with 'traditional' social democratic results. Although this should not lead to the denial of New Labour's success in reducing poverty and slowing the rise in inequality (Machin and Van Reenan, 2010).

As mentioned above, this mixed legacy is not based on the fact that New Labour diverged from the generally pragmatic approach of 'old' Labour. New Labour like 'old' Labour stuck with the prevailing economic consensus, a consensus built on the defeat of organized labour, and attempted with some success to pursue progressive objectives within these confines (Fielding, 2003; Rubinstein, 2000). As Rubinstein states, 'the Labour Party is now a party of consensus and so was it in the past. The difference is that "the new consensus leans to the Right"' (Rubinstein, 2000: 164). The Attlee, Wilson and Callaghan administrations were not radical challengers to the prevailing order, they all governed within the prevailing economic consensus. Fortunately for these governments, they governed at a time when the balance of class power made highly egalitarian concessions to a powerful working class, primarily in the form of full employment and high social expenditure, essential for political legitimacy, and even necessary for the maintenance of economic stability, as trade union cooperation was needed to control inflation, maintain competitiveness and avoid industrial strife. In contrast, New Labour inherited a society with a greatly weakened labour movement whose economic and political strength was arguably lower than at any time in the twentieth century. Demonstrated by the fact that Tony Blair became 'the first post-war Labour prime minister not to face serious industrial unrest' (Quinn, 2010: 372). In these conditions, a return to 1979 and the major concessions to the working class this entailed was not politically or economically necessary and therefore not part of the prevailing consensus. Because of this fact, it would have represented not the implementation of the 'general interest' and a demonstration of economic competence but a radical challenge to the prevailing order and class relations. A radical challenge that is unlikely to be politically desirable, for a Labour Party that has, like the majority of governing parties of the left, historically tended to prioritize consensual reform that shows the country that they 'are not under the domination of the wild men' (Former Labour Chancellor Philip Snowden, quoted in Allender, 2001: 128). Essentially, New Labour acted as social democrats have always done, and sought social reform (with substantial success) within the prevailing capitalist consensus; unfortunately the prevailing consensus made social democratic results hard to obtain.

Because of this it is concluded that any revival of the egalitarian and power relations shifting social democracy of the post-war golden age is dependent on the return of a strong labour movement that must be 'appeased' by all governing parties in their own electoral self-interest and desire to maintain a stable economy. Essentially, social democratic success was dependent on pressure from below, it was never dependent on the election of radical governments committed to breaking with the prevailing order and radically shifting the balance of class power. This success was based on the fact that British governments understood that political legitimacy and economic success/stability was dependent on granting major concessions to the working class. Without this understanding there will simply be little fundamental political or economic pressure for a future Labour administration to move away from humanizing neo-liberalism and massive pressure for it to stay in the new 'centre' ground, where all governing parties generally seek to remain.

THE LABOUR PARTY IN OPPOSITION, A RETURN TO THE 1980S?

In 2008 the economic crisis hit, this spelt the beginning of the end for a Labour government that had heralded the end of 'boom and bust', and which had so clearly privileged the City over industry (despite generally having been seen as effective in dealing with the economic crisis), but not in any way the end of the prevailing neo-liberal consensus. Instead of the neo-liberal economic model coming under political and ideological threat, Labour's public spending was very effectively framed by the parties of the Coalition (the Conservatives and the Liberal Democrats), both before and after the May 2010 general election, as reckless, apparently leaving the country in a more difficult position than if they had been running a smaller budget deficit or surplus. Thus, it has been the right that has politically 'won' the economic crisis, creating a substantial level of legitimacy for public spending cuts (Green and Lavery, 2015: 913). Labour in opposition was unable to counter this narrative. They felt that this was a debate that they could not win (they have now thoroughly lost it), and wanted to move on from the Blair-Brown years. Labour under the leadership of Ed Miliband (elected as leader in September 2010) was seeking to mildly move away from the all-out embrace of the neo-liberal economy that had characterized New Labour. With Miliband himself arguing for a move towards a more progressive version of capitalism, and placing a strong focus on tackling inequality. This mild return to more social democratic economic ideas can be seen in slogans and ideas such as pre-distribution, predators and producers, and 'One-Nation' Labour, the latter harking back to the era of social democratic Toryism. As well as in the numerous policies offered in their 2015 general election manifesto, including the abolition of non-domicile tax status (British residents whose permanent home is outside the UK currently have the opportunity to avoid tax on foreign earned income), the introduction of a mansion tax, the freezing of energy bills, the building of 200,000 houses a year by 2020, the capping of 'excessive' private sector rents, the abolition of zero-hour contracts and finally the bringing of the top rate of tax back to 50 pence in the pound (Labour Party, 2015). There was very clearly a cautious move away from the all-out embrace of neo-liberalism under the leadership of Miliband. Unfortunately for Labour and British social democracy the polls that had for months been predicting that the Labour Party was neck and neck with the Conservative Party proved highly inaccurate. The Conservative Party was returned with an unexpected majority and Miliband gained less parliamentary seats than Brown had in 2010, although Labour did marginally increase its share of the vote. Nevertheless, they remain in a position of electoral weakness not seen since the mid 1980s. The election result, while not necessarily a ringing endorsement of austerity, certainly demonstrated that the neo-liberal economic consensus is 'very much alive and kicking' (Glaser, 2015: 23). This leaves the question of where the social democratic left can go in an era where neo-liberalism remains the prevailing consensus and radical change appears to be off the political agenda.

Because of the continued weakness of the labour movement, demonstrated in the stagnation of living standards, and the electoral victory of the Conservatives, who actually increased their vote after five years in power (a very rare achievement for a governing party), this remains a defensive era for the forces of social democracy. Therefore, the social democratic left's objectives have to be limited and pragmatic, and since Labour continues to be a progressive force, albeit within the confines of the prevailing neo-liberal economic consensus, it is highly important for the social democratic left that Labour returns to power. But how can Labour return to power in the aftermath of such an unexpected and devastating defeat?

The disastrous 2015 general election result was driven by the Labour Party's failure in both Scotland and England. Labour's formerly safe constituencies north of the border have been lost to the Scottish National Party (Labour retained one seat in a Scotland they had previously dominated). But even with their traditional seats in Scotland, Labour would still have fallen far short of a majority. This was because they had also failed to perform in England, failing to take marginal seats from the Conservative Party, making a net gain of one from them. The reasons put forward for this major defeat have been strongly clouded by political allegiance and a desire to secure political advantage. The Blairites, including many ex-ministers, have very quickly pointed towards what they regard as Labour's predictable failure to win marginal seats off the Conservatives in England (seats that are essential for any Labour victory) as evidence that Labour should have moved towards the centre ground. By this they mean that Labour should have been perceived as less anti-business and more in-tune with 'aspirational' middle class voters. The left in a more defensive manner have argued that the loss of Scotland to the Scottish National Party (SNP) means that Labour must bring back its core voters by turning towards the left and truly distinguishing themselves from the Conservative Party. Neither of these narratives is particularly convincing. The Blairite argument is unpersuasive because many of the reforms proposed under Miliband were popular, people believe the government should regulate big business, tax the wealthy and place growth and investment over the need to immediately cut the deficit (GQRR, 2015). Labour essentially did not put off voters because its policies were perceived as too left wing. The primary problem was that Labour were seen as less able to provide economic stability, which is partly a legacy of New Labour (Curtice, 2015). Secondly, the Blairite argument cannot explain the loss of Scotland to what appeared to be a more leftist SNP, although the Institute for Fiscal Studies (IFS) has shown that 'the SNP's stated plans do not necessarily match their anti-austerity rhetoric' and were indeed very similar to those of the Labour Party (IFS, 2015: 4). The left narrative, established almost solely on the defection of Scotland to the SNP, is based on the assumption that the SNP vote was primarily a rejection of austerity, which would have been repeated across the country if such an alternative existed outside Scotland. While some of the SNP vote was no doubt such a rejection (but as the IFS shows, this would have been misplaced), it also clearly represented a populist nationalism, something not repeatable by a UK party and something that is next to impossible to compete with. This is demonstrated by the fact that 'nearly nine-in-10 of those who voted "yes" in the independence referendum in September 2014 had opted to back the SNP' (Curtice, 2015). Therefore, even a more radical, Corbyn-led Labour Party would have struggled to compete (although if Labour had not become New Labour in the first place it is arguably the case that the rise of the SNP would never have taken place). The argument is also pretty unconvincing when analyzing the election results in England, where fear over the control the SNP may have over a minority Labour government is seen to have pushed many people to vote Conservative. Surely, if there was a strong desire to end austerity and see more progressive economic policies, such potential control would have been an asset, rather than a grave threat to Labour's electability. Essentially for these voters, English nationalism and a desire for economic stability triumphed over a more progressive economic policy. Neither is a turn to the left likely to bring back core voters from the UK Independence Party (UKIP) concerned about immigration, or win over the Conservative-held marginal seats that in the First Past the Post electoral system are absolutely essential for any return to power in 2020. Labour's loss to the right in England is as worrying as its loss to the left north of the border. Neither a lurch to the left nor the right will solve Labour's electoral problems. So what can Labour do to win in 2020?

Post-election polling helps point the way forward for Labour. This polling shows that the primary problem for Labour was their apparent lack of economic competence (GQRR, 2015), an issue that the Conservatives have historically tended to benefit from. It is of course next to impossible to win an election if the majority of the population think the other governing party is more competent with something so fundamental to their lives. Especially as it is older voters with a greater tendency to turn out that are attracted to the most 'competent' party (Curtice, 2015). This helps explain Labour's terrible performance amongst those over 65, gaining the support of a shockingly low one in four people in this group (Ipsos MORI, 2015). This damaging lack of competence was arguably created by the fact that Labour never really put forward a coherent economic strategy, with easily digestible political appeal. As Alastair Darling, Labour's Chancellor between 2007 and 2010 stated, 'you can't win on a series of "retail offers" like 10 bob off your next electricity bill' (Quoted in Sylvester, 2015). Thus, Labour did not lose because of its centre left 'retail offers', many of these were popular. It lost because it was not seen as the safe option with regards to the economy (Curtice, 2015), especially as the population were expecting a Labour government to be a minority one reliant on the SNP. It therefore does not need to desperately abandon its progressive policies (such as the energy price cap, the mansion tax and the 50 pence top rate of income tax) to attract 'aspirational voters', what McKibben rightly calls 'a moth-eaten concept known only to journalists and New Labour politicians' (McKibben, 2015). Although the party must equally recognize that in this era of trade union weakness the achievement of the appearance of economic competence is unlikely to be compatible with a radically progressive strategy, with only 15 per cent of those polled by GQRR claiming to 'want political parties to offer a big vision for radical change in this country' (GQRR, 2015). Thus, the cautious reform of aspects of the neo-liberal economy put forward in the Miliband years probably contained the right approach to policy, especially as the Labour Party desperately needed to renew itself after haemorrhaging support in 2005 and 2010 (Curtice, 2015). Unfortunately, this was clearly not matched with a clear economic plan that exuded competence and made clear what Labour stood for. A clear plan and simple narrative must therefore be at the front and centre of Labour's programme for 2020.

POSTSCRIPT

The Labour Party have certainly not followed the cautious move to the left, advocated above and pursued during the Miliband years. The party has overwhelmingly endorsed the candidate of the 'hard left' Jeremy Corbyn, rather than the early favourites Andy Burnham and Yvette Cooper. Corbyn won the leadership election by a landslide, gaining an astonishing 59.5 per cent of the vote, his nearest challenger gained a measly 19 per cent. The Labour leadership election (conducted under a system of one member, one vote) had seen a massive inflow of members and affiliates during the period of the campaign (citizens had the ability to affiliate to the party for just £3). The Labour Party 'electorate increased from under 200,000 in May to 550,000 in September' (Quinn, 2015). Most of these were supporters of Corbyn, with polling suggesting that 84 per cent of those paying £3 to affiliate voted for him (Kellner, 2015a). This meant that long-term Labour members were rapidly outnumbered by this influx, with only 25 per cent of those eligible to vote being pre-2010 members (Kellner, 2015a). 'Had only they (the long term members) voted in the leadership election, it is touch-and-go whether Mr Corbyn would have won at all' (Kellner, 2015a). Thus, Corbyn had clearly galvanized and was dependent on strong support amongst new members and affiliates disaffected by New Labour, sweeping away and humiliating the mainstream candidates in the process.

The election of Corbyn has no historical precedence, never before has a radical backbencher, with no experience of government led the party. Other leftist leaders of the party have all had government experience, George Lansbury (1932–35) was a Cabinet member (First Commissioner of Works) between 1929 and 1931 and Michael Foot (1980–83) had been Deputy Leader of the Labour Party and Minister for Employment amongst other positions. The election of Corbyn due to a massive influx of membership and with virtually no support from the parliamentary Labour Party is a truly monumental and historically unprecedented event.

It is a monumental moment for the British left, but it is also a moment of extreme danger. An electoral loss of the Foot variety (a poorly qualified but principled leader, leading the party to electoral disaster) will lead to the delegitimizing of the left within the party and British society. The triumphalism of the Labour Party right after Miliband's 2015 general election defeat will pale in comparison to that which will inevitably follow a similar loss by Corbyn, leading to irresistible demands for a charismatic and popular leader who can appeal to 'middle England'. So, the core question is can Corbyn win in 2020? Left wing and relatively radical leaders can win elections, but these have usually been at times of acute crisis. The election of a relatively radical government in a highly stable democracy that also happens to be the world's fifth biggest economy (and is predicted to still be in this position in 2020) will clearly be a game changer (CNN Money, 2015).

Winning the 2020 general election will be extraordinarily difficult. Firstly, the Conservative Party will have a new leader, who will likely be a political heavyweight, with a national profile, such as Boris Johnson, Theresa May or George Osbourne. Secondly, the Conservatives now have a majority in the House of Commons, this will allow them to pursue boundary changes that are predicted to cost Labour around 20 seats in the House of Commons. Thirdly, the SNP are not going anywhere, their progressive nationalism offers everything Corbyn can and more. Fourthly, Corbyn suffers from the same problem that undermined Miliband. Corbyn like Miliband does not appear 'prime ministerial', and this is reflected in the fact that Corbyn has the worst initial rating of any new opposition leader in six decades of polling (Kellner, 2015b).

Clearly, the challenge is enormous, much greater than that faced by Miliband after 2010. The Labour Party have to put in a good showing in 2020, otherwise this remarkable victory by the left will be squandered for at least a generation. The first two months have not been particularly promising. Some of the actions taken by the leadership have been unforced errors. The giving of positions of influence to those on the 'hard left' does not help unite the party, or show that the leadership is representative of a broad range of opinion. John McDonnell as Chancellor of the Exchequer and Seamus Milne as Executive Director of Strategy and Communications are the most notable examples and are less than inspired choices. The latter was a particularly unnecessary indulgence. The leadership must attempt to be more inclusive. This would have been helped by giving a leading position to a representative of a rival faction (for example, Harold Wilson making James Callaghan Chancellor of the Exchequer in 1964), and of course this is not helped by the fact that many right wing members of the party have refused to serve in the Shadow Cabinet. Corbyn has also followed in the footsteps of Michael Foot and focused on issues of minute importance to the general public, the scrapping of Britain's submarine carried nuclear deterrent named Trident (a move not supported by the public or Britain's biggest union, Unite). Corbyn like Foot is strongly associated with the Campaign for Nuclear Disarmament, in fact he is the organization's vice president. This issue has already divided the party and distracted it from issues that the population actually cares about.

Thus, the start has not been great (reflected in low approval ratings for Corbyn), and the challenge remains daunting. So how does the party succeed where Miliband failed. Firstly, they need to develop a coherent and consistent economic policy that exuberates competence (very important to the population as a whole), at the same time as putting forward popular left wing policies such as the nationalization of the railways and the energy companies, increased corporation taxes and an increased minimum wage. These polices can be massive electoral assets as long as they are part of a greater whole. Secondly, they need to avoid symbolic issues of minute importance to the general public, especially if it involves foreign policy or defence. The last thing Labour needs is to oppose Trident, its continuation has virtually no effect on people's lives (it will also lead to job losses in the defence industry, the reason why Unite support Trident's renewal) and costs relatively little in the grand scheme of things, plus its continuation is popular amongst the general public. Thirdly, the party needs to be unified. We must hope that the Labour right don't commit political suicide again as they did in the 1980s by establishing a breakaway party.

A more progressive Britain is possible, many left wing policies are in isolation very popular, but its achievement will involve serious work and compromise. There is not a left wing majority patiently waiting for the opportunity to vote for a socialist. Electoral victory in 2020 will be based on convincing politically uninterested, relatively moderate and often socially conservative voters in England that Labour will improve Britain and their own living standards.

BIBLIOGRAPHY

Allender, P. (2001). *What's Wrong with Labour: A Critical History of the Labour Party in the 20th Century*. London: Merlin Press.

Bogdanor, V. (2007). 'Social Democracy'. In A. Seldon and D. Kavanagh (eds), *Blair's Britain 1997–2007*. Cambridge: Cambridge University Press: 164–84.

Chote, R., Crawford, R., Emmerson, C. and Tetlow, G. (2010). 'Public Spending under Labour: 2010 Election Briefing Note No. 5'. Institute for Fiscal Studies. Available at www.ifs.org.uk/bns/bn92.pdf (accessed May 2016).

CNN Money (2015). 'World's Largest Economies'. Available at http://money.cnn.com/news/economy/world_economies_gdp/index.html (accessed May 2016).

Cobham, D., Adam, C. and Mayhew, K. (2013). 'The Economic Record of the 1997–2010 Labour Government: An Assessment'. *Oxford Review of Economic Policy*, 29 (1): 1–24.

Coutts, K., Glyn, A. and Rowthorn, B. (2007). 'Structural Change under New Labour'. *Cambridge Journal of Economics*, 31 (6): 845–61.

Curtice, J. (2015). 'A Defeat to Reckon with: On Scotland, Economic Competence, and the Complexities of Labour's Losses'. *Institute for Public Policy Research*. Available at www.ippr.org/juncture/a-defeat-to-reckon-with-on-scotland-economic-competence-and-the-complexities-of-labours-losses (accessed October 2015).

Daddow, O. (2015). 'New Labour: A Witness History'. *Contemporary British History*, 29 (1): 106–36.

Daniels, G. and McIlroy, J. (2009). 'An Anatomy of British Trade Unionism since 1997: Strategies for Revitalization'. In G. Daniels and J. McIlroy (eds), *Trade Unions in a Neoliberal World: British Trade Unions under New Labour*. London: Routledge: 98–126.

Dell, E. (1996). *The Chancellors: A History of the Chancellors of the Exchequer, 1945–90*. London: HarperCollins.

——(1999). *A Strange Eventful History: Democratic Socialism in Britain*. London: HarperCollins.

Glaser, E. (2015). 'Post-politics and the Future of the Left'. *Juncture*, 22 (1): 23–31.

Goodhart, D. (2015). 'Globalisation, Nation States, and the Economics of Migration'. In I. Geary and A. Pabst (eds), *Blue Labour: Forging a New Politics*. London: I.B. Tauris: 246–84.

GQRR (2015). 'UK Post Election Poll for the TUC'. Available at www.gqrr.com/uk-post-election-2 (accessed May 2016).

Green, J. and Lavery, S. (2015). 'The Regressive Recovery: Distribution, Inequality and State Power in Britain's Post-crisis Political Economy'. *New Political Economy*, 20 (6): 894–923.

Gregg, P. (2010). 'New Labour and Inequality'. *The Political Quarterly*, 81 (s1): s16–s30.

Grimshaw, D. and Rubery, J. (2012). 'The End of the UK's Liberal Collectivist Social Model? The Implications of the Coalition Government's Policy during the Austerity Crisis'. *Cambridge Journal of Economics*, 36 (1): 105–26.

Fielding, S. (2003). *The Labour Party: Continuity and Change in the Making of 'New' Labour*. Houndmills, Basingstoke: Palgrave Macmillan.

Hay, C. (2004). 'Credibility, Competitiveness and the Business Cycle in "Third Way" Political Economy: A Critical Evaluation of Economic Policy in Britain since 1997'. *New Political Economy*, 9 (1): 39–56.

Heffernan, R. (2011). 'Labour's New Labour Legacy: Politics after Blair and Brown'. *Political Studies Review*, 9 (2): 163–77.

Hobsbawm, E. (1983). 'Labour's Lost Millions'. *Marxism Today*, October: 7–13.

Howell, C. (2005). *Trade Unions and the State: The Construction of Industrial Relations in Britain, 1890–2000*. Princeton: Princeton University Press.

Hyman, R. (2001). *Understanding European Trade Unionism: Between Market, Class and Society*. London: Sage.

Institute for Fiscal Studies (n.d.). 'Incomes in the UK'. Available at www.ifs.org. uk/tools_and_resources/incomes_in_uk (accessed May 2016).

—— (2015). 'IFS Briefing Note BN170: Post-election Austerity: Parties' Plans Compared'. Available at http://election2015.ifs.org.uk/uploads/publications/ bns/BN170.pdf (accessed May 2016).

Ipsos MORI (2015). 'How Britain Voted in 2015: The 2015 Election – Who Voted for Whom?' Available at www.ipsos-mori.com/researchpublications/ researcharchive/3575/How-Britain-voted-in-2015.aspx?view=wide (accessed May 2016).

Joyce, R. and Sibieta, L. (2013). 'An Assessment of Labour's Record on Income Inequality and Poverty'. *Oxford Review of Economic Policy*, 29 (1): 178–202.

Kellner, P. (2015a). 'An Anatomy of Corbyn's Victory'. YouGov. Available at https:// yougov.co.uk/news/2015/09/15/anatomy-corbyns-victory/ (accessed October 2015).

—— (2015b). 'Analysis: Could Corbyn become Prime Minister?'. YouGov. Available at https://yougov.co.uk/news/2015/10/20/analysis-could-corbyn-be-come-prime-minister/ (accessed October 2015).

Kitson, M. and Wilkinson, F. (2007). 'The Economics of New Labour: Policy and Performance'. *Cambridge Journal of Economics*, 31 (6): 805–16.

Labour Party (2015). *Britain Can Be Better: The Labour Party Manifesto 2015*. Available at www.labour.org.uk/manifesto (accessed October 2015).

Lee, S. (2008). *Best for Britain? The Politics and Legacy of Gordon Brown*. Oxford: Oneworld.

Lindley, J. and Machin, S. (2013). 'Wage Inequality in the New Labour Years'. *Oxford Review of Economic Policy*, 29 (1): 165–77.

Lord Ashcroft Polls (2015). 'Post-vote Day Poll 7 May 2015'. Available at http:// lordashcroftpolls.com/wp-content/uploads/2015/05/LORD-ASHCROFT-POLLS-Post-vote-poll-summary1.pdf (accessed September 2015).

Lupton, R. with Hills, J., Stewart, K. and Vizard, P. (2013). 'Labour's Social Policy Record: Policy, Spending and Outcomes 1997–2010'. Centre for the Analysis of Social Exclusion. Available at http://sticerd.lse.ac.uk/dps/case/spcc/rr01. pdf (accessed May 2016).

Machin, S. and Van Reenan, J. (2010). 'Inequality: Still Higher but Labour's Policies Kept it Down'. The Centre for Economic Performance. Available at http://eprints.lse.ac.uk/57989/1/__lse.ac.uk_storage_LIBRARY_Secondary_ libfile_shared_repository_Content_Centre_for_Economic_Performance_ Policy%20Analysis_ea015.pdf (accessed May 2016).

McKibben, R. (2015). 'Labour Dies Again'. *London Review of Books*, 37 (11): 11–12.

McIlroy, J. (2000). 'New Labour, New Unions, New Left'. *Capital & Class*, 24 (2): 11–45.

—— (2009). 'Under Stress but Still Enduring: The Contentious Alliance in the Age of Tony Blair and Gordon Brown'. In G. Daniels and J. McIlroy (eds), *Trade Unions in a Neoliberal World: British Trade Unions under New Labour.* London: Routledge: 165–201.

O'Hara, G. (2007). *From Dreams to Disillusionment: Economic and Social Planning in 1960s Britain.* Houndmills, Basingstoke: Palgrave Macmillan.

Panitch, L. (1977). 'The Development of Corporatism in Liberal Democracies'. *Comparative Political Studies*, 10 (1): 61–90.

—— (1979). 'Socialists and the Labour Party: A Reappraisal'. In R. Miliband and J. Saville (eds), *The Socialist Register 1979.* London: Merlin Press: 51–73.

Quinn, T. (2010). 'New Labour and the Trade Unions in Britain'. *Journal of Elections, Public Opinion and Parties*, 20 (3): 357–80.

—— (2015). 'Jeremy Corbyn Wins Labour Leadership Election – So What Next? The Conversation. Available at https://theconversation.com/jeremy-corbyn-wins-labour-leadership-election-so-what-next-47449 (accessed May 2016).

Rubinstein, D. (2000). 'A New Look at New Labour'. *Politics*, 20 (3): 161–7.

Sylvester, R. (2015). 'Ed Miliband's Five-year Suicide Note Left Labour Doomed'. *The Times.* Available at www.thetimes.co.uk/tto/news/politics/article4465656. ece (accessed September 2015).

Smith, M.J. (2014). 'Globalisation and the Resilience of Social Democracy: Reassessing New Labour's Political Economy'. *British Journal of Politics and International Relations*, 16 (4): 597–623.

Stewart, K. (2007). 'Equality and Social Justice'. In A. Seldon and D. Kavanagh (eds), *Blair's Britain 1997–2007.* Cambridge: Cambridge University Press: 408–35.

Stuart, M. (2014). *What if… John Smith had Lived?* Available at http://nottspolitics. org/2014/05/12/what-if-john-smith-had-lived (accessed August 2015).

Trades Unions Congress (1944). *Interim Report on Post-war Reconstruction.* London: TUC.

Tomlinson, J. (2010). 'Sick but Not Dying'. *Political Studies Review*, 8 (1): 67–72.

Upchurch, M., Taylor, G. and Mathers, A. (2009). *The Crisis of Social Democratic Trade Unionism in Western Europe: The Search for Alternatives.* Farnham: Ashgate.

Weldon, D. (2013). 'Beyond Living with Capitalism: The Labour Party, Macro-economics, and Political Economy since 1994'. *Renewal: A Journal of Social Democracy*, 21 (2/3): 21–33.

Whyman, P. (2006). *Third Way Economics: Theory and Evaluation.* Houndmills, Basingstoke: Palgrave Macmillan.

Worley, M. (2005). *Labour Inside the Gate: A History of the British Labour Party Between the Wars.* London: I.B. Tauris.

Part II
Peripheries

5

Till Death Do Us Part? Kirchnerism, Neodevelopmentalism and the Struggle for Hegemony in Argentina, 2003–15

Mariano Féliz

The extended Kirchnerist decade in Argentina (2003–15) is reaching its closure, and the political transition towards a new phase of the neo-developmentalist era has begun. This new phase will be earmarked by the heritage of Kirchnerism as a hegemonic political project and will reflect both the new policies introduced by it and the profound continuities with the neoliberal era, whose main traits were consolidated and perfected during this period (Féliz, 2012a). This transition occurs in a global and regional framework that has violently mutated in recent years since the beginning of the 2008 capitalist crisis in the centre, and the unexpected death of Venezuela's President Hugo Chávez.

This chapter analyzes how the era politically dominated by Kirchnerism came to mould the constitution and crisis of neodevelopmentalism in Argentina after the downfall of neoliberal rule. In this process, popular organizations struggled to push forward the organizational momentum that was built through clashes with neoliberalism in the late 1990s. But the limits of Kirchnerism as a progressive, 'social-democratic' movement became evident as it could not surpass the boundaries of dependent capitalism, thus becoming a farce of its own discourse of change.

The chapter is organized as follows. First, we present the basis of neoliberal crisis and the transition into neodevelopmentalism. We then show how Kirchnerism became the political force in office and attended to the need to build legitimacy and hegemony. This process required the neutralization of the potential destabilizing effect of unfettered popular struggles. Third, we explain how the neodevelopmentalist project entered into crisis as its barriers grew and its limits became evident. We also analyze the way in which Kirchnerism tried to displace such barriers without attempting to surpass those limits. Finally, we show how the crisis on neodevelopmentalism turned into a transitional crisis for Kirchnerism (a crisis for its own transcendence and survival, as it attempted to remain in the government).

KIRCHNERISM, NEOLIBERAL HERITAGE AND THE WEAK STATE

Neoliberalism, crisis and transition

Kirchnerism was born in the explosive transition away from the convertibility plan (CP). The CP (1991–2001) was the vernacular expression of the Washington Consensus in Argentina and expressed the highest form of neoliberalism, which began as a project in Argentina in 1975 (Féliz and Pérez, 2010). The long agony of neoliberal rule in the country (1998–2001) was the outcome of the 'Menemist radicalization' of the programme of structural reforms (1989–99), and the development of its contradictions to their maximum expression (Féliz, 2011).[1] After 1999 the coalition *Alianza* (centre-right leaning), which had won the presidential elections, took on the task of trying to avoid the explosion of increasing contradictions. This proved to be impossible (Féliz, 2011a).

This crisis developed within the regional and global framework of the disruption of the basis of the neoliberal project resulting from (a) the upsurge of popular struggles and economic and political crises in the peripheries; (b) the crisis tendencies in the centre (only displaced temporally by means of war and speculation); and (c) the progressive change in the axis of world hegemony towards the East (Féliz, 2011b: 247–8). In Argentina, the violent advancement of big capitals in the process of transnationalization, the increase in the concentration and centralization of capital and the displacement of living labour in the process of the valorization of capital created the material substratum for the crisis (Féliz, 2011a). At the same time, the political recomposition of the working classes in the country fed a cycle of social agitation that progressively undermined the basis for the legitimacy of the neoliberal programme and its state (Dinerstein, 2002). Led in struggle by the movement of the unemployed and factions of the organized labour movement, popular classes were able to erode the legitimacy of the neoliberal programme, leading to its final crisis in December 2001. The political transition included a record high vote abstention and blank votes in the national mid-term elections of October 2001, dozens of deaths by police repression after the 19 December 2001 popular uprising, the resignation of the president on 20 December and a rapid succession of interim presidents that would put Eduardo Duhalde in charge of the Executive power in early January 2002, not by popular vote but by decision of Congress. Being the governor of the province of Buenos Aires (the biggest, most populous province in Argentina) and having been Menem's vice-president, dominant political forces, led by the Peronist party, saw him as someone able to bring back order and perform the reforms that were needed to surpass the limits of the neoliberal programme.

The organic crisis of neoliberalism in Argentina was superseded through economic adjustment and repression. On the one hand, this was done through a political process marked by an economic programme that attempted to recompose the conditions for the profitability of capital (Bonnet, 2006). These policies involved a huge devaluation of capital in every form (as variable capital, as constant capital, as financial capital, as productive and merchant capital etc.) and a huge transfer of income from labour to capital (Féliz, 2012a; Schorr, 2005). Even if shock policies were able to jump start accumulation, political stability was limited. Mass popular struggles continued across the country as the negative consequences of exiting neoliberalism were significant for most of the population. Real wages plunged 18.1 per cent and employment fell 6 per cent in 2002 in comparison with 2001, as 52 per cent of Argentina's urban population was statistically income-poor in that year (Féliz, 2015: 75). In this context, the multiplication in the number of cash-transfer programmes and beneficiaries was promoted as a new policy of social control to attempt to satisfy immediate demands for income of millions of poor families while at the same time defuse the most radical political demands. In May 2002, the *Plan Jefes y Jefas de Hogar Desocupados* (plan for unemployed heads of households, PJJHD) reached almost 2 million direct beneficiaries. The coercion and repression of social struggles also played a key role in containing social conflict, reaching their highest point with the assassination of the *piqueteros* Darío Santillán and Maximiliano Kosteki by police forces on 26 June 2002.[2] These killings (and the reaction of popular organizations to them) became a limit to the political transition led by Duhalde, and gave momentum to the project designed to build a new political order that would reinstate the state as the representative of the 'general will' of the people, and could, once more, revive capitalism as a means to attempt to achieve development in the periphery. Mass mobilizations by popular movements forced a government that had come to stay for several years to call for early national elections in 2003. In the meantime, the new economic policy was beginning to be fruitful in terms of capital accumulation – in the third quarter of 2002 Argentina's economy was starting to grow again after 17 quarters of falling real gross domestic product (GDP) (Féliz, 2015: 74).

By chance, a little known Peronist candidate, Néstor Kirchner, won the presidential election in March 2003 with only 22 per cent of the votes. Kirchner had been a long-running member of the Justicialist Party (the main formal political organization of the Peronist movement) and was proposed by Duhalde as its 'successor'. In the national presidential elections, Kirchner came second (as candidate of the Peronist, social-democratic coalition *Frente Para la Victoria* (Front for Victory, FPV), after Carlos Menem (Peronist but neoliberal) who obtained 24.36 per cent of the votes. The party on the left spectrum with the best performance (*Movimiento de los Trabajadores Socialistas* (Movement of Socialist Workers, MST) gained only 1.75 per cent. However, Menem withdrew from the run-off second round, with the result that Kirchner was automatically elected, since opinion polls indicated that Kirchner would win with a landslide. With few initial allies in parliament and having won by default of its competitor, Kirchnerism as a political force in the state was born with poor original legitimacy.

Kirchnerism: making virtue out of necessity

Kichnerism appeared as a possible political solution to the capitalist governability crisis caused by the political and economic limits of neo-liberalism. Kirchnerism took on the task of amplifying its political base while at the same time looking to deactivate the more radical demands of the popular movements.[3] This was attempted within the pre-existing macroeconomic framework, characterized by an expensive dollar, low real interest rates, wages crushed by the inflationary effects of the initial devaluation of the national currency and the reorientation of aggregate demand towards the global market (Féliz, 2015). These were the canonic coordinates of the macroeconomic policy of neodevelopmentalism (Bresser-Pereira, 2010; Curia, 2007). Kirchner's first years were marked by continuities in economic policy, with Roberto Lavagna staying on in his post at the Ministry of the Economy, as did the president of the Central Bank, Alfonso Prat Gay.

Kirchner (as most political leaders within Peronism) had been an ally of Menem in the 1990s. However, in this new time he read the political situation as a period of higher levels of social conflict, a society rejecting the social consequences of neoliberalism, and a regional arena turning slightly to the left, with Chávez's government in Venezuela in the process of radicalizing the Bolivarian Revolution after the oil strike of 2002–03. With this understanding, one that recognized a definite but limited change in local and regional correlation of social forces, Kirchner was able to create a powerful new political coalition based on factions of progressive organizations (such as some from the human rights movement), several *piquetero* organizations (lured in by a combination of genuine political conviction and economic cooptation), the main organizations within the labour movement, particularly the backbone of the Peronist movement the *Confederación General del Trabajo* (General Labour Confederation, CGT). To be clear, Kirchnerism adopted a populist (not popular) strategy for it needed to recognize the organized presence of a part of the working people while at the same time attempting to limit their political autonomy (Mazzeo, 2010).

Kirchner's government moved forward on a political programme that in public statements rejected neoliberalism and allowed him to win additional constituents. The government rolled back some of the policies of the 1990s, and reasserted state ownership over some of the companies that had been privatized, such as the *Correo Argentino* (Argentine postal service) in 2003, *Aguas Argentinas* (Argentine Waters, the water and sanitation company of Greater Buenos Aires) in 2006 and *Aerolíneas Argentinas* (Argentine Airlines, the national airline) in 2008 (Féliz, 2014). But no significant decisions were made regarding privatized energy, phone, trains, social security and other strategic enterprises and areas, at least until 2009.

With lip-service to national-popular rhetoric (some of it limited by symbolically important decisions, as stressed in the previous paragraph), taking advantage of the improving economic conditions, and having access to the fiscal resources of the national state (that allowed it to favour allies in the different provinces, local governments and organizations), Kirchnerism attacked the two main sources of possible political instability at the time: new young rank-and-file activism in trade unions and *piquetero* organizations.

In the first instance, Kichnerism looked to channel labour struggles within the traditional institutions of Argentina's labour legislation, in particular through collective bargaining. A new generation of trade union activism had been born in the struggles against neoliberal adjustment, with wide and general demands for wage recovery, employment and improvement of working conditions, and willing to back up their demands with street struggles outside institutional regulations. Most of this activism was based in industrial manufacturing industries, and developed with the protection of the legislation that has historically given important autonomy to rank-and-file leadership on the shopfloor. Some of this new activism was tied to historical radical-left parties of Trotskyite tradition, in particular the *Partido de los Trabajadores Socialistas* (Socialist Workers' Party, PTS). To confront this disruptive activism, collective bargaining agreements (CCA) were reactivated. Capitalist enterprises demanded this in an attempt to fragment and institutionalize the demands of the radicalized bases of organized labour

(Campione, 2008). This process carried on in partial and conflictive ways, mediated by different levels of repression and accompanied by other forms of intervention, such as increases in minimum wages by executive decree (to be included later in future collective agreements). The government had to rely on a combination of bureaucratic control of union membership (mainly through the CGT leadership), the Ministry of Labour's intervention and targeted repression of relevant conflicts (for example, Buenos Aires' floating casino and the synthetic fibres manufacturer Mafissa in 2008, Kraft Foods in 2009 etc.). This strategy was successful in stealing control of the political initiative away from grassroots movements and allowed bureaucracies to channel demands within 'rational' boundaries (Féliz, 2012a).[4] Economic expansion resulting from the aforementioned changes in macroeconomic policies and the global situation gave way to growth in employment (and falling unemployment) and allowed the absorption of wage increases without affecting the general profitability of capital (Féliz, 2015: 77). This process produced a progressive systemic inclusion of a significant faction of the new working class, even if this process included varied forms of precariousness and informality.

At the same time, Kirchnerism actively operated to contain social conflict led by the *piquetero* movement. In early 2002, Duhalde's government had created the PJJHD to put down the social fire of the post-20 December 2001 popular uprising. The *piquetero* movement was at the time made up of three main political tendencies (Svampa and Pereyra, 2003). One was composed of 'autonomous' movements inspired by grassroots organizing, the construction of popular power and the New Left (NL) experiences. A second tendency was a grouping of movements mainly inspired by the national-popular tradition of Peronism. Finally, there was an aggregation of movements tied to radical-left parties, especially the other important Trotskyite organization in Argentina, the *Partido Obrero* (Workers Party, PO). This plurality of movements made them extremely difficult to deal with. Besides, most movements had been able to gain access to public resources through street struggles, thus gaining greater political autonomy.

President Kirchner's government promoted the implementation of a new generation of social policies, the so-called 'second generation' social policies promoted and financed by the World Bank and the Inter-American Development Bank (IADB) under the so-called 'Basic Universalism' paradigm. These policies helped neutralize the bases of the popular rebellion. On the one hand, these policies operated as complements to increasing inclusion through the labour market. The PJJHD, born as a quasi-universal plan, was progressively displaced by other plans that tended to emphasize the need for active requisites on the part of benefi-ciaries (Féliz, 2012a: 114). Some of these new programmes (such as the *Plan Manos a la Obra* (Hands-to-Work Plan, PMO)) were used arbitrarily to compensate with extra resources the more 'complacent' organizations, such as the new *Movimiento Evita* (Evita movement, in tribute to Eva Perón, historical leader of the Peronist party) that articulated the lot of the *piquetero* organizations allied to the government. With a combination of 'stick and carrot', Kirchnerism was able to dismantle most significant opposition to the new hegemonic project in the making.

New myth, new hegemonic project

In a favourable international and regional framework, with a successful combination of policies, Kirchnerism was able to rebuild the myth of capitalist development in the periphery. This was backed by the ascension of popular left governments in Venezuela and Bolivia (with Cuba constituting the radical axis of the *Alternativa Bolivariana para las Américas* (Bolivarian Alternative for the Americas, ALBA) and progressive neodevelopmentalism in Brazil, Uruguay, Ecuador and, for some time, Paraguay, and took advantage of favourable dynamics in world capitalism and the momentum of China's incursion into the world market. In such conditions, the neodevelopmentalist project in Argentina was able to create the material and symbolic conditions for the recon-struction of capitalist legitimacy without altering its foundational basis created through neoliberalism (Féliz, 2015): plundering of natural riches (extractivism) and superexploitation of the labour force, extended trans-nationalization of the cycle of local capital and dependency on global powers (USA, European Union) and regional sub-imperialisms (Brazil, China). These elements, which were part of the neoliberal heritage, were integrated as foundations into the neodevelopmentalist project.

In its first five-year period neodevelopmentalism, in its Kirchnerist version, was able to increase employment while maintaining high levels of work precarization (over 50 per cent of the labour force), partially recover real incomes for workers while keeping 20 per cent of the working population in poverty (Féliz et al., 2010) and maintain accelerated economic growth. This was the general dynamic of the first phase of the official process of 'growth with inclusion' (the neodevelop-mentalist version of the neoliberal trickle-down effect).

New hegemonic project with a new state?

In its first years, the neodevelopmentalist project, incarnated by Kirchnerism, was able to regain in a stable way the profit rate for big capitals, opening up space for its expanded reproduction. Sustained expansion in accumulation allowed for the creation of a great number of new jobs, albeit of a precarious nature. In parallel, the better organized factions of the working class were able to partially recover their real wages, while more informal workers as well as public employees suffered stagnation in their real incomes, which remained well under the average levels of the 1990s. Average wages grew in real terms by 4.0 per cent annually (7.8 per cent for registered wage-earners) between 2002 and 2006 (Féliz, 2015: 81). Social policies, multiplied under the support of international credit institutions, created a network of survival that, at this stage, allowed the government to contain social conflict.

Kirchnerism aimed at installing the idea that in this new stage the state would reappear as the great peacemaker in the class struggle, as an actor above all class actors. In the social-democratic tradition, the government attempted to recreate the ever-elusive class alliance between labour and the local bourgeoisie. While this had already been a difficult bet in post-war Argentina during the first round of Peronist governments (1945–55), it would turn into an impossible task in the post-neoliberal era (Féliz, 2012b). With no national bourgeoisie at hand, capitalist 'development' can only be attempted by fostering a local bourgeoise of transnational tendencies.

With a political programme of bourgeoise recomposition in the national-popular tradition of Peronism, Kirchner's government pushed the state to appear more permeable to the contradictory demands of the different social forces in dispute. The state was thus 'softer', more malleable to popular demands, in recognition of a correlation between social forces and a still fragile political equilibrium of classes. However, since the rules of capital had come to deeply permeate the whole realm of social relations, the neodevelopmentalist state was forced to limit emergent social conflict and popular demands within the boundaries of big transnational capital interests. This discourse of development as 'growth with inclusion' finds its proper place here to develop for a while as it served the attempt to build a new project with hegemonic capacity, even if in a contradictory fashion.

FROM RECOVERY TO STAGNATION

Consolidation and first transition

The 2005 legislative elections and the 2007 presidential elections were tests for the ability of the government to create a sustainable hegemony of the power of the state. In 2005, the governing FPV obtained almost 30 per cent of the votes for the House of Deputies (HD). While improving its position, the FPV was still weak in terms of representation in Congress since it had, on its own, only 94 of 257 seats in the HD. After 2007, this representation went up to 153 members of a total of 257 deputies and 44 senators of a total of 72. The left (in all its variants) had no representation.

The high point in political terms in this period was the Summit of the Americas in November 2005. Here, Chávez's political initiative was key to bury the *Alianza de Libre Comercio para las Américas* (Alliance for Free Trade for the Americas, ALCA) project proposed by the president of the USA (George W. Bush). For Kirchnerism, this was the chance to amplify its 'progressive' discourse. The rejection by most Latin American countries of this free trade agreement was a significant setback for US interests in the region.[5] In the 2007 presidential election, Cristina Fernández de Kirchner (Néstor Kirchner's wife) was elected with 45 per cent of the vote.

From 2007 on, the political project of Kirchnerism lacked the few achievements in economic results that had marked the initial stage of recovery after the neoliberal crisis. Economic growth became more unstable, price inflation accelerated and began to paralyze growth in salaries and wages of working families and the labour market strongly reduced its ability to integrate the labour force. There were different factors that contributed to this situation. On the one hand, capitalism in the central imperialist countries was going through a profound crisis of the neoliberal project. On the other hand, the South American region faced a combination of the loss of initiative of the countries in the ALBA project, deepened by Chávez's early death, the consolidation of the neodevelopmentalist projects (under the leadership of Brazil's sub-imperialist policies) and the regional advancement of China in its inter-imperialist dispute with the USA.[6] Last, but not least, internal contradictions particular to the neodevelopmentalist project were translating into ever growing barriers: high and sustained inflation, growing fiscal deficit and increasing foreign exchange deficit, amongst others (Féliz, 2015).

Adjustment on the move

In this context, the new government of Cristina Fernández de Kirchner introduced a controlled devaluation of the nominal exchange rate and more explicit caps on wage negotiations (Féliz, 2014). Inflationary tensions led popular organizations to renew their struggles. Several organizations from the NL, many of them born from the *piquetero* movement, initiated in 2008 a campaign against inflation that included the organization of 'popular markets' (to sell products at low cost, without intermediaries) and the demand for the elimination of Value Added Tax (VAT) on basic products.

The neodevelopmentalist myth began to crumble as it had difficulties living up to the expectations it had created. The objectives of progressive redistribution of income and reindustrialization began to reach their limits. By 2006, capital's response to higher wage demands was to increase inflationary pressure, actual inflation began to exceed 20 per cent of the annual rate. Real wages began to stagnate even for the more organized factions of the labour movement. The result was to bring to a halt the recovery in the share of labour in total income that, since 2007, had only marginally improved. However, while real wages stagnated and productivity growth picked up, the inflation rate has remained in the range of 20–30 per cent annually (Féliz, 2015: 81). A process of intensive accumulation (i.e. substantially higher investment rates and productivity growth) failed to succeed the 'easy' accumulation based on cheap labour (extensive accumulation) and high export prices.

In this phase of instability, Kirchnerism decided to displace the axis of its hegemonic constitution. With that aim, it attempted to confront a bleak economic situation with a Keynesian expansion in public expenditures through the flexibilization of monetary policy and the appropriation of available sources of non-tax income. The combination of a wider fiscal base and changing monetary policy was an attempt to articulate an expansive and compensatory economic policy in a framework of general contraction. The objective was to revalidate the 'growth with social inclusion' in this more adverse situation. In order to achieve this, the government needed to do two things. First, there was the need to reform the function of the central bank, which was still ruled by 1990s legislation that did not allow for easy credit to the government. In late 2009, it was decided to legally allow the central bank to pay public foreign debt. This decision created a political crisis in the government as the central bank's president (the neoliberal Martín Redrado, appointed in September 2004) refused to give course to such payments. He eventually resigned in January 2010. Furthermore, in 2012, the reform of the central bank's charter freed its hand to finance a growing fiscal deficit by pure monetary emission. This change would force the central bank to abandon its independent, inflation-targeting policy and make it more concurrent with neodevelopmentalist macroeconomic policy.

Second, the nationalization of the social security system provided the state with a new source of income without having to create new taxation. This decision came after the failed attempt in mid 2008 to raise taxes on soya exports. The mobilization of exporters and producers, which included roadblocks, generated a political crisis in the government with the vice-president having the swing vote in Congress that rejected the raise. The political consequence of the crisis was the consolidation of a centre-right political space formed by several parties, in particular the traditional *Unión Cívica Radical* (Radical Civil Union, UCR) and the new business-oriented, right-wing party *Propuesta Republicana* (Republican Proposal, PRO). In the 2009 mid-term parliamentary election the *Acuerdo Cívico y Social* (Civic and Social Accord, with the UCR as its main party) obtained 28.9 per cent of the vote, only slightly below FPV's 30.8 per cent. The coalition *Unión PRO* (PRO and allies) got 17.7 per cent.

TRANSITIONAL CRISIS OF KIRCHNERISM IN NEODEVELOPMENTALISM

These new instruments, designed to free economic policy from some (not all) of the remaining restrictions from institutions of neoliberal origin, proved to be of little success in inducing persistent growth. They were unable to displace the structural limits of the economy in the midst of a global crisis. As the world economy began to face its first downturn (2007–09) in this century, the Argentinian economy was well furnished to take the blow and avoid significant negative effects and an outright accumulation crisis. In 2007, international reserves topped 15.7 per cent of GDP (up from only 9.5 per cent in 2003), the current account ran a surplus of 2.8 per cent of GDP (down from 6.4 per cent in 2003) and the national government's primary fiscal surplus was 3.2 per cent of GDP (up from 2.3 per cent in 2003). As exports (mainly commodities) began to fall in late 2008, industrial production stalled. The impact of the world crisis was reflected in falling international reserves and a significant deterioration in the (already fragile) fiscal surplus. However, capital profitability was only slightly affected. After falling in 2008, the profit rate on circulating capital for big companies recovered in 2009 (Féliz, 2015: 84). Thus, a slight economic recovery was set in place for the period 2009–11. In the five years since 2008, average economic growth fell to half that of the previous stage: GDP grew only 4.8 per cent between 2008 and 2013, with at least two years with less than 1 per cent growth.

In spite of the political and social fragmentation of popular protest, the ghost of the upheaval of late 2001 remained as an influence on the form of the state along the entire period. For that reason, in an attempt to overcome the barriers to the hegemonic project in this bleaker stage, Kirchnerism accentuated its national-popular discourse to build the means for materially overcoming the ensuing transitional crisis. If left unchecked, such a crisis would erode Kirchnerism's support and force it out of government, even if that would not necessarily mean the end of the neodevelopmentalist project (or the demise of Kirchnerism as a political force within the Peronist movement).

Since economic growth was lagging, the government increased the use of basic universalism in its policies, which included increasing pension coverage for people without enough contributions, further generalization of cash transfer through the creation of the *Asignación Universal por Hijo* (Universal Benefit for Children) and promotion of popular credit (and indebtedness) to compensate for wage stagnation. The government also activated an existing but mostly unused programme of subsidies for companies in distress called *Programa de Recuperación Productiva* (Programme of Productive Recovery, REPRO), created in 2002 that permitted the government to subsidize the wage bills of almost 200,000 employees of big and medium sized corporations. This allowed companies to suspend workers – instead of firing them – and avoided a sizable political conflict. Finally, in 2009, the creation of the *Plan Argentina Trabaja* (Argentina Works Programme), consisting of about 100,000 jobs in cooperatives financed by the government, allowed the government to relieve the political pressure that social organizations – with origins in the *piquetero* movement born in the 1990s – were taking to the streets (Féliz, 2015: 84).

This 'populist' radicalization was successful in amplifying Kirchnerism's support in the polls in the October 2011 elections. Cristina Fernández de Kirchner was re-elected with 54 per cent of the votes. At the time, a change in electoral law had created compulsory and simultaneous primaries for all political parties (PASO), and had set a minimum of 2 per cent of total voters required for any party to be able to go on to the official election. This promoted the constitution of a radical left electoral front (*Frente de Izquierda y de los Trabajadores* (Front of the Left and Workers, FIT) from three Trotskyite parties (PO, PTS and *Izquierda Socialista* or Socialist Left, IS). They obtained only 2.3 per cent of the popular vote.

With the support of more than 50 per cent of the electorate, Cristina Fernández's last government found Kirchnerism confronting the systemic need to push forth the capitalist radicalization of the hegemonic project through devaluation, fiscal and external adjustment, with the aim of overcoming its barriers (inflation, stagnation in production, employment and wages, fiscal and foreign deficits etc.). This decision expressed its desire to search for its continuity in power for the management of the state. In October 2010, the unexpected death of Néstor Kirchner gave a blow to Kirchnerism's intentions of him coming back as presidential candidate in 2011 or in 2015 (after Cristina Fernández's last constitutional re-election).

The transition began in late 2011 (right after Cristina Fernández's re-election) with a heterodox adjustment policy, dubbed 'fine tuning' by the government. This new policy was marked by tighter controls of foreign currency markets. In late 2013, the new policies were consolidated by naming a new Minister of the Economy (the Keynesian Axel Kiciloff). A significant devaluation of the peso in early 2014, a progressive return to international financial markets, the amplification of the policies of popular credit for consumption and the strengthening of the strategy of implicit wage ceilings were the key tools in the new strategy. These instruments were used to try to adjust the macroeconomic disequilibria that were most evident and risky for the continuity of the neodevelopmentalist strategy (e.g. increasing foreign deficit and loss of productive activity) and in the development of an 'in the medium run' programme that would consolidate the structural bases of the hegemonic project. Due to this 'fine tuning' of economic policy, in 2014 for the first time in more than a decade real wages fell and so did, consequently, popular consumption.

Increasing fragmentation of the labour movement and growing uneasiness amongst the working people and popular organizations marked this new period. The two main labour organizations were divided into factions more or less distant from the government. In 2008 the CGT became divided in three ways, in 2010 the *Central de los Trabajadores Argentinos* (Argentine Workers Central Union, CTA, born in the mid 1990s and constituted mainly by state employees and teachers) was also formally divided. After many years, factions of the CGT and the CTA prepared a general strike for November 2012, several more strikes would come in the next few years. They would have disparate participation and political impact. Kirchnerism's political control was tested in this final stage since economic stagnation, instability and systematic deterioration of the living conditions of the population were fracturing its political coalition and base. This expressed the weakening of the hegemonic capability of neodevelopmentalism as a project of the dominant classes, and that of Kirchnerism as a privileged political actor that warrants its continuation.

Popular sectors are still lacking political alternatives that they recognize as their own and seem to keep betting for the 'lesser evil' that is, paradoxically, always the worst since it promotes the adaptation towards a historically regressive movement (Gramsci, 1999) and it negates the need to build real radical political alternatives and tends to support reformist options within capitalism (such as Kirchnerism). The promising electoral front of the anti-capitalist left around the FIT has not become an option for the masses of people in the field of elections. In the recent 2015 presidential elections, the FIT received only 3.27 per cent. With its limits, this convergence seems to be part of an 'in the medium run' political alternative for radical transformation, to build a political unity in the diversity of practices and traditions that can recover the best of popular 'good sense' (to paraphrase Gramsci) as part of a wide strategy for the construction of popular power. In fact, many popular organizations promoted and campaigned for FIT, even if not formally being part of it.[7]

The new economic policy puts Kirchnerism into crisis (since it needs to find ways to present itself as a dominant political force) and the radicalization (capitalist intensification, if you will) of neodevelopmentalism increases the alienation of its social bases, fragmenting class actors and political forces. The forces of succession within the 'parties of order' (to paraphrase Marx in the 18th Brumaire) are being set in a context quite unlike the one that gave birth to Kirchnerism in 2003. With an organic crisis in the making, the newly elected government of Mauricio Macri, candidate of the right-wing coalition *Cambiemos* (Let's Change) that was constituted for the 2015 elections, will deepen the tendencies to adjustment of the several disequilibria and limits facing the neodevelopmentalist project with the intent to recover the macroeconomic conditions for expansion within this project.[8] This will include acceleration of the devaluation of the local currency, reduction of the fiscal deficit and increasing indebtedness in global markets. The new government will confront the working people while they are in a situation of political disarray, which will be one of Kirchnerism's most important heritages. Only if the people and their organizations can recover the ghost and experience of the 2001 popular uprising will we be in a condition to confront the future with the chance of making it our own.

NOTES

1. Carlos Menem was elected president in 1989. He was a prominent member of the Peronist movement, a political movement characterized for its labour origins but also its pragmatism. Menem was elected on a developmentalist platform but as soon as he took office he embraced a neoliberal programme. Most of the elected members of the Peronist movement at the time defended this right-wing swing.
2. *Piquetero* is the denomination of a way of popular struggle that implies the use of roadblocks (*piquetes*) as an important means of direct action, especially for movements of unemployed people (Dinerstein, 2002). *Piqueteros* are

those people participating in such actions. Darío Santillán and Maximiliano Kosteki were members of the Movimiento de Trabajadores Desocupados (movement of unemployed workers, MTD) Anibal Verón.

3. These demands could be summed up in the expression *Trabajo, Dignidad y Cambio Social* ('Work, Dignity and Social Change', which at the time meant 'socialist' change) and *Que se vayan todos* ('They all must go', in the understanding that the political elite was to be ousted).

4. This does not mean that union leaders did not 'win' benefits for their constituency. However, their need for control over potential competitors within their unions led them to fight against more radical struggles.

5. The ALCA project would deepen Argentina's economic dependency, as it would promote imports from the USA and enhance the production of primary products for exports. Its rejection, however, didn't prevent Argentina's economy from increasing its dependent pattern of association in the world market through growing asymmetric relations with Brazil and China, amongst other economic spaces.

6. China still operates as a sub-imperialist power but it is increasingly becoming a neo-imperialist one.

7. While in social terms, the political forces from the left have significant weight through territorial organizations, unions etc. (although not dominant presence), they still lack sufficient electoral influence. There is much to work out in terms of unity and the ability to gain majority support of the population. But, as the writer Andrés Rivera says, 'revolution is an eternal dream'.

8. As we were closing this chapter, on 23 November 2015 the PRO candidate, Mauricio Macri, had won the presidency in the 2nd round against the Kirchnerist candidate Daniel Scioli, by a slim margin of 51.4 per cent against 48.6 per cent.

BIBLIOGRAPHY

Bonnet, A. (2006). 'Qué se vayan todos!: Discussing the Argentine Crisis and Insurrection'. *Historical Materialism*, 14 (1): 157–84.

Bressser-Pereira, L.C. (2010). *Globalización y competencia. Apuntes para una macroeconomía estructuralista del desarrollo.* Buenos Aires: Siglo XXI Editora Iberoamericana.

Campione, D. (2008). '"Reaparición obrera" en Argentina a partir de 2004'. In M. López Maya, N. Iñigo Carrera and P. Calveiro (eds), *Luchas contrahegemónicas y cambios políticos recientes de América Latina.* Buenos Aires: CLACSO: 279–98.

Curia, E. (2007). *Teoría del modelo de desarrollo de la Argentina: las condiciones para su continuidad.* Buenos Aires: Galerna.

Dinerstein, A.C. (2002). 'The Battle of Buenos Aires: Crisis, Insurrection and the Reinvention of Politics in Argentina'. *Historical Materialism*, 10 (4): 5–38.

Féliz, M. (2011a). *Un estudio sobre la crisis en un país periférico.* Buenos Aires: Editorial El Colectivo.

——(2011b). 'Neoliberalismos, neodesarrollismos y proyectos contrahegemónicos en Suramérica'. *Astrolabio*, 7: 238–65.

—— (2012a). 'Neo-developmentalism Beyond Neoliberalism? Capitalist Crisis and Argentina's Development since the 1990s'. *Historical Materialism*, 20 (2): 105–23.

—— (2012b). 'Sin clase. Neodesarrollismo y neoestructuralismo en Argentina (2002–2011)'. *Século XXI. Revista de Ciências Sociai*, 2 (2): 9–43.

—— (2014). 'The Neo-developmentalist Alternative: Capitalist Crisis, Popular Movements, and Economic Development in Argentina since the 1990s'. In S. Spronk and J. Weber (eds), *Crisis and Contradiction. Marxist Perspectives on Latin America in the Global Political Economy*. Leiden: Brill: 52–72.

—— (2015). 'Limits and Barriers of Neodevelopmentalism: Lessons from the Argentinean Experience, 2003–2011'. *Review of Radical Political Economics*, 47 (1): 70–89.

Féliz, M. and Pérez, P.E. (2010). 'Políticas públicas y las relaciones entre capital y trabajo. Contrastes y continuidades en la pos-convertibilidad a la luz de la historia argentina'. In C. Figari, P. Lenguita and J. Montés Cató (eds), *El movimiento obrero en disputa. La organización colectiva de los trabajadores, su lucha y resistencia en la Argentina del siglo XX*. Buenos Aires: CEIL-PIETTE/ CONICET, Fundación Centro Integral Comunicación, Cultura y Sociedad/ Ediciones CICCUS.

Féliz, M., López, E. and Fernández, L. (2010). 'Estructura de clase, distribución del ingreso y políticas públicas. Una aproximación al caso argentino en la etapa post-neoliberal'. Available at http://marianfeliz. iles.wordpress. com/2010/10/02-02-jec-2010-feliz-lopez- fernandez.pdf (accessed 16 May 2016).

Gramsci, A. (1999). *Cuadernos de la cárcel*, 9 (XIV). México: Benemérita Universidad Autónoma de Puebla: 294–5.

Mazzeo, M. (2010). *Poder popular y nación. Notas sobre el Bicentenario de la Revolución de Mayo*. Buenos Aires: El Colectivo/Ediciones Herramienta.

Schorr, M. (2005). *Modelo nacional industrial*. Buenos Aires: Capital Intelectual.

Svampa, M. and Pereyra, S. (2003). *Entre la ruta y el barrio. La experiencia de las organizaciones piqueteras*. Buenos Aires: Editorial Biblos.

6

Whither Social Democracy in Chile?

Ximena de la Barra Mac Donald

Following the 17-year dictatorship of General Pinochet, the 'transition to democracy' in Chile has continued a legacy of over 40 years of neoliberal entrenchment. Supporters of the Pinochet dictatorship managed to recycle themselves into a new political party and became a major political force. Selling out to the neoliberal model, the renovated Socialist Party and the Christian Democratic Party, now together in government, have turned Chile's eminently middle class society, which prevailed from the late 1930s to the early 1970s, into one of the most polarized societies in the twenty-first century. The indiscriminate opening of Chile to foreign trade and investment, and a relentless will to serve hegemonic interests dominating the region, have resulted in the loss of sovereignty over natural resources and lack of financial resources to allow for state involvement in the transformation of society. Social movements have been masterfully co-opted, or have been criminalized under the repressive laws dating back to the dictatorship. Democracy and a whole range of human rights have been the main casualties in this process.

Analyzing social democracy in Chile is no easy task since this political ideology is hard to find in the current political scene. In this chapter ideological shifts in the main political parties and in party coalitions are introduced, with the intention of finding the elusive social democratic traces within them. This is followed by a description of the recent evolution of equally elusive democracy in Chile, subverted by neoliberalism, corruption and the current Constitution. Even if a real presence of social democracy was found, it would offer no answer to Chile's structural problems and to the locks that currently block any possible solutions to them. Nevertheless, a note of optimism for the future, which emerges from past history and from current struggles led by social movements, concludes the analysis.

IDEOLOGICAL SHIFTS IN THE MAIN CHILEAN POLITICAL PARTIES

The Social Democratic Radical Party (PRSD)

We start by analyzing the only current party that nominally pays tribute to social democracy, the PRSD, founded in 1994 when the Social Democratic Party, dating from 1971, joined with the Radical Party (PR), which was created in 1863 with a centre-left orientation. Both parties were part of the Unidad Popular (UP), or Popular Unity, the coalition supporting socialist President Allende's electoral campaign and participating in the first part of his three-year government (1971–73). A split in the PR in 1971[1] destroyed the UP alliance with the middle class and the bourgeoisie, which the PR had represented. It was the left wing of the PR that remained in the UP rejecting bourgeois democracy and declaring themselves socialists. In 1983, the PR and the Social Democrats both joined an early coalition opposing the Pinochet regime. Since the transition to democracy in 1990, they both became part of the ruling neoliberal coalition, the *Concertación de Partidos por la Democracia (Concertación)*, now *Nueva Mayoría* (1990–2010, 2014–present), and they continued to be part of it after they merged to form the PRSD. Even though the PRSD is a minority party, it holds office in the Senate and the Chamber of Deputies, as well as in some municipal governments, courtesy of the flawed Chilean electoral system inherited from the dictatorship.[2] The PRSD is affiliated with the Socialist International, as is the Socialist Party.

The Socialist Party (PS)

Younger than the PR, the PS, founded in 1933, is now considered a centre-left party by the official press. While in exile, during the Pinochet years, people who currently call themselves progressives, formerly supporters of socialism, became enthused with European 'third way' reformed socialists. They hoped that European social democracy, with their new ideologies and financial support could potentially provide for those struggling against the dictatorship (Vitale, 1982: 1). Thus, the PS renovated itself by abandoning its Marxist and revolutionary roots and rhetorically becoming social democratic and claiming to reconfigure or humanize capitalism. In reality, while in government and contrary to social democratic principles, the PS has been a strong promoter of neoliberal policies – defending the interests of big business instead of the Chilean people. Rather than humanizing capitalism they have been perfecting it and defending it from popular revolt. Former radicals and

Marxists have abandoned their dreams of emancipation, transforming Chile into one of the most unequal societies in the world.

The PS became staunch defenders of impunity, most especially that of dictator Pinochet, and gladly accepted amnesty arrangements for him. The PS appointed one of its leading members, Jose Miguel Inzunza[3] to be in charge of the pantomime aimed at rescuing Pinochet from trial after he was arrested in London. The PS also came to serve the interests of the United States both in foreign and internal affairs.[4] This was a huge transformation, considering that during the Allende period the PS was more radical than the Communist Party (PC), so radical that they refused to support the president, a PS militant himself, when most needed.[5] Rather than supporting Allende's tactics, they perceived him as a conciliatory reformist (Moulian, 1998a: 89–99). Radical socialists at that time, were not willing to accept the political rhythms required by the process. They also did not understand the need to broaden the political base by making overtures to the left wing of the Christian Democrats (PDC), mostly followers of Liberation Theology. Since Allende believed that socialism ought to be an expression of perfected democracy, he did not act against the PS (Moulian, 1998a: 54–5).

Salvador Allende gave his life during the 1973 military coup, among other reasons because he was trying to show the world that the 'democratic road to socialism' was possible, a premise that the imperial power was not ready to allow. Equally unacceptable to these powers was the fact that Allende democratically nationalized the copper industry,[6] jeopardizing the interests of transnational companies, mainly those of the United States. During the presidency of renovated socialist Ricardo Lagos (2000–06), one of his many betrayals to what had been Chilean socialist principles was granting foreign interests full concession[7] to the copper mines, reversing nationalization and allowing the plunder of Chile's main natural resource, export commodity and foreign income source (Caputo and Galarce, 2011: 60). Lagos also betrayed people's trust by legitimizing with his presidential signature the dictatorship's 1980 Constitution, without consulting the people (Grez, 2011: 67–90). Eliminating only a few flagrant anti-democratic articles, such as the one relating to the 'designated' senators, he left the main body intact, including the enforcement of neoliberalism. It therefore comes as no surprise that he was considered by the business community to be 'the best right-wing president of all times' (Portales, 2014b). Lago's chameleonic nature was not apparent while he had a remarkable role in the opposition to the dictatorship from a democratic stand. His democratic credentials have now all but disappeared since he was not only willing to negotiate with the dictatorship but also became a supporter of the coup in Venezuela (Portales, 2015).

Current socialist president Michelle Bachelet is still to this day refusing to call for a Constitutional Assembly, to democratically draft a new social pact that would turn her own promises for social reform into something more than empty promises. It is hard to believe that with such a record, the PS can be considered social democratic, let alone socialist. Among the higher ranks, some socialists have become successful business entrepreneurs, others high level national or international bureaucrats. Most have enjoyed the personal benefits and privileges of the revolving doors between these two positions.

The Party for Democracy (PPD)

When outlawed during the dictatorship, some socialists formed the (PPD), an instrumental party to end the dictatorship, that still remains as a distinct party and mainly consists of renovated socialists and social democratic radicals, as well as people from diverse political origins. Its initial stated ideology was social democracy and liberal socialism. Currently, it self-defines itself as a left-wing, democratic and progressive party. The truth of the matter is that it is as neoliberal as the rest of the *Concertación*. Possibly the best-known member is former President Lagos, who holds double membership in the PS and the PPD.

The Christian Democratic Party (PDC)

The PDC is no suspect of social democratic inclination but, together with the PS, is one of the most blatant examples of ideological shifts and political transformation in Chilean politics. It also plays a prominent role, similar to the PS in the *Concertación* first and later in *Nueva Mayoría*. As the party in government prior to Allende and the UP under the slogan 'Revolution in liberty', they emphasized reforms and enhancement of local communities. But as soon as Allende was elected in 1970, an important PDC leader, who later became the first president of the transition to democracy, Patricio Aylwin (1990–94), undemocratically undertook negotiations with the Armed Forces to impede Allende from taking office (Garcés, 1993: 6). The PDC's alliance with the right wing to oppose the UP ended the tri-polar political situation existing in 1970 (Conservatives, UP, PDC), when the UP was voted into power. Even though fractions within the PDC, the Popular Unitary Action Movement (MAPU) and the Christian Left (IC), convinced of the need for more profound reforms, converged towards the UP, the PDC as a whole remained actively in the opposition, including taking aggressive actions, such as purposely causing a bank run to destabilize the new Allende government.

After wholeheartedly supporting the military coup in 1973, the PDC turned democratic again, opposing the dictatorship within an opposition coalition including some of their former arch-enemies. As soon as they took a stand against the dictatorship, their leaders too were murdered, including former President Frei Montalva (1964–70). The irony being that later, in a second twist, as *Concertación* members, they actively defended impunity for Pinochet as did the *Concertación* as a whole.

The Concertación

A coalition of political parties, the strongest of which are the PS, the PPD and the PDC, was formed with the aim to lead the transition to democracy after the 17-year long dictatorship (1973–89). A perpetual transition, as human rights lawyer Roberto Garretón rightfully calls it (Garretón, 2011: 73–92), since it is certainly far from completed. In essence, it was supposed to integrate social democrats and Christian democrats so it also included the PRSD and PPD. In negotiations with the dictatorship, reneging on their social rights-based programme and betraying the trust of their voters, the *Concertación* opted for maintaining and entrenching the neoliberal model and the institutional and political systems enshrined in the 1980 Constitution, which are to this day the main obstacles for democratic progress.

Edgardo Boeninger, a *Concertación* ideologue and former minister, later recognized that the *Concertación* had no intention of complying with their first electoral programme. He also stated that the *Concertación* leadership, by the end of the 1980s, had given an ideological U-turn, converging with the right wing's stand on economics, even though at the time they were not in a position to make this shift public (Boeninger, 1997: 368–70). This explains why instead of replacing the neoliberal economic model imposed by the dictatorship they proceeded to legitimize, consolidate and perfect it. The same explains why they opted to adopt the Pinochet Constitution – approved in a plebiscite under a state of siege.

The Constitution bans the state from competing with private enterprises and can only intervene in those activities in which the private sector does not have an interest. In those cases, it can either be involved by direct activity or by subsidizing private activity. This is what in Chile is called the 'subsidiary role of the state'. It is this provision in the Constitution that was used to dismantle state enterprises and privatize basic state functions from 1980, when the Pinochet Constitution was enacted, until this day. This is how the huge and powerful economic conglomerates and their intricate networks emerged and have become the real power governing the country. It is also how corruption and the power of money over politics began to reign.

Former presidential candidate Tomas Hirsch has stated, *Concertación* 'today is an enterprise where there are shareholders, where there are positions and where dividends are paid, but where there is no project for social transformation. Therefore, there is no leftist component in the *Concertación*' (Hirsch, 2006). Fully concurring with this view, it is worth adding that there is also no social democratic component. It has become very difficult for these centre-left progressives to prove that they are any different from the conservatives. The words of the current president of the Chilean Student Federation (FECH) say it all: 'now we see how the profound differences that the *Alliance* (right-wing coalition) and the *Concertación* say they have, in reality don't exist when at the end of the day they both receive funding and reach agreements with the same businessmen' (Saavedra, 2015).

The Chilean Communist Party (PC)

Even though originally not suspect of pledging to social democratic principles, recent transformations in the PC make it necessary to include this party at this point in this chapter in order to understand the current ruling coalition. The Socialist Workers Party, a PC precursor, was founded in 1912 and ten years later joined the Communist International, officially becoming the Chilean Communist Party (PC), of Marxist-Leninist ideology. The PC backed the Allende UP government until the very end. Decades later, in 2013, in order to overcome its isolation and have access to a handful of parliamentary benches and one or two ministries, it converged towards the centre and joined the *Concertación* – from that moment on renamed the *Nueva Mayoría* (New Majority). Rather than exercising a notable influence, this transformation has meant a significant loss of identity for the party. Sociologist Tomás Moulian, regarding the PC, has stated that 'in spite of its explicit commitment with a democratization programme – the sickle and the hammer in the midst of the neoliberal plot – looks more like a social democratic current advancing in the direction of an improved neoliberalism' (Moulian and Salazar, 2014).

As corruption scandals within the *Nueva Mayoría* begin to dominate the concerns of Chilean society, the PC becomes one of the great losers since its loyalty to its newly acquired coalition stains its previous good name. It has also become ineffective in leading unions as it feels forced to support the tepid government reforms, most of all labour reform that does not rescue trade unionism from the weak position it was left in by the dictatorship.

Nueva Mayoría

Nueva Mayoría, elected in 2014 with Bachelet as its leader, has turned out to be a mere electoral exercise based on Bachelet's now faded charisma and the use of slogans people were eager to hear, such as a promise to end the flagrant disparities, but with no larger vision of structural change for society as a whole.

Parties situated to the left of *Nueva Mayoría* remain excluded from the parliament because of the undemocratic binominal electoral system embedded in the Constitution. They have not managed to form their own coalition, the only way small parties can expect to enter office. Hope is now being placed on the student movement that has emerged with great strength and a comprehensive understanding of society, denouncing not only the model turning education into a commodity but the economic and political model as a whole. The *Concertación* earlier and the *Nueva Mayoría* currently has been diligent in their efforts to domesticate this movement (Mayol, 2014).

The Alliance

Even though conservatives have no relation to social democracy, several issues are addressed in order to understand the current democratic deficits. The right-wing parties in the opposition have been the only ones to remain faithful to their ideology, distancing themselves from democratic beliefs. Suffice it to say that among its ranks are those who take pride in considering themselves the true heirs of Pinochet's legacy, the Independent Democratic Union (UDI). Its main identity is the defence of the socio-economic and political institutional structures, including the binominal electoral system and the extremely high quorums required to modify constitutional laws contained in the 1980 Constitution. For electoral purposes, UDI formed a coalition, the *Alianza*, with *Renovación Nacional* (RN), a slightly more moderate conservative-liberal party claiming to represent the centre-right. This coalition managed to gain the presidency with business leader Sebastian Piñera (2010–13), mainly because Chileans felt betrayed by the *Concertación*. Forced to choose between two different right-wing coalitions, the more moderate *Concertación* and the *Alianza*, the Chilean people decided by a thin margin to punish the one that had pretended to be progressive and democratic as it governed during the preceding 20 years of 'neoliberal continuity' (de la Barra, 2011: 1).

It would be hard to find another country where actors with important roles within a dictatorship, including proven but not convicted torturers, manage to recycle themselves as elected officials or get appointed as high level public servants designated by their rival coalition, in this case, the *Concertación*. The two coalitions participating in the electoral game invariably end by exercising politics by consensus. The worst case of political consensus being the one providing impunity to Pinochet and other human rights violators, and also, as has now been found, that *Concertación* and *Allianza* are partners in crime regarding the corruption scandals and their cover-up attempts.

Media conglomerates make sure Chileans have little awareness of the magnitude of these ideological transformations and betrayals, so that people will continue voting as if they were electing politicians that would act on their behalf. The *Concertación* has been instrumental in destroying independent or alternative media, including their own (Portales, 2011a, 2011b, 2011c). Freedom of expression and information is thus distorted by the market and Chile ranks as number one in the concentration of media in Latin America (Ballantine, 2014). Chileans have been made to believe that their country is the most successful country in Latin America, and that those who are not thriving can only blame their own personal shortcomings. The myth that has been circulated worldwide and supported by the international financial institutions is that Chileans have undertaken an exemplary transition and have made a remarkable leap towards development. Chile has been designated as the showcase for neoliberalism in Latin America (de la Barra, 2011: 1).

SUBVERTED DEMOCRACY

The concept of democracy has been transformed in Chile, throughout the endless period of the still unfinished transition to democracy or democracy to the extent possible. Far from meaning equal rights for all, the shortfalls of Chilean democracy evolved towards the more restricted term of 'electoral democracy'. For those who were aware of the unfairness of the electoral system, this was the wrong term. Other more realistic terms for Chilean democracy followed: 'tutelage democracy' (Portales, 2000), meaning democracy under the guardianship of right-wing Pinochet supporters – whether military or civilian; 'low intensity democracy' (Punto Final, 2005); 'democracy without democrats' (Roitman, 2011); and so on.

The term 'negotiated democracy' would have been better, according to this author, in view of the fact that the main opposition and the dictatorship actually negotiated an end to the regime in exchange for secret concessions to the dictatorship, such as: amnesty laws; Pinochet's continuing as commander in chief of the Armed Forces; 10 per cent of copper sales earmarked to fund the Armed Forces; a certain number of designated rather than elected members of parliament; and non-compliance regarding a broad range of human rights. But it was worse, rather than negotiating between different positions, it turned out to be a commonly shared agreement.

Since all *Concertación* governments up to this date have ruled in overt or covert consensus with the right-wing coalition, and both have monopolized electoral results, the term 'consensus democracy' soon emerged (Moulian, 1997: 37–45). Though the *Concertación* claims that their proposals have been vetoed in parliament by the right-wing coalition, the fact is that whenever they found themselves constituting a majority, they did not bother to use their voting power in parliament to mend the flaws in the system (Portales, 2014a). Ricardo Lagos (renovated socialist) and Pablo Longueira (Pinochet supporter) gave Chileans a great show of what consensus politics could do when, in 2003, they worked together to create the most shameful impunity agreements to protect those who had allowed the secret topping up of salaries for high level government officers and the overall fraudulent funding of politics. The *Nueva Mayoría* is again, in 2015, negotiating a probity pact with the Alliance in order to approach, as business as usual, a new wave of corruption that has been made public.

Tomás Moulian coined the concept 'demobilizing democracy', not referring to repression but instead to apathy towards the electoral processes. This apathy is due to job insecurities and anti-union legislation, which has led to the atomization and decline of the former union movement. To this he adds the emergence of a 'neoliberalized left' that has substituted their former belief in socialism for a belief in democratic capitalism, contributing to legitimize the system and turning the masses into being more interested in consuming and entertainment than in public affairs (Moulian, 1995: 35). This is especially serious considering that with the sole exception of Sebastian Piñera's government (2010–14), the so-called left has been in government with the *Concertación* since the end of the dictatorship.

In view of the appallingly widespread corruption within state institutions and among government officers and politicians, going way beyond the revolving door between politics and big business, Chileans these days are reading headlines calling democracy oligarchic democracy, plutocracy and worse, 'cleptocratic' democracy. What is irrefutable is that the economic power has blatantly subverted democracy in Chile, adding a political debt to the social, economic and environmental debt that neoliberalism accumulates.

The fraudulent mechanism that was utilized to fund political campaigns worked as follows. The politicians or their front men would provide business conglomerates with false invoices for work that had never been undertaken, and covertly devote such funds to their campaigns or add to their personal wealth. Business would then proceed to deduct those amounts as expenses, paying less tax and in the long run defrauding the state and stealing from the Chilean people what the fiscal policies would have otherwise funded.

Politicians, thus oiled, would have to place their voting power at the service of their benefactors' interests, even though that could mean going against the programme they were elected for. This explains the extremely limited nature of the current government reform proposals. Students have come to realize they have wasted a year negotiating to improve the education reforms. Labour has been defeated in their right to negotiate by economic sector or branch and instead have seen their rights weakened, their jobs become more precarious and their leaders too close to the establishment to be willing to struggle for reasonable labour reforms, which now stand as pro-business and do not comply with international agreements. Illegal funding of politics has been the instrument to obstruct any possibility of transforming or regulating the corrupt neoliberal repressive and anti-democratic model inherited from the dictatorship. It also blocks any redistributive mechanism that would jeopardize the privileges held by the economic powers.

As people become aware of the corruption in which the institutional system is immersed, a new demobilizing factor emerges, and they increasingly lose their faith in elections, in current electoral laws and in representative democracy, as proven by extremely high abstention figures. Socialist President Michelle Bachelet was elected in late 2013 with 60 per cent of only 39 per cent of potential voters. She was opposed, among others, by a social movement calling for an electoral strike. News alerting of entrenched corruption in her government, and even within her family, are reflected in the latest surveys that show further declines in popularity and credibility for this president.

Chile can also not be considered democratic when it ranks as the most unequal of all countries with comparable data in terms of income distribution. Income inequality in Chile is determined in part by a lopsided tax system that taxes wages more heavily than capital. A study by a group of economists from the University of Chile's Faculty of Business and Economics found that if capital gains were to be properly included in income statistics, the level of income inequality would surge. The Gini coefficient, the standard measure of income inequality, would increase by 8 points, from 0.55 to 0.63. This research also confirmed that the imbalance rests primarily with the ultra-rich, the wealthiest 1 per cent and especially the wealthiest 0.1 and 0.01 per cent. Even when estimating their income conservatively, their share of total national personal income is extraordinarily high: over 30 per cent for the wealthiest 1 per cent, 17 per cent for the wealthiest 0.1 per cent and more than 10 per cent for the wealthiest 0.01 per cent, as an average, during the 2004–10 period (López et al., 2013: 24–5).

The disenfranchised are expected to become entrepreneurs as if they had the necessary tools or the resources to compete with that privileged 1 per cent. Those who fail or do not dare are considered to be irresponsible and forgers of their own ill fate (Mayol, 2013: 23, 135–7). Education is also seen as an answer for social mobility, ignoring the fact that education, too, is segregated. Entrepreneurship and easy credit are demobilizing factors that make people believe that because they are consumers, they are integrated within the system (Moulian, 1998b: 63–4). Individualism surges, but individualism does not help when education, health care, the pension system and other services needed for social reproduction have been sold to for-profit enterprises, further exacerbating income disparities among Chileans. A state that does not protect the human rights of those excluded from the system cannot be considered either developed or democratic. The fact that Chile was admitted into the Organisation for Economic Co-operation and Development (OECD), the club of developed countries, becomes void of any significant meaning when Chile ranks 36th and last among them in terms of income inequality.

In another show of undemocratic undertakings, Chile has been the champion in signing bilateral Free Trade Agreements but has remained only an observer in counter-hegemonic regional trade agreements such as MERCOSUR and has no intention of joining ALBA.[8] Faithful to its determination to serve hegemonic powers, Chile spearheaded the formation of the Trans-Pacific Partnership (TPP), which serves transnational corporation's interests, is subjected to the International Center for Settlement of Investment Disputes (ICSID) and has power over national policies, legislation and regulations. It therefore comes as no surprise that Chilean democracy has become a democracy without citizens, a democracy without sovereignty.

THE CHILEAN ROAD TO SOCIALISM

Chileans, however, have a history that can be used to muster strength. Chilean youth has become eager to unearth this history in order to guide them in their struggles. Salvador Allende (1908–73), who has been considered for years to be a loser by many in Chile, is now being vindicated as an example of dignity and democratic convictions. The *Chilean road to socialism* continues to be relevant even though neither the *Concertación* nor the *Nueva Mayoría* have made any attempts to honour it.

Allende emerged from within a welfare state tradition in a family of radical party militants. He was 25 when he became co-founder of the Chilean Socialist Party (Marxist) in Valparaiso, and 29 when he was elected to Congress, while simultaneously practising medicine. He became Health Minister in President Aguirre Cerda's (PR) Popular Front government (1938–41), integrating radicals, socialists and communists. The motto this government is proudly remembered for is: 'To govern is to educate', and educate at all levels they did (Amorós, 2013: 17–78). An egalitarian culture was thus being forged.

Inspired by the epic of the Spanish Republic and the horrors of fascism in Europe, Chile became the only country in Latin America to form a popular and anti-fascist front during the 1930s. It was this front that displaced from power the traditional oligarchic parties that had governed Chile since independence (Amorós, 2013: 63–9). The need to unite progressive forces became firmly embedded in Allende's political convictions, even though he continued his socialist militancy throughout his life and became the PS Secretary General in 1943.

Other popular fronts would follow, such as the UP that placed Allende in office in 1970, but with communists and socialists rather than radicals taking the lead. For the first time in Chile, the Marxist left, social democrats, Christians for socialism, progressive sectors and independents all joined forces around a UP Programme (Unidad Popular, 1969). Beyond addressing social needs, which was also done by earlier popular fronts, the UP made a substantial step forward in addressing the structural causes of these needs, namely, capitalism, imperialism, monopolies and heavily concentrated land tenure. Socialism was understood as enhanced democracy and became the guiding principle for the *Chilean road*. Executive power was to be reached without resorting to armed insurrection, believing that the peaceful way was also revolutionary as long as it included the masses and their class struggle (Corvalán, 1971: 32–4). The basic concepts contained in the programme were democracy, pluralism and freedom, and the way to achieve them was through the electoral process and the existing institutional arrangements (Garretón and Moulian, 1993: 184). Armed struggle was purposely avoided in view that the UP did not have a military apparatus of its own. Since the peaceful, legal option required the support of the majority of the population, the UP resorted to strengthening class-consciousness and workers' unity and to a coexistence with the middle class sectors within the opposition (Garcés, 2013: 57–9).

The originality of the *Chilean road* was not only that it was a pacifist road but did not call for the dictatorship of the proletariat, the overall nationalization of the economy or the destruction of the state. Allende saw the possibility of placing the state at the service of the people by changing the class character of the legal order. He initially attempted to utilize all available constitutional provisions to his advantage. For example, the wording of an agrarian reform law passed by a previous government allowed the president of the republic to intervene in the sector at the first sign of landowner resistance, enabling executive power to accelerate the purchase of farms on favourable terms for the government. Another legal decree dating back to 1932 allowed the government to nationalize industrial holdings that failed to comply with state norms concerning inventories when the government determined that a given commodity was in short supply (Amorós, 2013: 320–1).

In December 1970, Allende presented to the Congress a constitutional amendment that would give absolute, exclusive, inalienable and irrevocable control of the state over the Chilean copper mining industry, including the power to expropriate the assets of any foreign company that it deemed was in the national interest. Following extensive debate in both congressional houses, all parties unanimously approved the amendment, thus authorizing the nationalization of copper mining (Caputo and Galarce, 2011: 50). While the opposition was concerned that this would bolster Allende's presidency, it was a sober recognition of the nearly universal popularity of the measure.

This strategy could only stretch so far. The working class had not yet become the dominant class (Garcés, 2013: 129). The need to negotiate in order to broaden the social base so that the UP Programme would become a reality was the only viable alternative. Allende announced his plan to more comprehensively reform the Constitution so as to socialize it and to institutionalize workers' participation at all levels of decision-making. He believed that this could only be possible in conjunction with highly mobilized mass participation of popular forces so that support for the popular government could be sustained by its class base, rather than by its limited electoral base. Allende was aware of the risks involved in undertaking constitutional change and took pains in explaining these intentions, saying:

> We will submit to the people's sovereign will the need to replace the present Liberal constitution with one of a Socialist orientation, and the current two chamber system of parliament with a single house. In this institutional manner, the government's program is committed to respecting legal due process in carrying out its revolutionary project. (Allende, 1971: 38)

And:

> The Chilean people are conquering political power without resorting to the use of arms and legitimately aspire to complete the phase of the transition to socialism without having to resort to authoritarian forms of government. It is my obligation, however, to warn the people of the danger that threatens the trajectory of our emancipation ... This threat is that of the use of violence against the decision made by our people. (Allende, 1971: 41)

The greatest challenge was to advance towards socialism when only the executive branch of the Chilean state had been conquered (Harnecker, 2013: 12). By 1972, Congress, the arena for the two social bases in dispute, started decomposing and the Justice System opposed the executive power (Garcés, 2013: 132). The PS brought to the forefront the idea of the need to destroy current institutions, which Allende opposed with vigour. He argued that it is not in the institutions where the power of the bourgeoisie is lodged but in their economic power. He also reminded the PS that it was the Chilean people who had conquered state institutions in order to institute the UP Programme. State administration needed to be modified but not destroyed (Allende, 1972a: 157–68).

Opposition forces were by then using every legal means possible to put the brakes on the UP Programme, including filing a suit against the executive branch and blocking the national budget. A constitutional reform was passed designed to prevent the president from further nationalizing industries or companies without expressed approval from Congress. Allende vetoed the legislation, and the opposition was unable to muster a two thirds majority to override it. An economic war was also being waged with the support of the United States, a shortage of basic consumer items and inflation were manufactured artificially. By

September 1973, the level of social conflict was substantially elevated throughout Chilean society.

Once Allende completed his proposal for a new Constitution seeking to move forward in democratizing the state, he circulated it to each political party within the UP. It was later to be submitted for discussion by the entire Congress. By then, the right-wing opposition was leading a virtual insurrection against the government, resulting in a postponement of congressional debate. Allende's idea was to form a pact with the more moderate Christian Democratic elements on the main point of contention between them, namely, the relative importance to be accorded to state, private and mixed forms of property. But the nature of the negotiations convinced Allende that the only real solution would be to submit the project directly to the Chilean people for approval by plebiscite (Garcés, 1993: 7–8).

Allende's reformulated proposal responded to the demands and expectations of popular and middle classes, enhancing their level of control over power and economic surplus (Garcés, 1993: 7). He communicated to the Armed Forces his intention to call a national plebiscite on his proposed constitutional reform. But the Armed Forces were in reality already well advanced in the planning of a *coup d'état* and decided that timing was critical to pre-empt Allende's move. As the president was preparing his televised speech to inform the nation, the Chilean Armed Forces betrayed their constitutional obligations to the country and launched the coup of 11 September 1973. The attack on the presidential palace resulted in the death of the president and the birth of a new militarized state predicated on terror, torture and the dismantlement of all revolutionary programmes, with the enthusiastic backing of Washington. Ironically, the *Chilean road* was not armed but it was also not peaceful. While it relied on the Constitution, *the legal way* could not be contested legally by the opposition who had to resort instead to the destruction of the state (Garcés, 2013: 188–9), which Allende had struggled so hard to defend.

The scene was set for imposition at gunpoint of the first neoliberal experiment, influenced by Spanish rancid catholic *gremialismo* emanating from the Franco dictatorship and by Milton Friedman and the Chicago School of Economics laissez-faire neoliberal fundamentalism. Later, with the 1980 Constitution, the dictatorship made sure matters were so tied up that no matter who would govern in the future, the system would remain. A country historically known for its progressive social policies and active union movement soon lacked both. The guns started to become unnecessary, the dictatorship an embarrassment to the United States.

AFTERWORD

To this day, the institutional arrangements inherited from the dictatorship are impeding real democracy, that kind of perfected democracy that Allende dreamed of when pursuing the *Chilean road to socialism*. It has also become pathetically evident that the neoliberal economic model inherited from the dictatorship has not only not been replaced by a social democratic one but has also become entrenched, making any shade of welfare state impossible. People are forced to resort to the market to satisfy their basic needs and will only get government subsidies if they manage to overcome bureaucracy and prove they are extremely poor. The main consequence is that democracy, other than the right to vote in the framework of a skewed electoral system, is nowhere to be seen. Nevertheless, the one gain has been that unless you are a Mapuche,[9] you are demonstrating to demand your rights or you are randomly and baselessly considered an 'anarchist', you can sleep peacefully at night, provided, needless to say, that you have a decent salary and you are not deep in debt, as most Chileans are, courtesy of the neoliberal model.

Welfare state capitalism of the 1930s has been replaced by a deregulated crony capitalism that generates yet more intense subjugation pressures. As we have seen, the nature of the multiple crises smothering Chilean people is such that humanizing capitalism will not solve them, therefore social democracy, if it existed, would not be the answer. The worst crisis – the loss of credibility in state institutions and in the political system – will not be easy to overcome. The underlying causes embedded in the Constitution make the future uncertain, highlighting the urgency of the need to break the locks that the dictatorship firmly closed on Chilean people.

Unlike the *Chilean road*, this time, a totally fresh start is needed. Utilizing the existing legal order to benefit the people is currently impossible due to its illegitimate nature, which, among other absurdities, ties in neoliberalism as the model to perpetuate. The only possible new beginning is a Constitutional Assembly with supra-constitutional power that will return Chileans their lost sovereignty by democratically drafting a new Constitution to be ratified by universal vote. A process that current dominant powers will avoid at all cost because the aim would precisely be to regulate and limit their power. This conflict of interest grants constituted powers no legitimacy as constituting power. Therefore, citizens must take the floor.

Students are the best positioned to become the leaders in this process. They have already conquered the hearts and minds of many who join them, marching in their public demonstrations. They are young enough not to have been co-opted or corrupted. Most were born after the *coup d'état*, but have demanded that their elders help them understand the truth that is kept concealed. They are full of energy and enthusiasm. They are old and well informed enough to understand, as Allende did, that more socialism means more democracy, very much unlike democracy under the actually existing socialisms of the past century. They are well aware that there are alternatives to neoliberalism, and that it is their right as well as their will to struggle for those alternatives. They are realistic enough to understand that in Chile, the process of change depends on a new Constitution developed democratically through a Constitutional Assembly, and on recovering the mineral wealth that belongs to all Chileans, since that wealth will be instrumental as a source of funding to turn their dreams into a reality.

Political education, organization and popular unity are the name of the game. A comprehensive understanding of our current reality and the inspiration of our political heritage will lead our current struggles to fully integrate all Chileans into society.

> It is our trust in ourselves what reinforces our faith in the great values of humanity, in the certainty that those values will have to prevail, they cannot be destroyed.

(Allende, 1972b)

NOTES

1. The Radical Party, dating from 1863 when it branched out of the Liberal Party, has gone through many changes in ideology – from socialism, historic materialism and class struggle to social democracy and consequently split many times in history, especially to form anti-communist fractions. Currently, it is embedded in a neoliberal coalition.
2. The electoral law means that winners – the first two majorities – take all, which makes independent or minority representation impossible. It also means that in order to win, parties need to form larger coalitions. The 20 January 2015 proportional system reform is an improvement but still gives the upper hand to coalitions and to top party echelons.
3. Jose Miguel Inzunza later became head of the Organization of American States (OAS), also known as the Ministry of the Colonies.
4. Examples of this servile attitude towards the United States are: the privatization and denationalization of natural resources and basic public services such as social security and pension funds, mainly to the benefit of US transnational corporations; the opening up to additional US military presence, including a military base; the investment in US bonds rather than domestic social services; joining the United States in destabilizing the

Venezuelan government; and the leading role they are playing in promoting the Trans-Pacific Partnership and the Trans-Pacific Trade Agreement.

5. The socialists demanded that UP should 'advance without compromising', pressing for policies beyond the legal, political and military capabilities of the government, whereas the communists supported policies that would 'consolidate while advancing' in the transformation process within the existing political and institutional framework (Garcés, 2013: 197).

6. Chilean copper was nationalized with unanimous congressional approval on 11 July 1971 and was enshrined as an amendment to the last democratic Constitution dating from 1925.

7. Full concession, a concept created by the dictatorship but placed in practice by the *Concertación*, implying even greater benefits than private property.

8. ALBA is a counter-hegemonic integration mechanism based on cooperation, solidarity and complementarity.

9. The Mapuche people were the majority Indigenous tribe populating Chile before the Spanish conquest.

BIBLIOGRAPHY

Allende, S. (1971). *La vía chilena hacia el socialismo*. México: Editorial Fundamentos.

——(1972a). *Obras escogidas (1970–1973)*. 18 March. Barcelona: Critica. Available at www.geocities.ws/chileclarin/index-2.html (accessed 16 May 2016).

—— (1972b). 'Speech at the United Nations General Assembly'. *Obras escogidas (1970–1973)*. 4 December. Barcelona: Critica. Available at www.abacq.net/imagineria/cronol04.htm (accessed 16 May 2016).

—— (1979). *Un Estado Democrático y Soberano: Mi Propuesta a los Chilenos*. Madrid: Centro de Estudios Políticos Simón Bolívar/Fundación Salvador Allende 1993. Posthumous text. Available at www.elclarin.cl/images/pdf/allende_constitucion_1973.PDF (accessed 16 May 2016).

Amorós, M. (2013). *Allende la Biografía*. Barcelona: Ediciones B/Fundación Salvador Allende.

Ballantine, E. (2014). 'En Chile, la libertad de expresión está distorsionada por el mercado'. *Rebelión,* 25 November. Available at www.rebelion.org/noticia. php?id=191204 (accessed 20 April 2015).

Boeninger, E. (1997). *Democracia en Chile: Lecciones para la gobernabilidad*. Santiago: Andrés Bello.

Caputo, O. and Galarce, G. (2011). 'Chile's Neoliberal Reversion of Salvador Allende's Copper Nationalization'. In X. de la Barra (ed.), *Neoliberalism's Fractured Showcase: Another Chile is Possible*. Linden: Brill: 47–71.

Corvalán, L. (1971). *Camino de Victoria*. Santiago: Horizonte.

de la Barra, X. (2011). *Neoliberalism's Fractured Showcase: Another Chile is Possible*. Linden: Brill.

Garcés, J. (1993). 'Prologo'. In S. Allende (ed.), *Un Estado Democrático y Soberano: Mi Propuesta a los Chilenos*. Madrid: Centro de Estudios Políticos Simón Bolívar/Fundación Salvador Allende. Posthumous text. Available at www.

elclarin.cl/images/pdf/allende_constitucion_1973.PDF (accessed 16 May 2016).

——(2013). *Allende y la Experiencia Chilena: Las Armas de la Política*. Madrid: Siglo XXI.

Garretón, M.A and Moulian, T. (1993). *La Unidad Popular y el conflicto político en Chile*. Santiago: CESOC/ LOM.

Garretón, R. (2011). 'Chile: Perpetual Transition Under the Shadow of Pinochet'. In X. de la Barra (ed.), *Neoliberalism's Fractured Showcase: Another Chile is Possible*. Linden: Brill: 73–92.

Grez, S. (2011). 'La Ausencia De Un Poder Constituyente Democrático En La Historia De Chile'. *Tareas*, No. 139. September–December. Panamá: CELA. Available at www.revistas.usach.cl/ojs/index.php/izquierdas/article/viewFile/939/888 (accessed 16 May 2016).

Harnecker, M. (2013). 'Reflexiones sobre el gobierno de Allende: Estudiar el Pasado para Construir el Futuro'. *Crónica Popular*, Suplemento Especial No. 4.

Hirsch, T. (2006). 'La Otra Cara'. Interview by Carlos Salas. *ALAI*, 10 May. Available at www.alainet.org/de/node/115176 (accessed 25 April 2015).

López, R., Figueroa, E. and Gutiérrez, P. (2013). *La Parte del León: Nuevas estimaciones de la participación de los súper ricos en el ingreso en Chile*. Santiago: Facultad de Economía y Negocios, Departamento de Economía, Universidad de Chile. Available at www.econ.uchile.cl/uploads/publicacion/306018fadb3ac79952bf1395a555a90a86633790.pdf (accessed 20 April 2015).

Mayol, A. (2013). *El Chile Profundo: Modelos Culturales de la Desigualdad y sus Resistencias*. Santiago: Liberalia Ediciones.

——(2014). 'El derrumbe del derrumbe?'. *En Mostrador*, 18 August. Available at www.elmostrador.cl/opinion/2014/08/18/el-derrumbe-del-derrumbe/ (accessed 24 April 2015).

Moulian, T. (1995). 'Capitalismo, democracia y campo cultural en Chile', *Encuentro XXI*, 1 (2): 29–37.

——(1997). *La Anatomía de un Mito*. Santiago: Lom Ediciones.

——(1998a). *Conversación interrumpida con Allende*. Santiago: LOM ediciones/ Universidad ARCIS).

——(1998b). *El Consumo me Consume*. Santiago: LOM.

Moulian, T. and Salazar, M. (2014). 'La Nueva Mayoría como amenaza conservadora'. *El Mostrador*, 19 December. Available at www.elmostrador. cl/opinion/2014/12/19/la-nueva-mayoria-como-amenaza-conservadora/ (accessed 23 April 2015).

Portales, F. (2000). *Chile: una Democracia Tutelada*. Santiago: Editorial Sudamericana.

——(2011a). 'La Concertación debe explicaciones (XXXIII)'. *El Clarín*, 4 October. Available at www.elclarin.cl/web/la-concertacion-debe-explicaciones/2694-la-concertacion-debe-explicaciones-xxxiii.html (accessed 24 April 2015).

——(2011b). 'La Concertación debe explicaciones (XXXII)'. *El Clarín*, 6 September. Available at www.elclarin.cl/web/la-concertacion-debe-explicaciones/2460-la-concertacion-debe-explicaciones-xxxii.html (accessed 24 April 2015).

——(2011c). 'La Concertación debe explicaciones (XXXI)'. *El Clarín*, 16 August. Available at www.elclarin.cl/web/la-concertacion-debe-explicaciones/2240-la-concertacion-debe-explicaciones-xxxi.html (accessed 24 April 2015).

——(2014a). 'Falacia del Ministro Peñailillo'. *El Clarín*, 22 July. Available at www.elclarin.cl/web/opinion/politica/12462-falacia-de-ministro-penailillo.html (accessed 24 April 2015).

——(2014b). 'El profundo derechismo de Lagos'. *El Clarín*, 3 September. Available at www.elclarin.cl/web/opinion/politica/12943-el-profundo-derechismo-de-lagos.html (accessed 24 April 2015).

——(2015). 'Lagos respalda nuevamente golpe en Venezuela'. *El Clarín*, 20 April. Available at www.elclarin.cl/web/opinion/politica/15410-lagos-respalda-nuevamente-golpe-en-venezuela.html (accessed 24 April 2015).

Punto Final (2005). 'Editorial'. *Punto Final*, 14 December. Available at www.voltairenet.org/article132482.html (accessed 20 April 2015).

Roitman, M. (2011). *Democracia sin Demócratas*. Madrid: Sequitur.

——(2013). *Tiempos de Oscuridad*. Madrid: Ediciones Akal.

Ruiz, C. and Boccardo G. (2014). *Los Chilenos Bajo el Neoliberalismo: Clases y Conflicto Social*. Santiago: Fundación NODO XXI/Ediciones El Desconcierto.

Saavedra, V. (2015). Speech by the President of the Chilean Students Federation (FECH) at the closing of the demonstration of 16 April 2015. Available at www.theclinic.cl/2015/04/16/el-discurso-de-la-presidenta-de-fech-en-masiva-marcha-estudiantil-contra-la-corrupcion-este-debe-ser-el-momento-en-que-chile-entero-diga-basta/ (accessed 20 April 2015).

Unidad Popular (1969). *Programa Básico de la Unidad Popular*. Available at www.bicentenariochile.cl/index.php?option=com_content&view=article&id=19:progamabasico (accessed 16 May 2016).

Vitale, L. (1982). 'El Papel de la Socialdemocracia en América Latina' (Segunda Parte y Final). *ALAJ*, 6 (17). Available at http://mazinger.sisib.uchile.cl/repositorio/lb/filosofia_y_humanidades/vitale/obras/sys/aaml/r02.pdf (accessed 20 April 2015).

7

Does Social Democracy Hold Up Half the Sky? The Decline of PASOK and the Rise of SYRIZA in Greece

John Milios

After the outbreak of the global economic crisis in 2008, Greece was the first Euro-area country where the neoliberal 'shock doctrine' was imposed. This was an attempt to place all the fallout of the systemic capitalist crisis on the shoulders of the working people. These extreme austerity policies were not left undisputed. A series of mass demonstrations and strikes ensued. The most important result of these mass movements was the fast disintegration of the political system as we used to know it, mainly through the unravelling of the Socialist Party (PASOK) that has stayed in power for more than 20 years in the last three decades and which negotiated a Troika (International Monetary Fund (IMF)-European Central Bank (ECB)-European Union (EU) 'stabilization programme' for the country and introduced class-ridden austerity policies.[1] Mass movements and popular demonstrations finally led to national elections in May and June 2012, through which the Coalition of the Radical Left (SYRIZA) became the major opposition party in parliament.[2] In the early national elections on 25 January 2015, SYRIZA achieved a stunning victory with 36.3 per cent, as compared to 27.8 per cent of conservative New Democracy and 4.7 per cent of PASOK, the two government coalition partners until that time. This electoral result translated into 149 parliamentary seats for SYRIZA, out of a total of 300, and led to a coalition government with the 'Independent Greeks' (ANEL), an anti-austerity party stemming from the conservative political camp (4.75 per cent, 13 seats).[3]

However, the collapse of PASOK does not mean that social-democratic political strategies will be marginalized, or even cease to exist, in the Greek political scene.

After six months in office, the SYRIZA-ANEL government agreed on a third financing programme by the European Stability Mechanism (ESM) and the IMF, connected to a new austerity Memorandum. The secession of 25 SYRIZA MPs, who soon after formed a new anti-austerity parliamentary group called Popular Unity (LAE), led to the resignation of the government and to new national elections on 20 September 2015. SYRIZA won again with 35.4 per cent and 145 seats, as compared to 28.10 per cent and 75 seats for New Democracy, and formed a new coalition government with ANEL (3.69 per cent, 10 seats). LAE, with only 2.86 per cent of the vote, did not reach the 3 per cent electoral threshold and remained without any representation in parliament.[4]

This chapter approaches the stability and prevalence of social-democratic type policies in Greece on the basis of a Marxist approach to (European) capitalism, relations of class representation and the historical tradition of the Greek left.

A SHORT EXPOSITION ON THE HISTORY AND THE IDEOLOGICAL-POLITICAL TRANSFORMATION OF GREEK SOCIAL DEMOCRACY AND THE COMMUNIST LEFT

Greek socialists have a tradition of political coalition or even coexistence with the communist party(ies) of Greece, longer than in most West European countries.

During the German occupation (1941–44) in World War II, a massive mobilization and armed resistance of the Greek people took place, under the leadership of the leftist National Liberation Front (EAM) in which all socialist groups and parties coexisted with the KKE. After the national liberation in October 1944, the first phase of civil war broke out (December 1944 to January 1945) in which EAM fought united against 'national' Greek police and army forces (mostly former collaborators of the Axis occupation forces) and the British army. Greek socialists did not follow KKE and the 'Democratic Army of Greece' in the second round of civil war (1946–49), however most of them participated in or collaborated with the United Democratic Left (EDA), which was founded in 1951 (two years after the final defeat of the left in the civil war) as a coalition of communist and non-communist leftists, and remained a major political party until the military coup of April 1967.[5]

Soon after the outbreak of the civil war, in 1947, a special legal framework was created, which excluded leftists from certain facets of political and social life: communist organizations were banned, communists and 'fellow travellers' were deprived of certain civic rights, such as travelling abroad, being employed in the broader public sector, obtaining a driver's licence etc.

The questioning, by the democratic and labour movement, of this 'state of the nationally minded', that is, of the oppressive anti-communist state that emerged from the civil war, allowed EDA, in the 1950s and 1960s, to maintain a radical 'revolutionary' political physiognomy.

At the same time, the leadership of the left tried to reverse the nationalist-conservative propaganda about communist 'anti-national complicity', by presenting itself as *the* national political force par excellence. This was achieved through a discourse that presented the 'Greek society and economy' (i.e. Greek capitalism) as 'backward' and 'dependent', by means of which the left appeared as the self-appointed defender of the 'real' interests of the Greek economy (i.e. of Greek capitalism and its expanded reproduction). In this context, Greek capitalism's international economic links were interpreted as putting Greece in a state of 'dependence' and presented as a prime mover explaining and determining everything from the class relations of domination to the developmental tendencies of Greek capitalism. Social change was accordingly to be understood by the proscribed Communist Party (KKE) and EDA as the continuation of a struggle for 'national independence', the class struggle was consigned to the margins and capitalist power relations were conceived, falsely, as relations (and conflict) of 'Greek society' or 'the Greek economy' with 'foreign interests'.

As a result of this theoretical inversion, the traditional (post-Stalinist) communist left adapted to – and finally adopted – the bourgeois ideological motifs of 'all-round development of the country', 'rational organization of production' and the like, doctrines that extol the processes of capitalist accumulation and integration while concealing their essence, that is, their social content: the deepening capitalist exploitation. The left was thus gradually integrated into the capitalist strategy and tried to differentiate itself from other political currents through baseless assertions: (a) that only the left had the solutions for 'real development'; (b) that the 'existing strategy' of the Greek bourgeoisie and particularly its course in relation to Europe will inevitably lead to the 'downgrading' and perhaps even 'destruction' of the 'Greek economy'.[6]

This ideological shift of the left takes place in a historical era of rapid growth of Greek capitalism. After World War II the 'real convergence' between Greek capitalism and the more developed capitalisms of Western Europe is particularly marked in the period between 1960 and 1975 (when the per capita gross national product (GNP) of Greece increases at an average rate of 8.5 per cent annually and industrial production at 9.4 per cent annually, as against corresponding rates of growth for the (then) nine countries of the EEC of 3.8 per cent and 3.7 per cent, respectively). After the outbreak of the global overaccumulation crisis in the early 1970s, this convergence process is sustained, somewhat abated, through the succeeding decade and essentially suspended in the period between 1985 and 1994 (on account of the more intensive crisis of over-accumulation of capital in Greece, which, however, was overcome in the early 1990s through an upturn of profitability in the new framework of neoliberal policies)[7] and becomes evident again from 1995 onwards. In the period 1995–2008 Greece experienced a real increase of the gross domestic product (GDP) amounting to 61.0 per cent. In contrast, growth was much lower in the more developed European economies; 19.5 per cent for Germany, 17.8 per cent for Italy and 30.8 per cent for France and was only comparable to other countries of the so-called 'EU periphery' (Spain, 56.0 per cent and Ireland, 124.1 per cent).[8] Moreover, statistical evidence shows that higher growth in the 'EU periphery' was associated with both higher profitability and the deterioration in current account positions as a general tendency.[9] This evidence shows that current account deficits should not be taken as an indication of loss in competitiveness. If this were correct, then how can their positive correlation with growth and profitability be explained?

It can be safely argued, therefore, that the exposure to international competition that was effected through the process of European integration secured for Greece and other less developed countries of the Union satisfactory rates of growth and profitability.

It is evident that the internationalization of Greek capitalism and its orientation towards the processes of European integration (linkage to the EEC in 1961, admission of Greece as the tenth member in 1981, entry into the Euro Area in 2001) are not part of a downgrading or 'de-industrialization' of the 'Greek economy'. They are a strategic choice of the dominant forces of Greek capital to upgrade and reinforce their position both inside the country (against the workers' movement) and within the framework of the international division of labour: an upgrading and reinforcement of their position through exploitation of the 'opportunities' and 'challenges' of international capitalist competition, through attachment to the process of upgrading of Western European capitalisms in the international economy. The entry of Greece into the Economic and Monetary Union and the adoption of the euro thus came as the result of a long process of strategic convergence of Greek capitalism with the process of capitalist growth and integration of the Western European capitalisms.

Moreover, this process in Greece secured the consent of the governed to the project of European integration and thus the capitalist power relations. Given that the left does not speak of the irreconcilable contradiction between capital and labour but of the 'damage' that will be inflicted on 'our economy' by European integration and Monetary

Union, the interests of capital are successful in appearing as the interests of the community as a whole.

The resistance to the military junta (1967–74), however, radicalized a significant part of the Greek left and led to the creation of many new organizations and parties,[10] among which PAK, founded by Andreas Papandreou in exile, which, eventually was renamed as PASOK (Pan-Hellenic Socialist Movement), was going to play a very important role after the junta's collapse.

The restoration of parliamentary democracy in 1974 constituted a decisive event in the history of post-war Greece, since it brought a final end to the anti-communist 'state of the nationally minded' (legalization of all communist organizations and parties, abolition of all 'emergency laws' against the left).

Under the new circumstances, the political strategy of both communist parties (see footnote 10) that proclaimed a slow and gradual transition to socialism, which would include those incredible stages of the 'New Democracy', of the 'anti-monopolist Democracy' and so on fell short of the radicalism of the equivalent proclamations of PASOK, while both political currents self-annulled any of their socialist rhetoric, within the ideologies of the 'dependence' and 'inadequate development' of Greek capitalism. According to the conclusions of this perception, socialism will only become possible when the 'transformation' of 'economic development' and 'national independence' is completed, a transformation that requires the government of the country be assumed by the 'progressive forces'.

Simply put, the analysis about the 'backwardness' and 'dependence' of Greek capitalism, the theoretical 'gospel' of both the communist parties and PASOK, suggested the (supposed) irrelevance of anti-capitalist strategy, and the priority of 'economic development'.

Until the beginning of the 1980s, this ideology would conceal its apologetic character because it produced certain political results that improved the economic and social position of the popular classes: the 'welfare state', educational reform, redistribution of income to benefit wages (after their unprecedented reduction during the period of the dictatorship), the institutional strengthening of the trade unions etc., goals for which the left had struggled with apparent possibility of victory.

The same also occurred, however, until the middle of the 1980s with PASOK. Indeed, after 1981, when PASOK rose to power, it tried to implement the visions of 'redistribution of income', beyond which would supposedly lie 'development', boosted by increasing demand, and socialism. The traditional communist left assumed the unhappy role of defending the government programme of PASOK, which the latter systematically breached, when it assumed the government of the country. The left adopted PASOK's slogan of 'change' with a twist by demanding 'real change'!

Thus, radicalism of the first period of the restoration of democracy began to retreat in favour of a reformist ('social-democratic') govern-mentalism, which, as was evidenced in the case of PASOK, had no need of the labour movement in order to exist. The rhetoric of 'institutional reform', 'welfare state' and 'economic development' prevailed instead.

This process intensified after the mid 1980s, when the sharpening of the prolongation of recessionary tendencies convinced the PASOK government that the 'redistribution of income' could no longer constitute a 'realistic' policy for managing the system. Reducing 'entrepreneurial cost', liberalizing markets, combating 'monopolies', in short neoliberal policies were then seen as a necessary, supposedly temporary 'detour to economic stabilization'.

A portion of the cadres of the traditional post-Stalinist left also chose at that point the pragmatism and 'realism' of 'economic stabilization' over the 'utopia' of social reformism, and connected the rhetoric of development to the 'renewed' spouting about 'modernization' coming from the right wing. The ideological change of the traditional communist left thus coincided with the phase of the frontal (economic, political, ideological) attack of the ruling classes on the working class, which was implemented through a series of neoliberal austerity economic programmes (1986–93).[11]

Without this change in practical ideology of the traditional left (i.e. in the everyday political practice of left parties and the respective con-sciousness of party cadres and members, in actual non-conformity with the programmes of those parties), it would not have been possible to interpret the inertia of the party apparatuses of the two communist parties, which allowed the ultimate opportunism of their leaderships to become a reality in the summer of 1989: both traditional communist parties of the country participated then in a 'caretaker government' of the right (New Democracy), which was supposed to investigate the 'economic scandals' of the previous PASOK governments, and which practically opened up the way for the third in a row electoral victory of New Democracy in April 1990.[12] Only a few well-known cadres or party organizations of intellectuals offered resistance to this accession. The electoral victory of the right in 1990 stabilized and legitimized neoliberal policies, and in this sense was a turning point in the recent political history of Greece.

The domination of bourgeois ideology over the practical ideology of the left had, then, already been completed when the collapse of the regimes of 'actually existing socialism' in Eastern Europe took place, a historical event that further marginalized left rhetoric about socialist transformation of advanced capitalist societies and significantly contributed in the stabilization of neoliberal policies all over Europe in the 1990s and 2000s. For its part, PASOK managed to remain in power until 2004, despite its turn towards neoliberalism, as it exploited economic recovery and growth since the mid 1990s to create dense corporatist and clientelist networks on all levels of Greek society.

SYRIZA'S HISTORY, CONTRADICTIONS AND MUTATION

A political unity of different traditions

SYRIZA was formed in 2004 as a coalition of the left party SYN (see footnote 12) and twelve other political groups of the left, at least five of which belonged to the so-called 'revolutionary extra-parliamentarian left'. The formation of SYRIZA was the final step of a process that started in the year 2000, when most political groups that later formed SYRIZA coexisted in the Greek and European alter-globalization movement that was being shaped during that period. In the Genoa 'Group of Eight' Summit protest, from 18 to 22 July 2001, possibly the biggest European alter-globalization demonstration ever, several thousand Greek leftists participated, the majority being members of the political organizations that later formed SYRIZA.

SYRIZA started as a fairly loose coalition of different left currents, whose coexistence allowed them to be represented in the Greek central political scene and the parliament, as an assertive left pole beside the KKE. The national elections of 2012 were a turning point in SYRIZA's history, when it became the main opposition in the Greek parliament. It was soon after transformed into a unitary party comprising different ideological streams in July 2013, on the basis of the Resolution of its 1st founding Congress.[13] However, SYRIZA never developed an entirely new synthesis, but actually remained a 'party of political unity', resembling rather a united front of different fractions and influential cadres.

Although comprising more than ten tendencies or streams of thought, SYRIZA practically derives from four major traditions: (a) The EDA-KKE tradition (which also contains the tensions between former pro-Soviet and Euro-communist sub-traditions); (b) the extra-parliamentarian left tradition (which contains the tensions between the Trotkyist, the Maoist and the radical Euro-communist sub-traditions); (c) the tradition of the 'alter-globalization movement' of the early 2000s, which practically influenced most SYRIZA parts, as all parties and political groups that formed SYRIZA had participated in the Greek and European Social Forums;[14] (d) the reformist social-democratic tradition, which was strengthened after the 2012 elections and the disintegration of PASOK that followed: as SYRIZA became at that time the main opposition in the Greek parliament, a part of its leadership, mostly stemming from the EDA-KKE tradition, adopted a reformist stance, advocating that the party should shift towards 'pragmatism' in order to win the next elections. A new narrative emerged within the party, which distinguished between the 'old SYRIZA of 4%' and the 'new SYRIZA of 27% (after the 2012 elections)'. This tendency was further strengthened by the fact that many former PASOK cadres and members entered SYRIZA.

The June 2014 elections for the European Parliament and the 'Thessaloniki Programme'

In the June 2014 elections for the European Parliament, SYRIZA led with 26.52 per cent as compared to 22.78 per cent of New Democracy. It was clear by then that SYRIZA would form, or at least be the leading partner in, the new government to come after the next national elections.

With arguments about 'effectiveness' and 'for safeguarding electoral victory', the majority of SYRIZA's leadership started flirting with centre-left politicians and small centre-left political formations (e.g. with the Democratic Left, a party formed in 2010 after splitting from SYRIZA, a government partner with New Democracy and PASOK in the period 2012–13, gained 1.2 per cent in the elections for the European Parliament in 2014). At the same time, in the official language of the party in the mass media, the slogans, as well as the 'immediate political targets' of SYRIZA started changing: the slogan 'For a Government of the Left' was gradually replaced by 'Government of National Salvation'; 'Redistribution of Power, Wealth and Income to the benefit of the Working Majority' was displaced by 'Productive Reconstruction of the Country'; all programmatic positions regarding the democratic control of the society and the economy by the people, the development of self-directed, co-operative productive schemes, non-market 'social economy' etc. were put aside; even SYRIZA's proposition to tax the rich (the party's programme on the reform of the tax system, presented by the president of the party himself in March 2013) was cast aside.

This shift to pragmatism was included in SYRIZA's electoral programme presented in September 2014, the so-called Thessaloniki Programme.[15] As M. Lebowitz correctly argues:

In place of any anti-capitalist (let alone, socialist) measures was a National Reconstruction Plan which focused upon restarting the Greek economy through public investment and tax reduction for the middle class. Recovery and growth (along with a negotiated moratorium on debt servicing) would rescue the Greek economy and allow it to 'gradually' reverse all the memorandum injustices, 'gradually' restore salaries and pensions and rebuild the welfare state. Economically, the Thessaloniki Programme was based upon Keynesian (not even post-Keynesian) theory, and it supplemented its focus upon aggregate demand stimulation by proposed measures to deal with the humanitarian crisis (e.g. subsidies for meals, electricity, medical care and public transit for the poor and unemployed).[16]

It is true that a lot of SYRIZA cadres, members and supporters considered the Thessaloniki Programme to be a tactical move, in the sense that it described only the first steps of a radical programme of democratic change that would evolve gradually, albeit steadily. This programme was supposed to: (a) stop austerity policies and (b) secure a deal with the official lenders of the country (the EU, ECB and IMF, which were called the Troika and are now referred to as the 'Institutions') in order to cover the financing needs of the Greek public sector. The 'financial gap' of the Greek public sector mainly refers to money owed to the Institutions in the framework of the bail-out programmes of the previous years.

However, a few weeks after the formation of the new government and especially after signing the preliminary agreement of 20 February 2015, it became clear that the Greek government was negotiating with the 'Institutions' by proposing a milder version of the austerity Memoranda.

From the 20 February 2015 agreement to the third austerity Memorandum (the 13 July agreement)

In the government formed by Alexis Tsipras after the 25 January elections, several important Ministers were appointed, including the Minister of Finance Yanis Varoufakis, who did not originate from SYRIZA or any left tradition.

Shortly after his appointment as Minister of Finance, Varoufakis repeatedly declared publically that 70 per cent of the Memorandum (the austerity 'financial stability programme') is favourable for Greece.[17] However, the SYRIZA government did not come to power supporting 70 per cent of the Memorandum. If SYRIZA had pledged so, it would probably not be included on the parliamentary map today, let alone playing the key role. Such notions redefined the SYRIZA mandate and amounted practically to an attempt to change the social alliances, which had so far supported the historical experiment of a left government in Greece.

Moreover, the Ministry of Finance produced publicity that totally distanced itself from SYRIZA's programmatic positions. In its *National Programme of Reforms* (Ministry of Finance, April 2015), all main arguments of the neoliberal austerity agenda are being adopted: Economic growth relies on exports and every wage increase is automatically considered as being against competitiveness.

> Greece has proceeded to an unprecedented economic adjustment aimed at improving budgetary consolidation on the one hand, and on the other to enhance the competitiveness of the economy ... The shift to a development model with export orientation seems to have been achieved in the years 2013 and 2014, when the current account recorded a surplus of 0.6% and 0.9% of GDP respectively.[18]

Furthermore, the minister himself always advocated in favour of a strategy that would supposedly lead Greece to its so-called 'growth stage', which is going to be devoid of class bias. His following declaration at the 20th Banking Forum of the Union of Greek Banks, on 22 April 2015 is characteristic:

> In the year 2015, after five years of catastrophic recession, where ultimately everybody is a victim, there are only a few cunning people who have profited from this crisis. The era in which a government of the left was by definition contrary to the milieu of entrepreneurship has passed. If we get to a point when there is growth, we can start talking again about conflicting labour and capital interests. Today we are together.

In the midst of such an ideological and political climate, the Greek government reached an intermediate agreement with the lenders, on 20 February 2015, which included a four-month extension of the existing Memorandum, signed by the previous government. According to the 20 February agreement, the Institutions had the right to adjudicate on whether Greece's commitments had been reached or not, and so even scheduled instalments as they appeared in the previous programme were left pending, as there were no positive evaluation by the Institutions.

The 20 February agreement made clear that the Greek government was negotiating within the European neoliberal austerity framework, merely seeking a 'fig leaf' to conceal its compromises. This 'fig leaf', which has often been described as the 'red lines' of the Greek government, was, on the one hand, a moderate programme of 'ending the humanitarian crisis' (energy subsidies, food stamps etc. for the very poor) and, on the other, rejection of any direct nominal reduction of wages and pensions, maintaining the existing restrictions as regards mass lay-offs, and maintaining low VAT coefficients for certain mass products and in the Greek islands.

This became even more clear after the promulgation, on 5 June 2015, of the Greek proposals to the Institutions.[19] The government had surrendered its programme (even the Thesaloniki Programme) and was attempting to get an agreement that would simply leave intact the existing neoliberal institutional and economic framework, with no further austerity measures to be taken as regards low and medium incomes.

However, the Institutions never accepted the Greek government's 'red lines' and shaped a plan to further finance Greece under the conditionality of deepening the neoliberal policies (where wage and pension cuts were also included), which was codified as the 'Juncker plan'. The negotiations went on for five more months, during which the Greek government did not receive any of the owed tranches by its lenders, whereas it continued paying all of its debt obligations to the ECB and the IMF, that is, more than €7 billion, or over 3 per cent of GDP, until the final depletion of all public funds and the delay, by necessity, of Greece's payment to the IMF on 30 June 2015, as the government practically ran out of cash.

On 26 June Greek Prime Minister Alexis Tsipras proclaimed a referendum on the 'Juncker plan' and on 28 June the government decided to impose restrictions on withdrawal of deposits from the Greek banks ('bank holiday' and 'capital controls'), as the ECB refused any increase in the Emergency Liquidity Assistance provided to the Greek banks, which could meet the needs of anxious depositors who withdrew their savings after the proclamation of the referendum.

The election campaign for the referendum had clear class and social characteristics, which had not been seen in the Greek political scene for decades. There were two 'Greeces' fighting each other. On one side, there were roughly the poor, wage-earners, the unemployed and many small entrepreneurs fighting for No, while on the other were the capitalists, the managerial class, the higher ranks of the state and so on agitating for Yes.

Ultimately, a broad coalition of the social majority saw the referendum as a chance to express their commitment not to continue with austerity and neoliberalism. So, the Greek people voted with the banks closed and in an atmosphere of fear that declared voting No would lead to disaster. There was also intense mouth-to-mouth blackmail from employers pressuring workers to vote 'Yes'. Yet despite this fear and propaganda, 61.3 per cent voted 'No'.

However, the Greek government transformed the No vote of the Greek people into a Yes vote in the parliament, in consensus with the conservative and centre-left opposition, and on 13 July 2015 in Brussels signed an agreement with the Institutions that practically duplicated the 'Juncker plan'.[20] The government itself described the agreement as the result of 'blackmail' by the dogmatic European elites[21] and a 'defeat' due to the negative relations of forces in the 'struggle' between Greece and the Institutions. However, 32 out of the 149 SYRIZA MPs, mostly members of the party's 'Left Platform', voted against the agreement in the Greek parliament, while six abstained from voting. Finally, on 20 August 2015, the prime minister decided to resign, so that new elections would be proclaimed. In response, 25 until then SYRIZA MPs, under the leadership of former Energy Minister Panagiotis Lafazanis, broke away from the party, forming a new party, 'Popular Unity' (LAE).

The official SYRIZA approaches to the negotiations and the 'demands of the Institutions' perceived austerity and the Memoranda either as simply 'an economic mistake', in the sense that it constitutes a recipe that is unable to boost growth, or as an attack against the Greek economy and society by 'foreign interests'. In this framework, the final capitulation of SYRIZA to the Institutions is being interpreted as a 'heroic fall in an uneven battle', which can be reversed in the future through 'equivalent measures' that the 'left government' shall put forward, such as combating corruption and reforming the state apparatuses.

Is austerity a 'false policy'?

The question that arises from the above is the following: Why have the European Institutions never deviated from their austerity agenda, at least since the outbreak of the global financial and economic crisis in 2008? Why did the Greek capitalist forces and their allies fight with such a fanatic frenzy for the 'Yes' vote in the 5 July referendum, in support of the 'Juncker plan' and a third Memorandum?

The answer is clear: austerity is not a 'false policy' but a class strategy promoting the interests of capital against those of workers, professionals, pensioners and economically vulnerable groups. In the long run, it aims at creating a model of labour with fewer rights and less social protection, with low and flexible wages and the absence of any meaningful bargaining power.

On the surface, austerity appears as a strategy of reducing entrepreneurial cost. It reduces the labour cost of the private sector, increases profit per unit (labour) cost and therefore boosts the profit rate. It is complemented by economies in the use of 'material capital'[22] and by institutional changes that, on the one hand, enhance capital mobility and competition and, on the other, strengthen the power of managers in the enterprise and bondholders in society. As regards fiscal consolidation, austerity gives priority to budget cuts over public revenue, reducing taxes on capital, dismantling the progressive tax systems and downsizing the welfare state. However, what is cost for the capitalist class is the living standard of the working majority of society. This applies also to the welfare state, whose services can be perceived as a form of 'social wage'.

The institutional arrangement of the Eurozone, with the ECB being deprived the power of a lender of last resort, deliberately reinforces neoliberal policies. Member states will not always have the necessary liquidity to pay off bondholders, as is nowadays the case with Greece. This makes the downsizing of the welfare state a precondition for financial solvency. The ruling European elites have thus voluntarily acquiesced to a high degree of sovereign default risk in order to consolidate the neoliberal strategies. In other words, they have jointly decided to exploit the crisis as a means to further neoliberalize state governance.

The continuation of austerity is always a matter of the social relation of contending forces. Capitalist societies, first of all the inner workings of an enterprise, constitute a battlefield between antagonistic interests. As Karl Marx commented on the limits of the working day:

> The capitalist maintains his rights as a purchaser when he tries to make the working-day as long as possible ... On the other hand, ... the labourer maintains his right as seller when he wishes to reduce the working-day to one of definite normal duration. There is here therefore an antinomy, of *right against right*, both equally bearing the seal of the law of exchange. Between equal rights force decides.[23]

Beyond certain limits, the subjection of all parts of social life to the unfettered function of markets and the dictate of profitability may create a 'political risk' for the neoliberal establishment, since it can trigger uncontrolled social outbreaks.[24] This 'political risk' was a strong weapon in the hands of the Greek working class, SYRIZA and the government in order to stop austerity and guarantee an agreement with the lenders that would not violate the 25 January mandate. Under one precondition: that SYRIZA and the government stick to the class partisanship of its programme, the strategy of 'people before profits', i.e. a strategy with an anti-capitalist direction – redistribution of income and power in favour of labour, to re-found the welfare state, democracy and participation in decision making; a radical reform of the tax system (so that capital and the wealthy strata of the society finally bear the appropriate burden); a wave of radical domestic institutional changes in order to build the allegiance of the subordinate classes on a new basis.

However, as already discussed, this strategy had been abandoned at least since summer 2014, that is, after SYRIZA was victorious in the elections for the European Parliament.

THE EVOLUTION OF SYRIZA TOWARDS SOCIAL DEMOCRACY AND THE NEW POLITICAL LANDSCAPE AFTER THE SEPTEMBER 2015 NATIONAL ELECTIONS

From its very beginning, social democracy conceived capitalism as a system that can be politically managed so as to become beneficial to both capital and labour. In the words of Eduard Bernstein from the year 1899: 'Democracy is in principle the suppression of class government, though it is not yet the actual suppression of classes.'[25] On the basis of this approach, social democracy slid from its historic strategy of 'peaceful transition to socialism' to welfare politics and Keynesian demand-side macroeconomic growth policies, and further to centre-left neoliberal pragmatism.

Social democracy practically attempts to refute the notion of capitalism's inherently exploitative and contradictory character – the notion that it constitutes a system of class power and class exploitation (extraction of surplus value) of the labouring class by the capitalist class. It is aware of the reality of inequality and social exclusion but attributes it to the hegemony of the 'counterproductive' financial system and to 'false' policies, not to the class structure of the capitalist economy. It does not aim, therefore, at promoting mass movements and curtailing the class power of capital (which would mean the exacerbation of social conflicts), but at 'stabilizing the economy'.[26] It complies with the capitalist strategy of profit maximization as a presupposition of increased investment and creeps to neoliberalism as it conceives the maintenance of capitalist profitability as the presupposition of 'social justice'.

As Karl Marx has repeatedly stated, in the capitalist mode of production, the income of the working class, the wage and the 'social wage' (the welfare state), depends on the priorities of capital accumulation: 'To put it mathematically: the rate of accumulation is the independent, not the dependent variable; the rate of wages is the dependent, not the independent, variable.'[27] Given the low rates of capital accumulation after the 2008 crisis as well as the existing social relation of opposing forces, enterprises ('individual capital' in Marx's terminology) spontaneously 'choose' to cope with the profitability problem not by expanding production and demand but further squeezing the labour share.

The sketching of the post-war history of the Greek left has shown, however, that the traditional post-Stalinist left also shared a lot of the main strategic ideas and practices with social democracy. Most importantly, it shared the goals of 'national independence' and 'economic development', that is, this characteristic mixture of 'statism', or rather 'governmentalism'[28] and economism[29] that shaped the rhetoric of all dominant fractions of the Greek left since the civil war.

Instead of putting the interests and the power of the working people above this bourgeois 'common interest' rhetoric, SYRIZA finally complied with capitalist 'reality', which emanated from the internal 'laws' of 'economic growth', that is, the 'laws' of capital accumulation on an expanded scale. By signing the new Memorandum, SYRIZA agreed to clear the Greek institutional and labour market framework from 'rigidities' stemming from past workers' victories and gains.

SYRIZA always had two 'spirits': on the one hand, the radical 'spirit' of the alter-global movements of the early 2000s, and, on the other, the 'patriotic reformism' of the KKE-EDA tradition. As we have argued above, at least after it had become the strongest party in Greek politics and without doubt after its ascent to government, SYRIZA followed the 'reformist' path, in the social-democratic sense, of 'economic stabilization and growth' as a prerequisite for 'social cohesion and change'. The roots of this shift are to be found not only in the 'new situation' of becoming a governing party, i.e. a party that is called to manage the capitalist state but also the 'old situation', that is, the ideological and political tradition of the post-Stalinist left.

SYRIZA as a governing party is thus in a process of transformation into a neoliberal centre-left party, practically belonging in the camp of contemporary social democracy.

The Greek political landscape continues, of course, to be unstable. The centre-left (liberal social-democratic) camp, in which SYRIZA enters at fast pace, also comprises a conglomeration of small parties (To Potami, PASOK), political groups (Democratic Left) and cadres, the majority of whom stem from the milieu of the formerly powerful PASOK. The final configuration of this political camp cannot be forecasted.

The success of SYRIZA in the September 2015 national elections has to do, on the one hand, with the political 'inertia' of the 'lesser evil' (a majority of the working class still believes that SYRIZA clearly differentiates itself in a positive manner from the 'old political system'), and, on the other, on the lack of a clear political alternative.

The political narrative of LAE (as well as that of KKE, to a large extent) bases itself on statist-economistic arguments, in many aspects similar to that of governing SYRIZA: 'We have *the* plan to stop austerity, as a prerequisite for the productive restructuring of the economy.' The *economistic* bent of LAE's political intervention can be fathomed from the importance given to acquiring a national currency (as a decision to be taken by a prospective *progressive government*). The introduction of a new national currency is seen as a means for boosting competitiveness of the Greek economy on the international level. There is a case to be made whether currency devaluation can guarantee the same level of (labour and material) cost reduction, but with lower unemployment, to the type of 'internal devaluation' being pursued at present by austerity policies. However, it is clear that devaluation is mainly seen as a means of favouring national capitalist interests (competitiveness of the domestic economy) and less a socialist or anti-capitalist perspective.

SYRIZA remains prevalent in the Greek political scene. However, not as a movement of the radical left. After its two electoral victories in seven months, 'order prevails' again in Greece, and social democracy continues to hold up half the sky.

ACKNOWLEDGEMENT

I thank Professor Vassilis Droucopoulos for his comments on an earlier version of this chapter.

NOTES

1. PASOK stayed in power during the following time periods: 1981–89, 1993–2004, 2009–11. In the period 2011–15 PASOK participated in coalition governments with various parties, the conservative New Democracy being the main partner.
2. SYRIZA was until then a small radical left party (4.6 per cent in the national elections of 2009) (see also below).
3. New Democracy elected 76 MPs and PASOK 13 MPs. Other parties in the parliament: Golden Dawn (Nazis) 6.3 per cent and 17 seats, To Potami (liberals) 6 per cent and 17 seats, KKE (Communist Party of Greece) 5.5 per cent and 15 seats.
4. Other parties in the new parliament: Golden Dawn 6.9 per cent and 18 seats, PASOK 6.28 per cent and 17 seats, KKE 5.55 per cent and 15 seats, To Potami 4.09 per cent and 11 seats, Union of the Centre 3.43 per cent and 9 seats.

5. M. Mazower (ed.) (2000). *After the War Was Over. Reconstructing the Family, Nation, and State in Greece, 1943–1960.* Princeton and Oxford: Princeton University Press.

6. From this viewpoint the following announcement by the Administrative Committee of EDA, at the time of acceptance of Greece's application to join the European Economic Community (EEC) in 1959, is entirely typical: 'The desire and the aspiration of our partners in the Common Market is that Greece should remain a backward agricultural country, a source of raw materials and a market for their industrial products ... For 75% of our backward and over-protected industry ... it is the difference between life and death' (Avgi, 1 August 1959). Three days before this (29 July 1959) the editors of *Avgi* had forecasted an even less auspicious future: 'No business is going to survive this relentless competition. Any that are not absorbed by the trusts will become their appendages and will be annihilated.'

7. See E. Ioakimoglou and J. Milios (1993). 'Capital Over-accumulation and Economic Crisis: The Case of Greece (1960–1989)'. *Review of Radical Political Economics*, 25 (2) (June): 81–107.

8. See J. Milios and D.P. Sotiropoulos (2010). 'Crisis of Greece or Crisis of Euro? A View from the European "Periphery"'. *Journal of Balkan and Near Eastern Studies*, 12 (3): 223–40. J. Milios and D.P. Sotiropoulos (2009). *Rethinking Imperialism: A Study of Capitalist Rule.* London and New York: Palgrave Macmillan.

9. See D.P. Sotiropoulos, J. Milios and S. Lapatsioras (2013). *A Political Economy of Contemporary Capitalism and its Crisis. Demystifying Finance.* London: Routledge: Chapter 9.

10. In February 1968, the exile Communist Party of Greece (KKE) was split into two parts: the pro-Soviet 'KKE' and 'KKE (interior)', which shortly after espoused the Euro-communist line.

11. For an analysis of the class character and the inner rationality of neoliberalism and austerity as profit raising and power redistribution strategies, see S. Lapatsioras, J. Milios and D.P. Sotiropoulos (2015). 'Addressing the Rationality of "Irrational" European Responses to the Crisis. A Political Economy of the Euro Area and the Need for a Progressive Alternative'. In A. Bitzenis, N. Karagiannis and J. Marangos (eds), *Europe in Crisis.* London: Palgrave Macmillan: 67–76. D.P. Sotiropoulos, J. Milios and S. Lapatsioras (2014). 'An Outline of a Progressive Resolution to the Euro-area Sovereign Debt Overhang: How a Five-year Suspension of the Debt Burden Could Overthrow Austerity'. Levy Economics Institute of Bard College, Working Paper No. 819. John Milios, (2015). 'The Class Logic Behind Austerity Policies in the Euro-area: Can SYRIZA Put Forward a Progressive Alternative?'. *Socialist Project*, e-bulletin No. 1124, 1 June, www.socialistproject.ca/bullet/1124.php. See also Ioakimoglou and Milios, 'Capital Over-accumulation'.

12. In 1987, KKE (interior) was renamed Greek Left (EA) and in 1989 formed the Coalition of the Left and Progress (SYN) with KKE and some non-communist (social-democratic) groups. In the same year, SYN participated in a

'caretaker government' with New Democracy. After its poor electoral result in the 1990 general elections (10.3 per cent as compared to 13.1 per cent in the June 1989 elections), KKE pulled back from SYN and is following a sectarian isolationist policy, initially condensed in the party's slogan 'five parties, two policies' (meaning 'KKE against all other parties', which supposedly follow converging policies). However, a large number of KKE cadres and members left the party and remained SYN members. SYN was then converted from an alliance to a unitary political party (1991).

13. See www.syriza.gr/article/id/53894/The-political-resolution-of-the-1st-congress-of-SYRIZA.html#.Vb9GBov9Ld4 (accessed August 2015). Also http://links.org.au/node/3466. For more details on the history of SYRIZA, see http://en.wikipedia.org/wiki/Syriza (accessed August 2015).

14. See http://en.wikipedia.org/wiki/Social_forum (accessed August 2015).

15. www.syriza.gr/article/id/59907/SYRIZA---THE-THESSALONIKI-PRO-GRAMME.html#.VcCvqYv9Ld4 (accessed August 2015).

16. M.A. Lebowitz, 'Social Democracy or Revolutionary Democracy: Syriza and Us'. *The Bullet, Socialist Project*, e-bulletin No. 1149, www.socialistproject.ca/bullet/1149.php (accessed August 2015).

17. Varoufakis declared on 9 February 2015: 'We will implement deep reforms in coordination with the OECD, which is why its secretary general Mr. Gurria is coming to Athens tomorrow in order to help us design these reforms and control their implementation in a transparent way. To these reforms we will add about 70% of the reforms or commitments that have already been laid out in the current memorandum. As wise people, we don't object to these reforms as long as the other 30% of reforms, which we deem unacceptable, are either suspended or removed.' See http://investmentwatchblog.com/greece-eu-medicine-is-toxic-fm-varoufakis-slams-eu-austerity-programme/#T7Lcg9pYPRzdoLjv.99 (accessed August 2015).

18. http://ec.europa.eu/europe2020/pdf/csr2015/nrp2015_greece_el.pdf (accessed August 2015).

19. 'Agreement on the Economic Policy, the Reforms of the Period 7/2015–31/3/2016 and the Completion of the Current Programme', see www.enikos.gr/data/files/3145c3ab732cf8cb3fc45710a9d806f9.pdf (accessed August 2015).

20. Full Statement of Eurosummit Agreement with Greece, 13 July 2015, see www.consilium.europa.eu/.../20150712-eurosummit-statement-greece/ (accessed August 2015).

21. The Greek government alleged that if it had not accepted the agreement the Institutions would have proceeded in expelling Greece from the Euro Area, a development for which the country was not prepared. The same argument was put forward after the 20 February intermediate agreement. However, as Gerry Rice of the IMF clearly stated on a press communiqué on 23 July 2015, 'as we've said before repeatedly, our baseline assumption has always been that Greece would remain a member of the euro area'. See www.imf.org/external/np/tr/2015/tr072315.htm (accessed August 2015).

22. Alas, another demand curtailing policy.

23. K. Marx (1990). *Capital*, Volume 1. London: Penguin Classics: 344, emphasis added.
24. As Franklin D. Roosevelt stated in his speech at Madison Square Garden, New York City on 31 October 1936: 'We know now that Government by organized money is just as dangerous as Government by organized mob.'
25. E. Bernstein (1961). *Evolutionary Socialism*. New York: Schocken Books: 143. Rosa Luxemburg criticized this approach as follows: 'Bourgeois legality (and parliamentarism as the legislature in process of development) is nothing but the particular social form in which the political violence of the bourgeoisie, developing its given economic basis, expresses itself.' Cited in T. Cliff (1959). *Rosa Luxemburg*, www.marxists.org/archive/cliff/ works/1959/rosalux/R. Luxemburg (accessed August 2015). Also in R. Luxemburg (1990). *Gesammelte Werke*, Volume III. Ost-Berlin: 361ff. See also L. Kolakowski (1978). *Main Currents of Marxism*, Volume 2. Oxford and New York: Oxford University Press: 56–7.
26. See W. Müller and C. Neusüss (1972). 'Die Sozialstaatsillusion und der Widerspruch von Lohnarbeit und Kapital'. *Prokla*, Sonderheft-1, Berlin.
27. Marx, *Capital*, Volume 1: 790.
28. Governmentalism: the idea that forming a government of the left is an *adequate and sufficient* condition for a change in enforceable policies, especially as regards 'the reconstructing of the productive basis of the economy' in order to be better able to compete and 'to bring Greece out of the crisis'. This can only sideline the central tasks of building a movement towards the ends of social change and socialism, with a level of active partic-ipation that historic experience shows is a vital prerequisite for making the best use of government.
29. Economism perceives social evolution as the result not of class struggle but the 'development of the productive forces' that (supposedly) comes into conflict with the relations of production, and thus 'makes inevitable' the transformation of the latter.

8

Social Democracy in Romania

Lucian Vesalon

The evolution of social democracy in Central and Eastern Europe is unique simply because new left-wing discourses emerged in the unprecedented context of the transition from socialism to capitalism in the 1990s. Recalling Lipset's comment from the 1960s, Kitschelt notes, 'social scientists are more inclined to write about the Left than the Right' (1994: 1). And yet, in the literature on post-communism, little attention is devoted to left-wing parties and ideologies in comparison to common transition issues: democratization, economic liberalization, European integration etc. (Pickles, 2008). Existing studies on social democracy in Romania usually focus on its place in national politics and in the party system, on electoral outcomes, internal organization of social democratic parties and more recently on the Europeanization process (Soare, 2012, 2013). A critical analysis of the social democratic ideology in the post-communist space is particularly underdeveloped, and discussed even less are social democratic policies in the context of the political economy of transition.

This chapter puts ideologies in a more central position than conventional analyses of parties in the literature on post-communism, and considers that political discourses are constitutive for economic and political change (Smith and Swain, 1998). As post-Marxist discourse theory suggests (Laclau and Mouffe, 1985), if the function of ideologies includes the construction of new political identities, then the role of social democratic parties is not only to secure votes, win elections, produce policies and ultimately govern, but also (re)construct political identities on the left side of the spectrum. This chapter therefore looks at social democracy as a terrain on which new social identities are constructed in political contexts defined by the presence of antagonistic political forces (Howarth and Stavrakakis, 2000).

By the beginning of the twenty-first century many voices lamented that 'the social democratic movement in Europe has become a shadow of its former self' (Berman, 2006: 210). The hope of a reinvigorated left movement 'from the East' was therefore alluring after the fall of communism. After all, a socialism liberated from the burden of totalitarianism could have produced a new alternative to both Soviet-style communism and neoliberal capitalism. This alternative was never produced. The optimism regarding the post-communist left-wing alternatives to Western social democracy soon dissipated (Gowan, 1995). The Third Way appeared as a 'normal' path for Central and Eastern European social democracies. Moreover, Eastern European social democrats didn't succeed in strengthening or reinvigorating social democracy in Europe.

In this context, the situation of Romanian social democracy is paradoxical. Although social democratic parties have won the majority of the parliamentary elections, social democratic ideology has a marginal position in the public space and did not succeed in establishing itself as an alternative to the dominant discourse, intellectual and political elites being rather socially conservative and economically hyper-liberal. The situation is even more puzzling given that the country experienced harsh neoliberal reforms and, as a consequence, has one of the largest vulnerable populations in the European Union (EU). Romania was one of the few cases where the left, then represented by the National Salvation Front (Frontul Salvării Naționale, FSN), won the first election after 1989. Following this, the FSN and its successors attempted to navigate through at least two complex and, to some extent, mutually exclusive tasks: constructing a social democratic alternative to neoliberalism and 'doing the transition' to capitalism. The first consisted of the complicated mission of positioning the party to the left, while offering assurances of a radical break with the communist past (including the break with the former communist party structures/members). The second consisted of the economic liberalization agenda of 'reforms', which largely contradicted the traditional values of social democracy.

A proper understanding of the evolution of Romanian social democracy should take into account the tension between the electoral success of the reformist left in Romania and its internalization of neoliberalism and certain elements of social conservatism. Changes in the structure of society, particularly the decline of the working class, changes in the structure of the economy and the regional political context are certainly important explanatory factors. However, of fundamental importance are its use of the anti-communist revolution as a legitimizing principle, and the failure to provide to the massive working class of the previous socialist regime a political identity in the new post-communist society.

SHORT HISTORY OF ROMANIAN SOCIAL DEMOCRACY AFTER 1989

The apparently basic question of which political parties represent the social democratic ideology in Romania hides theoretical controversies and ideological pre-commitments. The conventional narrative says that in the ex-socialist states, communist parties (CPs) have reinvented themselves as new social democratic parties. On one hand, this was an opportunity for the communist parties to reform their ideology and become key players in the new democratic arena. On the other hand, 'this "social-democratizing" of the CPs pre-empted the space for freshly created social democratic parties' (Eley, 2002: 453). The Romanian case presents a somewhat different story. Before the Second World War, a Romanian Social Democratic Party existed (Partidul Social Democrat Român, PSDR) and was dissolved at the beginning of the communist regime. It was re-established after 1989 and had only a limited political impact, being eventually assimilated into the larger post-communist Social Democratic Party.

The main route of post-communist social democracy began with the National Salvation Front (Frontul Salvării Naționale, FSN), self-titled the 'emanation of the Revolution', which emerged in the days that followed the 1989 revolutionary events. FSN was led by the controversial former communist second-rank leader Ion Iliescu, who was seen during the 1980s as a potential socialist reformist alternative to the autocratic regime of Nicolae Ceaușescu. The dominance of the FSN was from the beginning contested by the 'democratic opposition', which gravitated around the newly re-established 'historical parties', the most important being the National Liberal Party (Partidul Național Liberal, PNL) and the National Peasants' Party (Partidul Național Țărănesc, PNȚ).

In 1992, following internal elections, the FSN split and Ion Iliescu, together with a large number of members who contested the new leadership and policies of the FSN, formed the Frontul Democrat al Salvării Naționale (FDSN). One year later, the FDSN had been transformed into the Social Democratic Party of Romania (Partidul Democrației Sociale din România, PDSR), the largest political organization struggling to represent the social democratic parties. At the same time, the FSN had been transformed into the Democratic Party (Partidul Democrat, PD), which for several years presented itself as the social democratic alternative to the 'neo-communist' PDSR, and which was a member of the Socialist International starting in 1996. The PD later adopted a right-wing ideology and affiliated to the European People's Party, withdrawing from the Socialist International. In June 2001, the PDSR united with the PSDR and formed the Social Democratic Party (Partidul Social Democrat, PSD), led by Adrian Năstase, followed by Mircea Geoană between 2005 and 2010, and then by Victor Ponta until 2015. The PSD thus established itself as the dominant social democratic party and has appropriated the political history and tradition of Romanian social democracy.

The interpretation of this history, especially the use of social democracy in this context, is still politically and ideologically controversial. The very inclusion of the FSN and later the PDSR in the social democratic family is contested (Soare, 2013). Especially in the 1990s, many considered that only the re-established PSDR, and later the PD, are genuinely social democratic, while the FSN/FDSN/PDSR is a 'neo-communist' party. The FSN, after several initial hesitations in the first months of 1990, claimed to be anti-communist and officially denied any connections with the Romanian Communist Party (Partidul Comunist Român, PCR). Numerous social democratic parties, or those using social democracy as a formal political identification or denomination, have been established since 1989. Apart from the FDSN/PDSR and the FSN/PD, they had a short existence and have won less than 0.5 per cent of votes in parliamentary elections. The use of social democracy as a political identifier by the FDSN/PDSR was contested both by the left and the right. From the left, the PSDR and the PD formally identified with the social democratic ideology, and both claimed to be the true representatives of social democracy in Romania. In fact, it was the PD that was a member of the Socialist International and began collaborations with social democratic parties from Europe.

The 1990s were the most dynamic years for Romanian social democracy in organizational terms, with splits and mergers between several parties and factions. The 2000s were then a period of organizational and ideological consolidation. Similar to its predecessors, the PSD has struggled to consolidate itself within the social democratic arena and to define its use of social democratic ideology. In contrast to right-wing parties, the PSD was comparatively better equipped to internalize its divisions, preserve the monopoly of representing social democracy in the party system and act as an ideological regulator. Although the FDSN/PDSR/PSD had consolidated its social democratic principles at an organizational level, its unilateral association to social democracy is problematic. For example, during the last 25 years numerous other parties have used the denomination, political principles and policies of social democracy, and after 1989 various cabinets followed social democratic policies.

As the history of the party relates, 'after the 1989 Revolution, the transition period has been, for the most part, managed by parties of social democratic vocation' (Statutul Partidului Social Democrat, 2015). The quasi-official history of the PSD shares with the narrative of its political opponents the idea that the party and its ideology have developed linearly from the FSN to the current PSD. While the complex organizational transformations of the party are acknowledged, the discontinuities in its ideology and policies are largely obscured in this history. Even though this chapter discusses mainly the largest social democratic party in the country, it also warns against reductionist unilateral identification of social democracy with the PSD and its predecessors. Returning to the initial question of who are the 'true social democrats' in Romania, it is obvious that no 'essence' of social democracy (Powell, 2004) is to be found in its history, but rather a highly dynamic organizational evolution and a set of discourses and practices that are constantly rearticulated in specific political contexts (Adamson, 2000).

ELECTORAL RESULTS

The first elections following the fall of communism were seen as 'exciting referenda on democracy' (Eley, 2002: 449). For the FSN it was an opportunity to frame ideologically the 1989 revolution through a confrontation with the so-called 'historical parties', the PNȚ and PNL, and by defining its relation with the former communist regime. In the 1990 elections, the FSN obtained 66.31 per cent of the votes for the Chamber of Deputies, the lower chamber in the Romanian parliament. The PSDR, the 'historical' social democratic party, won less than 1 per cent in the same election. In the 1992 elections, the FDSN had registered a comparatively modest 27.72 per cent of the votes, although Ion Iliescu, its candidate, won the presidency with 47.34 per cent in the first round, and in the second with 61.43 per cent of the votes. In 1996, the PDSR received 21.52 per cent, and the Social Democratic Union (Uniunea Social Democrată, USD), which included the PD and the PSDR, 12.93 per cent of the votes (Project on Political Transformation, 2002).

The 2000 elections brought 36.61 per cent for the PDSR, which formed the government led by Adrian Năstase. The PD, on the other hand, got 7.3 per cent in the same elections. A similar score, of 37.16 per cent, was won by the PSD in an electoral alliance with the Romanian Humanist Party (Partidul Umanist Român, PUR) in 2004. However, given that the right-wing candidate Traian Băsescu won the presidency, the Justice and Truth Alliance (Alianța Dreptate și Adevăr, DA) was nominated to form the government. A similar story was repeated in 2008, when the PSD in alliance with the Conservative Party (Partidul Conservator, PC) won 2,279,449 votes, but one seat less in the lower chamber than its main competitor, the PDL, which got 2,228,860 votes, a situation made possible by a change in the electoral system. In 2012, the PSD, in alliance with the National Liberal Party, that is, the Social Liberal Union (Uniunea Social Liberală, USL), secured 58.63 per cent of the votes (Autoritatea Electorală Permanentă România Website, 2015; Project on Political

Transformation, 2002). One year before the parliamentary elections scheduled for 2016, the Prime Minister Victor Ponta had resigned from office and the social democratic government was replaced in November 2015 by a so-called technocratic cabinet led by Dacian Cioloş, the former EU Commissioner for Agriulture and Rural Development in the Barroso Commission. Ponta is under legal investigation for activities dating back to 2007–08, when he was a lawyer, being charged of forgery, tax evasion and money laundering. His resignation, however, was precipitated by the street protests following a fire in a Bucharest club, which killed 60 people and injured more then a hundred.

These electoral results demonstrate that social democratic parties, either alone or in coalitions, won all elections since 1989, with only one exception, in 1996. On the other hand, they were not able to form the government in two electoral cycles, mainly because the social democratic candidates for presidency lost the elections in 2004, 2009 and 2014. The incapacity to win presidential elections after 2004 is in stark contrast with the 1992 and 2000 elections, when Ion Iliescu obtained a much higher score than his party. This situation pointed to the high degree of person- alization, the party relying heavily on the so-called 'electoral locomotives', a role performed especially by Ion Iliescu until 2004 (Consiliul Naţional al PSD, 2003). After 2000, the social democrats have preferred to run in elections as part of electoral alliances. In terms of party membership, the PDSR and the PSD have outperformed all parties, with 309,000 party members registered in 1995 and approximately 700,000 in 2005 (Soare, 2013).

Romanian social democracy is a post-communist ideological development decoupled from the pre-communist socialist democratic experiences. The lack of a continuous development and the discon- nection from a well-established social democratic tradition had a fundamental impact on its evolution. Its organization as a party (FSN) was deeply connected to the first political structures of the post-com- munist period, when state structures and political structures were not well differentiated. The PDSR and then the PSD became the largest party organizations, which were well adapted to winning parliamentary elections and forging governing alliances, but less successful in winning the presidency. On the other hand, the significant electoral capital gained during the last two decades has not been used for consolidating the core principles of the left, but rather for navigating between neoliberal reforms and provisional protection of the population against the effects of free market policies. This has led to a peculiar situation of the left in Romania: it won the majority of parliamentary elections, but failed to provide an encompassing left-wing ideological platform as an alternative to right-wing ideologies and policies.

THE ELECTORAL BASE OF SOCIAL DEMOCRATIC PARTIES: THE 'UNMAKING OF THE WORKING CLASS'

Romanian social democracy seemed to be in the ideal environment for becoming a dominant ideology after 1989. Indeed, the country had a massive workforce employed in industry, in industrialized agriculture and in the state sector. This could have formed a solid and stable social base for left-wing parties. Such expectations soon proved unrealistic for at least two chief reasons. Firstly, as a general principle, the evolution of political parties in the twentieth century, and of social democratic parties in particular, proves that 'there is no "natural relationship" between social structure and voting behaviour' (Schmidt, 2012: 23). Secondly, the traditional social base of social democratic parties in Central and Eastern Europe had been rapidly eroded after 1989 by the process of post-communist transition (Gowan, 1995).

The relevance of traditional political cleavages is a key debate in political studies (Mair, 2001: 28–30), with the 'obsolescence' of the workers'/ employers' cleavage being particularly under scrutiny in post-industrial societies (Bartolini, 2000). Indeed, in the second half of the twentieth century, the percentage of (industrial) workers and farmers in the total workforce was steadily declining, which led to the questioning of the political importance of the working class in Western societies (Dogan, 2001: 95–101). The erosion of the traditional working class base is a highly relevant factor for the evolution of Romanian social democracy. The working class of the former communist regime had rapidly diminished after 1989, both in size and political weight. The dismantling of the socialist economy through privatization and the collapse of the large industrial plants had not just economic but also significant political consequences (Greskovits, 2008; Pickles, 2008). A massive process of de-industrialization and a significant de-urbanization had deeply transformed the social structure, leading to the retreat of the working class from its former central social, economic and political position. Not only had the number of industrial workers been drastically reduced but the numbers of employed persons in general had dramatically fallen as a result of economic transition: '[in 2010] the employees are less than 60% (4.6 million) of their numbers in 1989, while the pensioners are 55% (5.5 million) per cent more than in 1989' (ICCV, 2010).

Being in government in key moments of the post-communist transition, the dismantling of the communist heavy industry was, at least partially, produced by left-wing governments. Although initially the FSN had claimed to represent the workers and former state employees of the communist regime, these workers have been gradually displaced from their central position by the very party that, in the wake of the 1989 revolution, invested them with such a key role in the making of the post-communist society. The largest wave of 'big privatizations' was coordinated by the PDSR government during the years 2000–04. Apparently generous 'exit packages' and 'early retirement' offers for workers also led to a sharp decline of the working class, both as an economic and a political subject. The Romanian social democracy thus contributed significantly to a true process of the 'unmaking of the working class' (Schmidt, 2012).

The erosion of the working class fuelled the opinion that left-wing parties in Romania have a stronger social base in the rural world and among the elderly. Indeed, the PDSR/PSD has a stronger organizational base and, in general, higher electoral scores than its competitors in rural areas. However, the fact that 'rural areas remained the PSD's almost exclusive preserve, challenged only recently by the PDL' (Soare, 2013) shouldn't be overestimated. Especially after 2000, the electoral differences between left-wing and right-wing parties in the rural areas were less significant, and local elections have been won by right-wing candidates and parties in numerous villages and small towns. On the other hand, the preference of rural voters for the PDSR/PSD signals the perceived association of social democracy to welfare state policies in a context of dramatic poverty, inequality and social exclusion induced by the post-communist neoliberalization of the economy rather than the closeness of the PSD to the rural world. The rural-urban dichotomy and the generational dimension of social democratic politics remains nonetheless relevant because they had an impact on the adoption of rather conservative social values by the PSD and have contributed to the disconnection of the party from the new 'progressive' social movements (environmentalists, feminists etc.).

The Romanian case illustrates very well the decline of class politics in Eastern Europe. With the dissolution of the communist society, political parties had the historical opportunity to produce new ideologies and political identities, an opportunity that was more successfully taken by right-wing parties. The neoconservative strategy was to use anti-communism as an ideological ground-zero for future articulations of socio-political identities: the entrepreneur, the public intellectual, the self-employed etc. On the contrary, social democratic parties have been less successful in offering alternative identities to this dominant ideological horizon. Interestingly, the PSD acknowledges the importance of this process for parties in post-communism: 'the relation was from the political towards the social and not the opposite, as it would have been normal in the activity of constituting political parties. Under such circumstances, the path of social democracy in transition was that of political formations seeking adherents and supporters in civil society' (Consiliul Naţional al PSD, 2003: 27). Its traditional social base was often labelled pejoratively as 'state-dependent' and 'electorally bribed' persons in right-wing discourses. The idea of 'a nation of socially assisted persons' continues to be used in Romania in connection to the perceived attempts of social democrats to preserve welfare state policies. Finally, the (neo) communist/anti-communist dichotomy has remained as one of the most enduring ideological legacies of the post-communist transition and has had a fundamental impact on Romanian social democracy.

IDEOLOGICAL ARTICULATIONS OF SOCIAL DEMOCRACY

Western social democratic parties made fundamental contributions to the evolution of the social democratic doctrine, with leading socialist intellectuals being also party activists (Berman, 2006). Romanian social democracy not only has a much shorter and fragmented history but has also made a less significant contribution to the regional, not to mention global debates on social democratic ideology. The PSD and its predecessors provided, on the other hand, the main elements for the articulation of social democracy in Romania, the party eventually establishing itself as the key actor in the construction of social democratic discourses and practices. Its ideology was challenged both from the right and, more recently, the left. The so-called 'democratic opposition' in the 1990s, mostly formed by centre-right parties and right-wing public intellectuals, charged the FSN/FDSN/PDSR of being a 'neo-communist party' and considered its ideology as a 'communism with a human face'. Only very recently, and in a marginal way, have social democratic ideology and policies been criticized for their neoliberal orientation.

According to a dominant interpretation, former communist parties went through 'superficial cosmetic changes' in order to become social democratic parties (Soare, 2013). While relatively accurate in the case of the majority of former communist states from Central and Eastern Europe in relation to party structure and organization, this interpretation contributes little to illuminating the ideological profile of social democratic parties in Romania. The right-wing label 'neo-communist' obscures, for instance, the neoliberal turn of social democratic parties in post-communist states. Moreover, such generalizations erase the shifts and turning points in their ideology. A more nuanced mapping of the evolution of social democratic ideology is therefore needed.

The first stage in the formation of social democracy in Romania began with an attempt to produce a hegemonic discourse on the 1989 revolution and on the profound changes that followed after the collapse of the communist regime (Adamson, 2000). The most difficult struggle carried out by the FSN was to be recognized concomitantly as the key revolutionary agent and as the stabilizing political force in the post-communist order. It was a unique case in the former communist space where former communist elites embarked on an (at least formally) anti-communist revolutionary project. They did so in the first instance by putting revolution as a central signifier in their discourse and by presenting themselves as the true inheritors of the revolutionary ideals: 'The platform of the FSN is written in the blood of the revolution' (Adevarul, 25 January 1990, in Adamson, 2000: 122).

In order to achieve the political goal of governing the post-communist change, the FSN had to capitalize on its self-defined role in the revolution and to fix the meaning of a plethora of signifiers that emerged after the revolutionary events: democracy, transition, reform, capitalism etc. Immediately after 1989, some of the FSN leaders continued to refer to 'socialism' and attempted to offer an interpretation of the revolution as anti-Ceauşescu but not anti-socialist. Adamson (2000) proposed the term 'revisionist socialism' to define this stage, the continuity with the former socialist model being the most sensitive issue during this period. Facing an increasing opposition, the FSN gradually abandoned this interpretation. A decade later, the PSD holds that 'no organisational nor logistical structure was there to be inherited [from the Communist Party]' (Consiliul Naţional al PSD, 2003: 26). Currently, the PSD discourages the use of the term 'socialism' in connection to its ideology or policies and uses 'communism' in a pejorative sense.

The second stage in the making of social democratic ideology is connected to the course of the post-communist transition during 1992–2000. Ideologically, the FDSN/PDSR attempted to offer an alternative to the neoliberal model of economic transition implemented in the majority of Central and Eastern European countries. In practice, however, this was translated into just a more gradual programme of privatization and liberalization (Ban, 2014). In several areas though, such as labour policies, specific social democratic social policies were still preserved. This led to a hybrid model that can be labelled as a reformist neoliberalism. The ideological distance to right-wing parties thus diminished considerably. Other interpretations would consider such evolutions as an expression of 'managerialism', a key element in the ideological profile of the post-communist elites (Eyal et al., 1998: 86).

The hypothesis of 'ideological contagion' can also explain the gradual neoliberal turn of Romanian social democracy. Volkens (2004: 38) argues that processes of 'contagion', both from the left and the right, can be rationalized in terms of electoral strategies, given that parties import perceived successful policies from rival parties. In Europe, this led to a 'contagion from the left' affecting major right-wing parties in the first two decades after the Second World War, and to a 'contagion from the right' that affected social democratic parties in the 1980s and 1990s (Volkens, 2004: 23–4, 37). The Romanian case is unique to the extent that the 'ideological contagion' from the right took place even though there was no electoral success of right-wing parties and following the unpopular policies of the right-wing government during 1996–2000. The 'contagion from the left' was also fundamentally weaker than in Western Europe. Despite this fact, the PDSR and the PSD were accused by their political opponents of being the successors of the Communist Party and their policies were frequently criticized for being too 'socialist'. Given that the right-wing discourses still use as a political weapon the connection of their adversaries with the communist past, the social democrats make constant efforts to distance themselves from any association with communism or socialism.

A third stage in the development of social democratic ideology begins in 2000, when the PSD became the governing party. The priorities during this stage were the consolidation of its pro-market orientation and pro-European position, in the wake of the bid for EU membership and during the first years of membership. The main challenge for the social democratic ideology remains the construction of a credible fusion between a 'social economy' and the completion of the transition to a capitalist economy. Even though it assumes that 'accusations of crypto-communism, neo-communism or communist continuity represent a useful falsehood for a certain electoral campaign approach' (Consiliul Naţional al PSD, 2003: 28), the PSD continues to internalize right-wing ideological elements in its discourse. In fact, the party initially associated with the slogan 'we do not sell our country' has produced the most comprehensive privatization programmes in Romania after 2000.

The current political programme of the PSD is summarized in eleven points, the content and order of which are reflective of the party's ideological positioning. The first article clarifies the orientation of its economic programme (protection of private property and commitment to free market), while the second articulates the imperative of 'restructuring and modernization of the national economy' and the reform of the state administration (Statutul Partidului Social Democrat, 2013: 10–11). The third point reiterates the principle of 'economic and social reforms', followed by a reference to the idea of 'social equity'. This was a key element in the discourse of transition, which the PSD had tried to articulate within a neoliberal reformist perspective. 'Reform' has indeed been one of the main empty signifiers in post-communism (Adamson, 2000). It has been invested with multiple functions in the social democratic discourse, including the signalling of a clear-cut separation from the communist past, but also from other forms of left-wing politics.

The principles of social protection and social justice are included in the fourth point and represent the main source for the social democratic orientation of the party (Statutul Partidului Social Democrat, 2013: 10–11). As shown in the next section, this reference is in stark contrast to the fact that welfare state policies in Romania are among the least developed in comparison to other EU states. The next five points define general commitments to the development of science and education, support for family, equality of opportunity, the protection of rights and liberties and other general political values. Clearly, there are differences between the description of the general social democratic values and the political objectives to which the party is committed. For instance, a social economy is presented as a fundamental value in the general introduction to the party doctrine, whereas in the programme the focus is on combining free market policies with social protections (Statutul Partidului Social Democrat, 2015).

The last point in the party programme refers to the adoption of the political principles defined by the Socialist International and by the European Socialist Party. Following Romania entering the EU in 2007, this commitment was reflected by a high degree of support for the decisions of the socialist group in the European Parliament (Votewatch Website, 2015). On the other hand, in national politics, the PSD had imported only a very limited agenda from the European Socialists group. Even in the context of European elections, the PSD preserves its reformist neoliberal vocabulary and focuses on domestic political issues. In addition, in the European elections in 2009 and 2014 nationalist slogans were highly present in the electoral discourses. The main slogan in 2014, for instance, was 'Proud to be Romanians', used in parallel with Romanian ethnic symbols and graphics.

In fact, the nationalist dimension has accompanied Romanian social democracy from its early formation. As Adamson (2000) demonstrated, the nationalist platform was an important ingredient of the post-communist Romanian left wing in the effort to reconstruct the idea of the nation after its disconnection from the national communist ideology of the

Ceausescu regime. The nationalist appeal was again heavily used in the presidential elections of 2014, when the same 'Proud to be Romanian!' slogan was also present, together with 'The President who unites'. The nationalist appeal was integrated into a conservative dimension of social democratic ideology, one that favours traditional social values at the expense of more progressive 'liberal' values.

On a final note, the neoliberal turn of Romanian social democracy is far from being a unique case, it actually confirms the European trend of social democratic parties. References to the retreat and even 'death of social democracy' are common in the literature (Powell, 2004: 5) and among political commentators. Other authors speak bluntly about 'the neoliberalization of social democracy' (Lavelle, 2008), the internaliza-tion and normalization of neoliberalism being considered one of the fundamental features of 'new social democracy' (Evans, 2012: 1). It is interesting that in the Romanian case it is rather the opposite perception: the PSD is still being dubbed 'neo-communist', despite the overwhelming evidence of an ideological commitment to deregulated capitalism and support for policies that weaken and even dismantle the welfare state.

SOCIAL DEMOCRATIC POLICIES AND
THE ROMANIAN WELFARE STATE

Social democracy has long been seen as a set of policies designed to defend society against the consequences of the free market. Albeit of limited value for understanding the social base of centre-left parties (Escalona et al., 2013: 9), this Polyanian representation provides useful insights into the formation of the social democratic ideology. But the post-communist context again provides a different story. In policy terms, the degree of support for the welfare state and for economic lib-eralization differentiated post-communist parties without producing a clear-cut separation in cross-national analyses between left- and right-wing parties (Kitschelt et al., 1999). The position on the pace and scope of privatization essentially became the post-communist equivalent for the workers'/employers' cleavage in Western Europe.

In the Romanian context, the FSN/FDSN had initially tried to build a more gradual model of economic liberalization and offer an alternative path of transition to the neoliberal 'shock therapy' approach followed in the majority of the ex-communist states (Adamson, 2002; Ban, 2014). However, the slower pace of reforms advocated by centre-left parties in Romania was never intended to offer a hybrid model of 'social capitalism'. This was evident especially after 2000, when they abandoned the gradualist approach and followed policies of economic liberalization and dismantling of the welfare state, which resulted in one of the most pronouncedly neoliberal projects in the region.

The political economy of Romanian social democracy has been intertwined with the main stages of its ideological development. The first stage consisted of the initial attempts to offer an alternative to the radical reforms applied especially in Central European ex-communist states. During 1992–96, the social democratic government adopted development policies based on what Ban (2014: 136) calls 'populist neodevelopmentalism', a hybrid policy that combined neoliberal measures with social protection, fusing together 'the demands of left wing populists' with the expectations of 'right wing demands for protecting the internal capitalist class'. The contradiction of a capitalist system being constructed in post-communism in the absence of a capitalist class (Eyal et al., 1998) could thus be resolved. Besides the modest results in protecting the 'national economy', the actual outcome of such policies provided the conditions for the emergence of a national class of capitalists and paved the way for a development path dependent on global and regional capital.

The first wave of free market reforms thus led to 'nomenklatura capitalism' (Adamson, 2000: 125). Commenting on the first wave of free market reforms in post-communism, Sassoon notes that it brought 'a bazaar capitalism of unusual proportions' (1997: 732). Similar conclusions were formulated by numerous social scientists. In a reference to the Romanian and Bulgarian initial course of transition, Eley comments that 'these were strategies of nationally protected capitalism, with modified welfare states and practical corporatisms based on post-Communist trade unions', concomitant with 'the region's brutal subjection to the global capitalist system' (Eley, 2002: 451). Such conclusions shouldn't be understood, though, as erasing the significant differences in the transition paths followed by post-communist economies and in the models of capitalism implemented during transition (Greskovits, 2008).

Commenting on the negative economic impact induced by the politics of 'shock therapy', Kolodko identified as its main causes 'ignorance of development policy, exaggeration of the significance of transition as such, and a confusion of transition with liberalization and privatization' (2000: 148). To this should be added at least two other factors, both of which are connected to the policies adopted by Romanian social democratic parties. One belongs to the arena of political economy and was termed 'cornered state', namely, a state that is *cornered by a coalition of hyper-mobile trans-national business with small- and medium-scale domestic capital* that is highly dependent on the opportunities to serve the former as subcontractor or labour contractor' (Greskovits, 2008: 39, emphasis in the original).

This basically assumes that 'there was no alternative' to neoliberalism for cornered states like Romania. The second factor refers to the constitutive role of social and political factors for economic systems (Ban, 2014; Smith and Swain, 1998). It stresses the importance of ideology and, in our case, of party doctrines and discourses in constructing economic alternatives. It implies that alternatives were available, and that specific political choices were responsible for the social and economic costs of transition. Such costs were therefore produced by particular political decisions, were largely avoidable and were not so much the outcome of reportedly inevitable circumstances. Romanian social democrats were key actors in the process of neoliberalization, during 1992–96 and especially after 2000. Alternative social democratic policies were pursued by left-wing parties from Central and Eastern Europe, for instance, in Slovenia and the Czech Republic (Ban, 2014).

There was certainly a tension between liberalization and social protection to be found in the economic policies pursued by social democrats in Eastern Europe after 1989. They seemed to be the only political force in post-communism that presented 'a commitment to social protection and a suspicion of market forces' (Sassoon, 1997: 754). Indeed, this was the case especially for the left-wing parties in Hungary and Poland in the 1990s, but such a conclusion cannot be generalized for the entire post-communist space. In Romania, the FSN/FDSN/ PDSR struggled in the 1990s to offer a 'local' alternative to the shock therapies, only to succumb after 2000 to the general neoliberal trend that was followed, albeit with significant adaptations, by the majority of the Central and Eastern European countries. This was the second stage in the socio-economic policies of social democracy, which produced one of the most radical free market reforms in the former post-communist space. There are numerous examples that help to understand the dimension of the neoliberalization process in Romanian, with the social democratic governments being directly involved in either formulating or applying such 'reforms'. Notorious cases include, for instance, the privatization of the national oil company, together with oil and gas deposits in 2004, and of the largest steel plant in 2001.

The third stage in the development of a social democratic political economy was the consolidation of a reformist neoliberal model after the EU accession in 2007. It consisted of socio-economic policies that followed a more conventional route of European social democracy in respect to social policies, while continuing the economic liberalization. The privatization drive of the 2000–04 PSD government continues to this day and benefits from justifications related to the *acquis communautaire*. Currently, there are discussions and attempts to engineer 'big' privatizations including of the national postal services, the railways, the remaining state-owned electricity production and the sell-off of shares in several state-controlled companies, such as the airways company or various industrial companies. Other liberalization measures were not taken directly by social democratic governments, but received their support. Illustrative examples include the compulsory private pensions system and the flat tax of 16 per cent. The latter was enthusiastically supported by right-wing parties and has more recently found a supporter in the social democrats. The alliance with the liberals and conservatives in the USL between 2011 and 2014 reinforced the consensus on a liberal approach to taxation.

Contrary to a widespread preconception in Romania, the country has one of the most liberal tax systems in the EU. The scale of the neo-liberalization process should be evident from the following data. Total taxes including Social Security Contribution (SSC) from 2000–2012 in Romania have been reduced by 1.9 per cent from 30.2 per cent in 2000 to 28.3 per cent in 2012. This ranks Romania in 25th position in the EU28, with only Latvia, Lithuania and Bulgaria having lower levels of taxation in 2012, and in sharp contrast with the EU28 average weighted gross domestic product (GDP) of 39.4 per cent (Eurostat, 2014). The direct taxation as a percentage of the GDP was 6.1 per cent in 2012, situating Romania again in 25th position, compared with 13.2 per cent EU28 average weighted GDP (Eurostat, 2014a). This taxation system was coupled with very low spending on social policies. State spending on pensions, health and education are constantly situated at about half of the EU average, for instance, 6.2 per cent of the GDP on pensions, compared to 12.4 per cent EU15 average during 1996–2007 (ICCV, 2010).

Besides their modest contributions measured by state spending, social welfare policies have also had a modest impact. Thus, the rate of relative poverty 'before social transfers' was 48 per cent of the population, with a reduction of 53 per cent after social welfare policies were applied during 2004–08 (ICCV, 2010: 32). Territorial disparities are also very high, both within the country and compared with other regions in the EU. Taking into consideration the NUTS 2 regions, we find the poorest region is North-East Romania (Eurostat, 2014b). In political economic terms, Romania has produced a 'capitalism without compromise' and has entered a 'neoliberal developmental trap' based on 'the consolidation of low wages, anti-labour regulation of industrial relations, poor work conditions, and ultimately a degradation of human capital' (Greskovits, 2008: 40).

As already mentioned, these conditions are the direct outcome of policies either produced or supported by social democratic governments and based on a neoliberal consensus in which the social democrats participate. Redistributive policies remain among the weakest in Europe, even when social democrats are in government. Romania has had one of the most radical dismantlings of the welfare state in Europe, despite the fact that 'shock therapy' policies were initially postponed, but then were, at specific stages, implemented by social democrats. Given the social context, with high poverty rates, low income and high inequality, the political and ideological consensus on rolling back the welfare state should be surprising. Despite such dim social records, the dominant representation is still of a state that is 'too big' and of social welfare policies as being 'too generous'. The idea of a 'nation of socially assisted persons' and the metaphor patented by the former President Băsescu, of the fat man ('the state') on the shoulders of a thin person ('the economy') is ad nauseam repeated by economists, politicians and political commentators (Vesalon, 2010). Having been in power for a long time and managing the transition process, Romanian social democrats contributed to the construction of one of the most neoliberal capitalist systems in Europe and provided the ideological background for its support.

BIBLIOGRAPHY

Adamson, K. (2000). 'The Construction of Romanian Social Democracy (1989–1996)'. In D. Howarth, A. Norval and Y. Stavrakakis (eds), *Discourse Theory and Political Analysis. Identities, Hegemonies and Social Change*. Manchester: Manchester University Press: 119–33.

Autoritatea Electorală Permanentă România Website (2015). www.roaep.ro/istoric/ (accessed May 2015).

Ban, C. (2014). *Dependență și dezvoltare. Economia politică a capitalismului românesc*. Cluj-Napoca: Editura Tact.

Bartolini, S. (2000). *The Political Mobilization of the European Left, 1860–1980. The Class Cleavage*. Cambridge: Cambridge University Press.

Berman, S. (2006). *The Primacy of Politics. Social Democracy and the Making of Europe's Twentieth Century*. Cambridge: Cambridge University Press.

Bonoli, G. and Powell, M. (eds) (2004). *Social Democratic Party Policies in Contemporary Europe*. London: Routledge.

Consiliul Național al PSD (2003). *110 ani de social-democratie în România*. București: Institutul Social-Democrat 'Ovidiu Șincai'.

Dogan, M. (2001). 'Class, Religion, Party: Triple Decline of Electoral Cleavages in Western Europe'. In L. Karvonen and S. Kuhnle (eds), *Party Systems and Voter Alignments Revisited*. London and New York: Routledge: 91–110.

Eley, G. (2002). *Forging Democracy. The History of the Left in Europe, 1850–2000*. Oxford: Oxford University Press.

Escalona, F., Vieira, M. and De Waele, J.-M. (2013). 'The Unfinished History of the Social Democratic Family'. In J.-M. De Waele, F. Escalona and M. Vieira (eds), *The Palgrave Handbook of Social Democracy in the European Union*. Houndnills, Basingstoke: Palgrave Macmillan: 3–29.

Eurostat (2011). *Taxation Trends in the European Union. Focus on the Crisis: The Main impacts on EU Tax Systems*. European Commission.

—— (2014a). *Taxation Trends in the European Union. Data for the EU Member States, Iceland and Norway*. European Commission.

—— (2014b). *Eurostat Regional Yearbook 2014*. European Commission.

Evans, B. (2012). 'Introduction. The New Social Democracy'. In B. Evans and I. Schmidt (eds), *Social Democracy After the Cold War*. Edmonton: AU Press: 1–11.

Eyal, G., Szelényi, I. and Townsley, E. (1998). *Making Capitalism Without Capitalists. Class Formation and Elite Struggles in Post-communist Central Europe*. London and New York: Verso.

Gowan, P. (1995). 'Neo-liberal Theory and Practice for Eastern Europe'. *New Left Review*, I/ 213: 3–60.

Greskovits, B. (2008). 'Leading Sectors and the Variety of Capitalism in Eastern Europe'. In J. Pickles (ed.), *State and Society in Post-socialist Economies*. Houndmills, Basingstoke: Palgrave Macmillan: 19–46.

Howarth, D. and Stavrakakis, Y. (2000). 'Introducing Discourse Theory'. In D. Howarth, A. Norval and Y. Stavrakakis (eds), *Discourse Theory and Political Analysis. Identities, Hegemonies and Social Change*. Manchester: Manchester University Press: 1–23.

ICCV (2010). *Dupa 20 de ani: optiuni pentru România*. Raportul social al ICCV. Bucureşti: Academia Română. Institutul Naţional de Cercetări Economice. Institutul de Cercetare a Calităţii Vieţii.

Kitschelt, H. (1994). *The Transformation of European Social Democracy*. Cambridge: Cambridge University Press.

Kitschelt, H., Mansfeldova, Z., Markowski, R. and Toka, G. (1999). *Post-communist Party Systems. Competition, Representation, and Inter-party Cooperation*. Cambridge: Cambridge University Press.

Kolodko, G.W. (2000). *From Shock to Therapy. The Political Economy of Postsocialist Transformation*. New York: Oxford University Press.

Laclau, E. and Mouffe, C. (1985). *Hegemony & Socialist Strategy. Towards a Radical Democratic Politics*. London and New York: Verso.

Lavelle, A. (2008). *The Death of Social Democracy. Political Consequences in the 21st Century*. Aldershot: Ashgate.

Mair, P. (2001). 'The Freezing Hypothesis. An Evaluation'. In L. Karvonen and S. Kuhnle (eds), *Party Systems and Voter Alignments Revisited*. London and New York: Routledge: 25–41.

Pickles, J. (2008). 'The Spirit of Post-socialism: "What is to be Understood by it?"'. In J. Pickles (ed.), *State and Society in Post-socialist Economies*. Houndmills, Basingstoke: Palgrave Macmillan: 1–16.

Powell, M. (2004). 'Social Democracy in Europe. Renewal or Retreat?'. In G. Bonoli and M. Powell (eds), *Social Democratic Party Policies in Contemporary Europe*. London: Routledge: 1–20.

Project on Political Transformation and the Electoral Process in Post-Communist Europe (2002). University of Essex. Available at www2.essex.ac.uk/elect/database/indexCountry.asp?country=ROMANIA&opt=elc (accessed May 2015).

Sassoon, D. (1997). *One Hundred Years of Socialism. The West European Left in the Twentieth Century*. London: Fontana Press.

Schmidt, I. (2012). 'It's the Economy, Stupid! Theoretical Reflections on Third Way Social Democracy'. In B. Evans and I. Schmidt (eds), *Social Democracy After the Cold War*. Edmonton: AU Press: 13–43.

Smith, A. and Swain, A. (1998). 'Regulating and Institutionalising Capitalisms. The Micro-foundations of Transformation in Eastern and Central Europe'. In J. Pickles and A. Smith (eds), *Theorising Transition. The Political Economy of Post-communist Transformations*. London and New York: Routledge: 24–50.

Soare, S. (2012). 'The Romania Party System's Europeanization: An Open Bet'. In E. Külahci (ed.), *Europeanisation and Party Politics. How the EU affects Domestic Actors, Patterns and Systems*. Colchester: ECPR Press: 145–56.

—— (2013). 'Romania'. In J.-M. De Waele, F. Escalona and M. Vieira (eds), *The Palgrave Handbook of Social Democracy in the European Union*. Houndmills, Basingstoke: Palgrave Macmillan: 526–49.

Statutul Partidului Social Democrat (2013, 2015). www.psd.ro/wp-content/themes/psd/pdfs/Statut-PSD.pdf (accessed May 2015).

Vesalon, L. (2010). 'Populism şi neoliberalism în discursul modernizării statului'. In S. Gherghina and S. Mişcoiu (eds), *Partide şi personalităţi populiste în România postcomunistă*. Iaşi: Editura Institutul European: 191–232.

Volkens, A. (2004). 'Policy Changes of European Social Democrats, 1945–98'. In G. Bonoli and M. Powell (eds), *Social Democratic Party Policies in Contemporary Europe*. London: Routledge: 21–42.

Votewatch Website (2015). 'Cohesion of (Trans-national) Political Groups in the European Parliament'. Available at www.votewatch.eu/en/term8-political-group-cohesion.html#sthash.jY8b1QgX.dpuf (accessed May 2015).

9

Slovenian Social Democracy: Long March Towards Irrelevance

Anej Korsika

Following the break-up of Yugoslavia, the League of Communists of Slovenia transformed itself into a classical social democratic party. Together with a couple of other parties it formed a new party, the United List of Social Democracy (SD). As such, it remained the second most powerful left-wing party (second only to the Liberal Democracy of Slovenia (LDS)). It held this position from 1992 until 2008 when it won the election and formed the government (winning 30.4 per cent of the votes or 29 seats out of 90). It did not manage to finish its mandate though. Early elections were held in 2011, a couple of months before the regular elections should have taken place, and the SD lost a great deal of support, they went down to 10.52 per cent of the votes, that is, 10 seats. But the real blow came in 2014 when another early election was held. The SD plummeted to its historical low of only 6 per cent, or 6 seats. In these elections a new political force emerged that explicitly argued (and still does) for democratic socialism, that is, the Coalition of the United Left (ULC). It, too, achieved 6 per cent.[1] What follows is an account of more than two decades of political life in Slovenia (1990–2015) and the complex and intertwined trajectories of social democracy and democratic socialism.

We argue that 2014 is an important historical as well as symbolic point that marks the end of an era. It is a point in time when the two trajectories crossed paths, both achieving almost identical election results. However, while social democracy is still on a clear downward trend, democratic socialism is clearly on the rise. While the latter has just entered the level of state and parliamentary politics, the former is most likely to exit it for the first time in its history.

Slovenian Social Democrats (SD) have undergone at least three major transformations that define their development over the last three decades and are essential for coming to terms with their current situation. It goes without saying that the internal dynamics of the party were greatly affected by both domestic and foreign political processes. We shall, therefore, try to analyze each respective period in the timeline of the development of the SD in terms of the interplay between inner-party dynamics, foreign affairs and domestic policies. The three periods can be roughly defined as:

1. The time of metamorphosis (1990–2008)
2. The time of government (2008–2011)
3. The time of decline (2011–?).

It goes without saying that such a periodization is only provisional and does not pretend to describe completely homogeneous periods. On the contrary, especially the first period, as the name suggests, was one of great changes. Firstly, there was a change from a communist party to social democracy, and then a change to Third Way ideology. These fundamental changes were also expressed by the changes in the leadership. Perhaps the second period, the time of government (2008–11), when SD was the ruling party, is the most distinct and one that justifies (even demands) a periodization that explains the development of SD before being the ruling party and after being the ruling party. The latter period, the time of decline, is still ongoing and, as we already suggested, might even end in the failure to enter the parliament in the next elections.

When Yugoslavia began breaking up, the Yugoslav League of Communists and its republican branches also began fragmenting, such was the case with the Slovenian League of Communists (SLC) as well.[2] The League and its constituent organizations, first and foremost, the League of Socialist Youth of Slovenia, were the catalysts of political changes. These organizations, with their already existing structures, provided a fertile ground for establishing new political parties. The majority of parties that played dominant roles in Slovenia's transition were established in this way, to be more precise, they were building blocks that merged later on. Though only social democracy was the official heir of the SLC and as such maintained a special position. Together with other familiar groups, the United List of Social Democrats (ULSD) was established and bore this name until the 2005 party congress, when it changed its name to the still existing Social Democrats.

TRANSITION: THE ERASED AND REVOLT
AGAINST SHOCK-DOCTRINE

In the first multi-party elections in April 1990, one of the founding parties of the United List participated as the Party of Democratic Renewal and achieved the highest result among individual political parties (17.28 per cent). However, it did not become the governing party because several other parties, uniting as the coalition Demos, formed the government. In the next elections, 1992, the already established United List got 13.58 per cent of the votes and entered a grand coalition with the LDS and the SKD (Christian Democrats). It remained in this coalition until 1996 when it resigned as a coalition member. The official reason for the resignation was that the government implemented socially harmful reforms, especially regarding pensioners. It remained in opposition until 2000, thus the SD spent the first decade mostly as an opposition party (six years), and had a limited impact on the Slovenian political scene. The transition from the Yugoslavian system of workers' self-management to a market economy was the core socio-economic process of this period. In comparison to other ex-Yugoslavian republics, especially Bosnia and Herzegovina, Slovenia was able to exit Yugoslavia without major bloodshed. The war with the Yugoslavian National Army lasted for only ten days and the number of casualties was relatively low.

Slovenia, having the most homogeneous, ethnically speaking, population amongst these republics, was fortunate in the sense that bloodshed experienced in the ten-day war with the Yugoslavian National Army was nothing compared to the wars in Croatia and Bosnia and Herzegovina. However, one must bear in mind that immediately after gaining independence Slovenia conducted an ethnic cleansing of its own. It was much subtler than the one in Srebrenica, no blood was spilled and instead of guns and tanks, passports, identity cards and other personal documents were used, i.e. they were confiscated and destroyed. The 'Erased of Slovenia' were a group of people that ceased to exist as citizens of Slovenia, while not gaining any other citizenship. In the administrative sense, it is estimated that some 18,000 people ceased to exist after 1991. The process took place immediately after the break-up and was concluded before the first multi-party elections were held in the newly independent Slovenia, in 1992. In this period approximately 200,000 residents were instructed to decide whether they wanted to keep their Yugoslavian citizenship or change it to Slovenian citizenship. A majority of people decided to change it to Slovenian, but 18,000, for various reasons, failed to do so. These were people who had lived in Slovenia for decades, even people born and raised in Slovenia that were literally overnight stripped of their existence. 'Bureaucratcide'[3] was thus inscribed into the very birth of Slovenia as an independent state. What have the SD done about it?

When they entered the grand coalition in 1992 the erasure was already done, however, as a governing party they didn't do much about it and did not try to solve this issue in any meaningful way. Although the Constitutional Court issued numerous 'rulings' regarding the situation of The Erased, the problem was addressed seriously only in 2008. To the merit of the SD, it was their coalition that finally began to legislate a solution for this issue, although the interior minister that pushed through the implementation of the Constitutional Court's ruling was not from their party. Prior to that a referendum had been held asking the general populace whether The Erased should be guaranteed all the rights that were taken from them.

The privatization process in Slovenia was fundamentally different from the one in other Eastern European countries. Though Jeffrey Sachs had a certain following and visited Slovenia after independence, a 'shock-doctrine' or blitzkrieg privatization did not take place in Slovenia. The period of 1990–92, or the so-called 'wild privatization' when the legislature was not yet adopted and the privatization process was not yet regulated, resembled the shock-doctrine the most. It is estimated that the state was deprived of up to €1 billion worth of property in such a way. What followed was the process that made the Slovenian socio-economic transformation special, a gradual privatization that the incumbent government is still trying to finish, more than 20 years later. The crucial element in following a much more gradual path was not an epiphany or benevolence of the political elites after the experience of the 'wild privatization', but a well-organized and mobilized working class. Throughout the 1980s Yugoslavia went through a wave of strikes, mainly due to the worsening economic situation that began to show in everyday life. This process was fueled, by and large, by the International Monetary Fund and its condition of political reforms (especially market liberalization) in order to receive any loan extensions. Though there shouldn't be any doubt that Yugoslavia also suffered from internal contradictions.

Unemployment in Slovenia was virtually non-existent before the break-up but skyrocketed immediately after gaining independence.[4] Where possible, the newly or soon to be unemployed were offered the option of early retirement. That provided for a socially less harmful way of decreasing the surplus labour force. Still, unemployment increased dramatically and stood at around 13 per cent throughout the 1990s. Workers already being mobilized took to the streets and massive strikes occurred throughout the country. Mainly because of such pressure from below, the gradual transition was implemented. Instead of overnight privatization, all citizens were given certificates in the formerly state-owned companies, effectively making them the shareholders, i.e. owners, while the state also remained an important shareholder itself. A class compromise was achieved in this way. Only a few cases have seen workers using this opportunity to actually gain control of the companies and implement workers' self-management. In the majority of cases people eventually sold their shares and spent them on consumer goods. Generally speaking, this potential economic power (wielded by citizens owning shares) never really achieved a qualitative transformation into political power. While workers were selling their shares, capital was buying them, thus slowly but continuously shifting the work-capital balance of power in the latter's favour.

STRUGGLE AGAINST THE NEOLIBERAL WAVE

By the end of the 1990s, capital was already in control of the majority of the companies. Class compromise began to gradually fall apart. Still, major political decisions were made in the Socio-Economic Council, a tripartite body where state, labour and capital would negotiate and agree upon policies. The Council was a concession to the working class after its show of power in 1993, but it was also a way in which to pacify and demobilize it. It gave the side of capital time to gradually develop and gain the upper hand. The much more dramatic and aggressive assault came in 2004 when the newly elected right-wing government of Janez Janša came to power and tried to implement a flat tax. After twelve years of almost uninterrupted rule of liberal democracy in Slovenia, this was the first time the conservatives came to power. Janša, as a prime minister, employed a couple of openly neoliberal economic advisors that advocated for a 'long overdue' shock doctrine that would come in the form of radical tax reform. Instead of the existing progressive taxation of five different tax classes, one universal tax level would be implemented for all. Trade unions were quick to realize that this would shatter the welfare state and cause social havoc. In an impressive performance of power, they were able to once again mobilize the working class and, in the midst of the November 2005 snow blizzard, more than 40,000 protestors marched through Ljubljana, Slovenia's capital. The government then withdrew its plans for a flat tax, but still made some changes and reduced the number of tax classes from 5 to 3. In a way it was the last great victory of the working class that was then forced on to the defensive. As in many other European countries, it was actually the SD that 'succeeded' in implementing some of the most neoliberal measures, and most 'successfully' undermined the strength of the trade unions.

Traditionally, trade unions, especially the biggest association, were strongly affiliated with the social democratic party. This relationship had its ups and downs, but it was actually after the SD won the elections that it became the most strained. When the SD won the parliamentary elections in 2008, the financial crisis was not that visible, it took a while to fully unravel. The right-wing government of Janez Janša worsened the situation during its time in office by pushing through pro-cyclical economic policies. The year 2007 saw the highest rise in gross domestic product (GDP) at 7.2 per cent, but public debt and budget deficits also grew to record heights exactly during this period. In just five years Slovenia's deficit almost tripled from 2.4 per cent of GDP in 2004 to 6.1 per cent of GDP in 2009. From 2008 to 2013 unemployment more than doubled, from 4.4 per cent to 9.6 per cent. Accordingly, the government debt to GDP ratio started to dramatically increase, from 22 per cent in 2009 to 78.1 per cent at the end of the third quarter of 2014.

The mandate of 2004–08 was also a time of what could be termed the second phase of privatization. As we've already seen, the company stocks had changed hands by the end of the 1990s as the majority of workers sold their shares. Because of record capital returns (i.e. profits) many managers saw this as an opportunity to go through with so-called manager buyouts. In essence, they indebted their respective companies and used their assets as collateral for loans they took from the banks. Banks had been very aggressively pushing and advocating for such loans as they saw it as a great business opportunity. Anticipating that record returns would continue, managers were confident in this scenario of buying out/privatizing companies. Such hopes were shattered with the onset of the crisis, when the majority of these loans became non-performing and banks experienced a change of heart and became much more conservative in their loan policies.

Since the manager buyouts failed, banks had to be rescued by public bailout. This, as we've already seen, further fuelled the debt and deficit. The SD government thus didn't inherit a very promising situation to start with, but their management of the crisis made matters worse. Although the problems of the banking sector were solved (for the time being) by being bailed out and socialized, banks then denied similar solidarity to the general population. Getting a loan as an individual without a secure and permanent job was not easy before the crisis and became next to impossible afterwards. This caused, and still causes, grave problems, especially for youth that are predominantly employed in so-called precarious jobs. The biggest issue was student jobs, a special type of employment that was initially meant as part-time jobs for students to increase their income. As the student job was never meant as a permanent position, it had basically no workers' rights attached to it, in essence a student worker had no social benefits, his working time was not counting towards pension entitlements, he or she just had a permit to work. Thus student workers could be fired overnight without any of the 'inconveniences' otherwise required by the labour law that regulated most working contracts. Another aspect of student jobs was that a certain percentage of the students' earnings were transferred to student organizations. This brought about an unprincipled coalition that had a common interest in not just maintaining but expanding these precarious student jobs.

Student agencies, the middlemen in providing students with student jobs, were of course interested in keeping this lucrative business. Student organizations themselves were vitally tied to this inflow of money, and employers were more than eager to keep this extreme form of precariousness. The state turned a blind eye, while trade unions simply never seriously dealt with this issue. There never was (especially at the time) a union of precarious workers. So, when the SD government tried to regulate the student jobs market it faced this powerful coalition of groups that each had their share of interests tied to student jobs. More importantly, the solution that social democracy proposed did not do away with student jobs but envisioned its universalization, something similar to mini jobs in Germany. The major change would thus be that instead of student jobs being tied to student status, they would now become available as a general type of employment. The government argued that pensioners could use such part-time work, and that the unemployed would benefit by making it easier to re-enter the labour market. Instead of stabilizing the situation of the student labour market, the government's 'solution', if accepted, would destabilize the whole labour market. In the end, the proposal was rejected in a referendum. What social democracy did manage to 'achieve' was a change of the whole structure of social dialogue.

TRADE UNIONS IN SLOVENIA

Trade unions have been losing their power, both quantitatively through the loss of membership as well as qualitatively through trade union fragmentation. Unionization of the labour force stood at around 40 per cent at the beginning of the 1990s and is currently below 20 per cent. While membership of unions was on the decline, the number of unions was on the rise. Currently, some 2000 trade unions exist and represent around 180,000 unionized workers. This fragmentation, the old 'divide and conquer' tactic, undermined the strength of trade unions. Because of neoliberal propaganda, unions themselves became susceptible to ideas about the division between the so-called real, i.e. private, sector and the public sector that doesn't produce anything. Some unions, even in the public sector, began to openly and exclusively fight for their members' interests while completely disregarding the situation of workers in other sectors (e.g. the union of doctors is such an example). As one of the foremost leaders of trade unions in Slovenia has said, unions have now entered their third stage of development since the break-up of Yugoslavia.

The first stage was when unions were quite militant working class organizations. They were able to quickly and easily mobilize workers and played a crucial part in securing an alternative path to the market economy. The last great show of this strength was the protest against the proposed flat tax reform. Generally, though, trade unions were mainly a partner in the social dialogue from the first half of the 1990s and onwards. This second period lasted until the crisis occurred and the social democracy government made the whole social dialogue obsolete. In the third period, social dialogue still exists but the balance of power has changed so much that the unions are now in a clearly subjugated position. Both objectively because of the financial crisis and subjectively because of the above-mentioned qualitative and quantitative fragmentation of the unions. Because of this, unions are now forced to play the role of fighting to minimize the most harmful policy proposals but are not really able to effectively oppose them, the so-called 'concession bargaining' tactic. Future prospects are equally bleak as union membership continues to decline and solidarity between unions gets ever smaller. From the perspective of the social democracy party, it is important to underline the crucial shift in strategy that they made when they were the ruling party. Consciously, they decided to abolish any meaningful social dialogue and even tried to push through socially harmful legislation. The historical alliance between the SD and unions, though having its ups and downs, was now gone. There is now a new political force, the United Left, which openly advocates for democratic socialism and has managed to forge strong ties with the unions. The United Left entered the parliament for the first time in July 2014 in the early elections. How is it that the United Left managed to get the same result as the SD, both getting six MPs? For the United Left this was a historical breakthrough and a huge success. For the SD this was a historical defeat, the worst result they'd had since the break-up of Yugoslavia, and a dramatic fall from the 29 MPs they'd had in 2008 when they had won the elections. How is it possible that this historic victory and defeat came about?

POWERFUL CIVIL SOCIETY

During the 1980s it was not just the workers that were mobilized, the civil society was also very vibrant and was, generally speaking, something that Antonio Negri would probably characterize as a multitude. In any case, the scene was very strong and diverse. It included a very powerful punk movement that had begun in the late 1970s. The theoretical scene was also very much alive, the two dominant currents were Marxism and Psychoanalysis with many important authors contributing to both. In the first case, authors used critique of political economy to grasp contemporary social processes but also to criticize the official party line and policies. This, one could provisionally term an ultra-leftist critique of the official party line, was centred on various newspapers and magazines. Though there were cases of censorship and, on a few occasions, even confiscations of entire issues, these publications never ceased to be funded by the official structures. The second, psychoanalytical or more precisely Lacanian, current has a much wider recognition. Especially thanks to Slavoj Žižek, Ljubljana's Lacanian School is known throughout the academic world and is still very much alive in Slovenia as the second generation is becoming ever more prominent. LGBT (lesbian, gay, bisexual, transgender), environmentalist, feminist and various other movements all either began or experienced a revival throughout the 1980s. This diverse and powerful civil society wave is essential for understanding the later development of both civil society as well as official politics in post-Yugoslav Slovenia.

Generally speaking, people that were the most visible throughout the 1980s remained so during the 1990s and in many cases up to the present. This is important for at least two reasons. Firstly, the protagonists generally remained a social liberal orientation. Secondly, because of such continuity, certain institutional arrangements were made that allowed critical thought and practice to remain alive, to a much smaller extent but alive nonetheless. One of these institutions was the Peace Institute in Metelkova City. It played, and still does, a significant role on the civil society scene. It was responsible for pushing the issues of The Erased, giving them a voice through various publications, research papers and public interventions. In 1997 another important project was launched as part of the Peace Institute, The Workers and Punks University (WPU). The name was chosen as a kind of homage to the 1980s but the WPU was, from the very beginning, a theoretical research project, a kind of para-university without any official affiliation to the university as such but a very productive platform for the development of critical thought. The WPU functions by way of annual project cycles, each being devoted to a certain cluster of problems. Among the first were radical left, radical right and revolution. Later on, the issues addressed were a mixture of more speculative philosophical matters such as sin, stupidity etc., and more politically engaged themes such as totalitarianism, ecology etc.

The third period, the current one, brought about more focused work on the critique of political economy. The annual series of lectures thus addressed financial crisis (2012), double crisis of euro integrations (2013), socialism (2014), the state (2015) etc. Apart from weekly lectures, two other activities complemented the work of the WPU. The first activity was reading seminars that dealt with various classics that were simply not dealt with seriously, or not at all, in the university. These authors and texts included Marx's *Das Kapital* and Hegel's *Phenomenology of Spirit*, while also concentrating on more contemporary issues such as the development of capitalism in China, theories of social capital, theories of financialization etc. Another important endeavour that the WPU organizes is the May Day School conference, an international conference with a special focus on leftist thinkers and activists from the region, especially ex-Yugoslavian republics. The May Day School provided a much needed platform for engaged theoretical and political discussions. Already in 2013, the School was devoted to the leftist strategies regarding the European Union, the main dilemma being one of exit (as advocated for by Costas Lapavitsas) versus reform (as argued for by Michel Husson).

People most active in the development of this third period of the WPU, devoted especially to the critique of political economy, knew one another from many years of political, especially student, activism. They have opposed the Social Democrat government and their proposal of 'mini jobs', organizing instead the 'Front of precarious workers' and the 'Working group against work' that were both very vocal in their opposition to the planned precarization of the labour force. This interconnection of theory and practice, one informing the other, was crucial and brought about very valuable experiences that proved essential in later development of the United Left, especially its core part, the Initiative for Democratic Socialism. By the end of 2011, Marxism was experiencing a certain comeback and interviews with certain members of the WPU were already making their way into the mainstream media. The year 2011 was also when the financial crisis began translating into a political crisis, it was the year of the Occupy Movement, Indignados Movement, Arab Spring, London riots etc. To a certain degree, all of this resonated in Slovenia as well and fuelled the debates among activists. By the end of 2011, an occupation of part of the Faculty of Arts at the University of Ljubljana began and lasted for three months. During the same time there was also the local expression of the Occupy Movement that occupied the square in front of the Stock Exchange. Both provided very valuable experiences and spaces for critical discussion among activists, academics and the general public (both happening during the time of the Social Democrat government).

ALL SLOVENIAN PEOPLE'S UPHEAVALS
AND CRISIS OF TRANSITIONAL PARTIES

The WPU collective was very active in the occupation of the Faculty of Arts and held its weekly lectures and reading seminars in the occupied lecture halls. Although certain professors expressed solidarity and even actively supported the occupation, the occupation didn't succeed in its three main objectives (gaining an autonomous student space, abolishing European Union's Bologna system and abolishing the fees for PhD students). This experience, however, had a profound impact and initiated a fundamental discussion in the midst of the WPU collective, it raised the ever-present question: 'What is to be done?' The occupation of the Faculty of Arts clearly showed the limits of the student and university struggle, out of which rose the dilemma of how to move forward in a meaningful way. To put it into a short formula, the burning question was: how to make the transition from a university struggle to a universal struggle? At the time, though, there was no consensus about the necessity and viability of such a transition. The WPU formed a new sub-body, the Working Group on Political Strategy, to exclusively deal with this dilemma. The group underwent several months of intense discussions on how to go about such fundamental transformation from a civil society subject to an explicitly political subject within the sphere of the state.[5]

A great many different scenarios, that is, diverse entry points, were worked through. Among these were ideas of entering already existing institutions that enjoyed certain public recognition and social power, and trying to 'subvert them from the inside'. Three such institutions that were considered were trade unions, partisan organizations and the SD. It quickly became obvious that both unions and partisan organizations, while very much sympathetic and supportive of the cause, are by definition organizations that have clearly defined borders of political engagement. Such limitations of course did not apply to the SD, and the Working Group for Political Strategy actually held some discussions with their official representatives. These talks, the ambition being to establish a radical socialist wing inside the SD as a kind of inner party sub-body, didn't come to fruition. This goal was perhaps naive on the part of the WPU, but on the side of the SD (especially having the presidency at the time) it was a very short-sighted dismissal. Another factor that contributed to the development of the political project was the experience of Anti-Kapitalistički Pokret (AKP) in Croatia. This project already had strong ties with similar organizations throughout the time of the WPU activities, therefore there was a lively and strong exchange of opinions and experiences during this period. This was thus a formative experience that had an important impact on the foundation of the Initiative for Democratic Socialism (IDS).

First and foremost, the experience of the AKP was very telling in regards to forging an organization out of various already existing organizations. For them, it proved to be almost impossible and eventually led to the break-up of the movement. Reflecting on this experience, the group building the IDS was very careful to first build a homogeneous ideological foundation, and then base its organizational development on that. In any case, this was much easier in Slovenia than it would have been and still is in other ex-Yugoslavian republics. Some of the factors that contribute to somehow more favourable circumstances for a revival of a socialist project include prolonged and much more gradual transition and privatization of state assets. Another factor is that there was no break-up war, as in Croatia, Bosnia and Herzegovina and Serbia. Slovenian trade unions were relatively stronger than in other ex-Yugoslavian republics, they were able to halt the most harmful social reforms. Finally, there was a general openness of media space for progressive ideas. Despite much more favourable circumstances, this process of self-clarifying as to what the renewal of the socialist project should look like would probably last too long, exhausting its protagonists and eventually coming to a standstill if not even a dead-end. Fortunately, the process was accelerated when in the autumn and winter of 2012/13[6] Slovenia was shaken by unforeseen anti-austerity protests.[7]

This protest movement was unique in its magnitude and timespan as well as from the perspective of qualitative political change. Firstly, the movement was second only to the working class demonstrations that took place at the beginning of the 1990s. And it differed from the massive protests of the trade unions against the flat tax reform by the fact that there never were any official organizers, just various support groups and self-organized movements. It lasted from November 2012 until February/March 2013, when it then slowly lost its breath. Most importantly, it was a protest against the political class as such, fuelled by the austerity measures but nonetheless directed against all existing political parties. This sentiment was embodied in the slogan: 'They are all the same!' Still, there were, broadly speaking, three different political agendas present in the protest movement. Most widespread was the narrative of corruption and the necessity for ethical renewal. This perspective found the gravest of problems to be the corruption of the ruling elite (both political as well as financial) and advocated that such representatives should be changed with ethical personas that have an impeccable record of public service. Leading by example, they would provide for a much needed return of trust into public affairs. Incidentally, incumbent prime minister, Miro

Cerar, was already being mentioned as such a person and later on formed a political party, the Party of Miro Cerar, that won the early elections of 2014. It goes without saying that recent political developments have shattered any belief in an ethical messiah.

The second narrative was a reformist one, which argued that problems go beyond individuals or groups of people and are of a political nature. Changing the harmful social policies was thus the proposed solution argued for by this part of the protest movement. One would imagine that the SD, especially after a severe loss in the elections following the resignation of their government and due to the fact that they were an oppositional party, would use this opportunity to capitalize on the sentiment of the protest movement. However, this was not the case for at least two reasons. One being that the SD was perceived as part of the problem,[8] not part of the solution, but even more importantly that the SD itself, and especially its president, did everything in its power to ridicule the protest movement and distance itself from it. Among the more visible groups that did participate in the protests and were vocal advocates of social reforms were two political parties that later on formed a coalition of the United Left, together with the IDS, the Party of Sustainable Development of Slovenia (TRS) and the Democratic Workers Party (DSD).

BUILDING A SOCIALIST ALTERNATIVE

It was only the third narrative, one of democratic socialism, which proposed more radical, in the last instance revolutionary, transforma-tions. The group around the WPU argued that capitalism cannot be reformed, that what was perceived as corruption and mistaken policies all had the same systemic root that resulted in the implementation of socially (and environmentally) harmful policies by the people in leading positions. As long as capitalism is the mode of conduct, all social relations will be employed to augment the profits of the ruling elites. Therefore, a more radical solution, one that would grasp the problem at its very core, would be needed. The WPU collective argued for such a solution, and that the alternative to the existing system would be democratic socialism – a socialism that would build on the experience of the so-called actually existing socialisms but also, and more importantly, learn from their mistakes. Thus, the accent is on the democratic, although socialism by its very definition is and should be democratic. Since members of the collective have considered the theory of such issues and have been involved in various struggles, the opportunity and readiness of the media to better elaborate on the idea of democratic socialism was used eagerly.

In a span of half a year, more than 100 media interventions were made (either through TV or radio interviews, articles, public statements, speeches at protests etc.) that gave democratic socialism a stronger momentum and broader recognition.[9]

What followed was the most intense political year that the renewed socialist movement had experienced to date. In 2014, one year after the protest movement and at the time when democratic socialism was already strongly present in the public and media discourse, the government experienced a crisis that brought about yet another early parliamentary election. On 8 March 2014, the IDS finally held a founding congress and became an official political party. This was just a week before it formed a United Left Coalition that consisted of three parties, the IDS along with the above-mentioned Party for Sustainable Development and the Workers Democratic Party. The formation of the coalition was a very successful public event, attended by representatives from Die Linke and by Alexis Tsipras, which gave the whole event huge media recognition. After that a series of three consecutive elections followed. Firstly, there were elections for the European Parliament. Though not succeeding in gaining an MEP, the United Left nonetheless showed a surprisingly good performance[10] that boosted its efforts on the second in the series of elections, the early parliamentary elections. The coalition achieved roughly the same result but this time it meant entering parliament and was a historic breakthrough. At the beginning of autumn local elections followed. The coalition managed to get a couple of dozen city council members throughout Slovenia, though no mayors.

Since entering parliament, the United Left Coalition has proved itself to be a political actor that has long-term goals and perceives parliamentary policies only as a means and not a goal in itself.[11] It gained wider public recognition and support through various proposals, such as the proposal to officially recognize the state of Palestine, the legislative initiative to write off the debts of the most vulnerable parts of the population etc. Without doubt the single most successful project was the law regarding same sex marriage. Instead of half-hearted ideas of solving the legal status of same sex couples that gave same sex couples some rights but by all means not all of the rights, the United Left proposal was unique in granting same sex couples completely equal rights as enjoyed by heterosexual couples. All of these efforts are being continuously recognized and awarded by the general public. Since entering parliament, the United Left is perhaps the only one among all parliamentary parties to steadily see a rise in its support. While equated with the SD when entering parliament, it is now firmly in third place among all the parties, while the SD (at certain times) is not reaching the threshold anymore (4 per cent).

Thus, it seems that Slovenian social democracy is about to reach the end of the road and disappear from the political scene completely. Successes and growth of the United Left show that it is not so much social democratic ideas that are in crisis. These are, after all, currently proposed by a variety of 'left of social democracy' parties throughout Europe, but a crisis of social democratic parties as such. While the SD were busy rejecting the ideas of social democracy, these ideas were saved and adopted by newly formed left-wing parties. The original sin was when the SD began seeing their ideas as irrelevant as this has led them on a path of themselves becoming irrelevant.

NOTES

Websites were last accessed 24 May 2015.

1. See G. Kirn (2014). 'A Groundbreaking Result: Slovenia's United Left Coalition Gets 6 Seats in the Parliament'. *LeftEast*. Available at www. criticatac.ro/leftteast/historic-victory-united-left-slovenia-6-seats/.

2. See L. Centrih (2014). 'The Road to Collapse. The Demise of the League of Communists of Yugoslavia'. Rosa Luxemburg Stiftung, Belgrade. Available at http://arhiv.rosalux.rs/en/artikl.php?id=410.

3. See J. Dedić et al. (2003). 'The Erased. Organised Innocence and the Politics of Exclusion'. Peace Institute, Ljubljana. Available at www2.mirovni-institut. si/eng_html/publications/pdf/MI_politike_erased.pdf.

4. See M. Stanojević (2011). 'Social Pacts in Slovenia: Accomodation to the EMU Regimes and the Post-euro Development'. *Warsaw Forum of Economic Sociology* 2 (1): 3 (Spring). Available at http://kolegia.sgh.waw.pl/pl/KES/struktura/ IFSISE/Documents/6.Miroslav_Stanojevic,Social_Pacts_in_Slovenia. Accomodation_to_the_EMU_Regime_and_the_Post-euro_Development. pdf.

5. See 'Building a United Left in Slovenia: Interview with Miha Kordiš MP' (2014). *Links* (international journal of socialist renewal). Available at http:// links.org.au/taxonomy/term/853.

6. See G. Kirn (2014). 'Slovenia's Social Uprising in the European Crisis: Maribor as Periphery from 1988 to 2012'. *Stasis*. Available at www.stasisjournal.net/all-issues/24-1-2014-revolutions-and-protest-movements/60-slovenia-s-social-uprising-in-the-european-crisis-maribor-as-periphery-from-1988-to-2012.

7. See B. Gračner (2013). 'Slovenia's "Zombie Uprising"'. Counterfire. Available at www.counterfire.org/index.php/articles/international/16323-slovenias-zombie-uprising. Also A. Slameršak (2013). 'Slovenia on the Road to Periphery'. International Marxist-Humanist Organization. Available at www.internationalmarxisthumanist.org/articles/slovenia-road-periphery-aljoa-slamerak.

8. See A. Korsika (2012). 'Slovenia – United in Austerity'. Rosa Luxemburg Stiftung. Available at http://arhiv.rosalux.rs/sr/artikl.php?id=209.
9. For more background, see A. Korsika (2014). 'The Formation of a European Movement is Key'. *LeftEast*. Available at www.criticatac.ro/lefteast/interview-anej-korsika-ids-1/. Also A. Korsika (2014). 'The Fight for Socialism in Slovenia'. *LeftEast*. Available at www.criticatac.ro/lefteast/fight-for-socialism-slovenia-interview-anej-korsika/.
10. For a more in-depth analysis of European elections, see A. Korsika (2014). 'Impressive Performance of Socialist Forces in Slovenia'. Available at www.transform-network.net/de/fokus/ep-14-die-europawahlen-aus-linker-perspektive/news/detail/Programm/slovenia.html.
11. On contradictions of parliamentary work, see A. Korsika (2015). 'Perils of Parliamentary Immersion'. Scriboman. Available at https://anejkorsika.wordpress.com/2015/04/07/perils-of-parliamentary-immersion/.

Part III

Regional Powers

10

The Workers' Party in Brazilian Governments: From Left Neoliberalism to Left Austerity

Jörg Nowak

The Partido dos Trabalhadores (PT), or Workers' Party, was first elected into government in 2002 (the term started on 1 January 2003), and has now been in government four consecutive terms (the last term started on 1 January 2015, six months before this chapter was written). PT rule began with high expectations for creating a new kind of democratic socialism, but the political effects and consequences of the policies implemented by PT governments contributed to the demise of the popular credibility of the party. The positive balance of the 2003–10 government coalitions gave rise, in part, to the situation that created problems for the PT-led coalitions from 2011 on.

At the time that the first PT government, led by the charismatic Luiz Inácio da Silva, better known as Lula, entered into office, Brazil was one of the most unequal country in the world with the Gini coefficient for per capita income distribution of the economically active population and the Gini coefficient for per capita household income consistently around 0.60 until the mid 1990s. Thus, the first progress made was in the context of catching up to the standards of 'normal' inequality that exists in capitalist political and social systems. The first and the second Lula governments were able to combine economic growth with an expansion of social security: extreme poverty decreased from 36 to 16 per cent between 2003 and 2012, the median income rose, the minimum wage saw considerable increases, informal employment went down in favour of regular jobs and unemployment decreased to 6 per cent (Krein and Baltar, 2013). But since the onset of the global crisis in 2008, economic growth in Brazil has plunged and has not yet picked up again. Growth has remained way below other emerging economies, being basically non-existent at 0.2 per cent in 2014. Inflation started to become a problem in 2013 at 6.2 per cent over the year, with an 8 per cent increase in food prices. In May 2015, general inflation reached a twelve-year high at more than 8 per cent.

The upward social mobility of parts of the population, which was encouraged by the policies of earlier Lula governments, and an increased political awareness, due to more education, led the working classes to have higher expectations. At the same time, a considerable part of the middle classes turned away from its sympathies for redistribution and supported the old elites and their neoliberal solutions. Thus, Lula's successor, Dilma, is now facing an impasse: her government is not able to deliver on the new expectations of the working classes, and is facing stiff resistance from the elites and middle classes who are against policies for more equality.

The protests against fare hikes in the public transportation system in June 2013 were quite symbolic of this dilemma: after more people could afford to buy automobiles due to less unequal distribution (the Gini coefficient of the distribution of family income fell from around 0.60 in the mid 1990s to 0.55 in 2001 and 0.52 in 2012), traffic broke down in Brazil's major cities and the extension of public transportation based on rail systems lagged considerably behind. The fare hikes aroused the anger of those who had to commute in overcrowded buses for hours every day.

THE PT, ITS ELECTORATE AND THE SYSTEM OF ALLIANCES

The PT in Brazil emerged directly from the enormous strike wave in the automobile and metal industry in the São Paulo region between 1978 and 1980 (Antunes, 1988). It was formed in 1980, three years before the formation of the trade union federation Central Única dos Trabalhadores (CUT). The leader of this party, Luis Inácio Lula da Silva (Lula), was the leader of the metal workers until 1994 and was in and out of jail during the years of the big strikes. Like the bulk of the workers in the metal industry in São Paulo, Lula came from a poor family in the Northeast of the country. The PT saw itself in its early years as a party to the left of social democracy, since the classical social democratic approach was represented by the Partido da Social Democracia Brasileira (PSDB). In the early 1980s, the founding members of PSDB could not agree with the leaders of the PT. Thus, they joined the larger liberal-bourgeois democratic party, Partido do Movimento Democrático Brasileiro (PMDB), but then left the PMDB in order to found the PSDB in 1988. The PSDB's original social democratic phase lasted only six years. After its leader Fernando Henrique Cardoso became president in 1994, he and his government embarked on a neoliberal course, characterized by a wave of privatizations of state companies and a flexibilization of the labour market. The PSDB did not have much influence in the trade union movement at that time.

Thus, the absence of an original social democratic party in Brazil in the 1980s and 1990s left a lot of political and ideological space on the left. The PT started as a left socialist party. Due to the struggle against the military dictatorship that ended with a smooth transition to democracy during the mid 1980s, and the international conjuncture in Marxist debates at that time, the PT adopted a neo-Gramscian approach that entailed a specific emphasis on democracy and distanced itself from traditional revolutionary strategies. This orientation went along with the negation of the socialist nature of the regimes in the countries of the Soviet bloc and the creation of a certain distance from the traditional left-wing parties Partido Comunista Brasileiro (PCB) and Partido Comunista do Brasil (PCdoB).

The PT was strong in establishing a wider bloc of alliances with the trade union movement and social movements that blossomed during the 1980s: the landless workers' movement Movimento de Tra-balhadores Sem Terra (MST), the women's movement, the Indigenous and ecological movement and the different trade unions united in CUT all had strong links with the PT, and the vast majority of leaders of these social movements had been members of the PT during the 1980s. The central demands of the PT during that time and well into the 1990s were no payments of debt to the International Monetary Fund (IMF) and expansion of a public system of education and health. This strong alliance between the PT and various social movements was gradually weakened during the 1990s by two developments. First, the presidential elections in 1989 were seen as a real possibility for Lula to win the presidency, but he failed with 44 per cent of the vote. The 1989 elections were instead won by the Conservative Party's Fernando Collor de Mello, who then initiated the first wave of privatizations. During his presidency, hyperinflation of 1200 per cent plagued the population, and Collor became the first and only president to be impeached in 1992 due to a corruption scandal. The failure of the PT to win the presidency in 1989 was a major blow and had a decisive impact on the party leadership. As a result, the PT sought to pro-fessionalize itself and become more moderate. The second development, the neoliberal attack during the 1990s, flowed from the first one. In the course of these years, the relationship of the PT to organizations like the MST did not completely break down, but a distance grew because of stances often taken by the PT. For example, actions like occupations of agricultural land were frequently condemned in public by the PT leadership in the late 1990s as 'illegal acts'. In the presidential elections of 1994 and 1998, the PT and Lula could not match the 1989 result of 31 million votes. Lula received only 17 and 21 million votes, respectively. It was only in 2002 that Lula could win the presidency with 39 million voters in the first round, and 52 million in the second round, representing 61.3 per cent of the votes. The PT finally came to power because the project of Fernando Henrique Cardoso entered into a severe crisis that affected the economic wellbeing of large parts of the population in the late 1990s, and because Lula softened his political stance and attracted many voters who felt alienated by the former socialist discourse.

One of the critical issues in the project of the PT being in government power is the weakness of the PT, and of Brazilian parties in general. Usually, political parties in Brazil are only able to enter into government in coalitions of a significant number of parties. Since the new republic was finally inaugurated with the passing of a constitution in 1988, there has never been a party with an overwhelming share of the votes, and there has been widespread practice of deputies moving from one party to another during their term. The huge number of parties in parliament reflects the underlying system of domination: clientelism, and the domination by a few wealthy families in the regional states, both of which give rise to the importance of certain political leading figures that tend to change parties and from time to time also found new parties. Ideological stability is not very entrenched in the party system, thus parties tend to change their political orientation if important *caziques* (regional leaders that exercise power like a feudal lord) enter their party.

The nature of this system of political domination had a certain impact on the presence of the PT in the two chambers, the Congress and the Senate. While the PT conquered some regional states in the 1990s, most notably the city-state of the capital Brasilia and Rio Grande do Sul, its presence in the two chambers remained low. In the elections in 1989, when Lula got 44 per cent of the votes, the PT got only 10.2 per cent of the votes for the Congress, which resulted in 35 out of 502 seats. These numbers improved slowly to 49 in the Congress in 1994, 60 in 1998 and, finally, 91 in 2002. The 91 seats in 2002 was the highest number of seats obtained in the Congress, clearly below 20 per cent, going down to 83 in 2006, 88 in 2010 and 70 in 2014. The representation in the Senate remained low, too, with 14 seats of 81 in the elections in 2002, 10 in 2006, 15 in 2010 and 12 in 2014. Thus, the PT had to enter into alliances, as did other parties. Usually, these alliances comprised the two communist parties and the smaller left-socialist party, Partido Socialista Brasileiro (PSB). But in 1998, the PT cooperated for the first time with one of the parties that is generally perceived to belong to the camp of 'Vargas-era' trade unions, the old corporatist system, the Partido Democrático do Trabalho (PDT), led by Leonel Brizola.

The electoral coalition led by the PT in 2002 contained a pact with the Liberal Party, Partido Liberal (PL), led by Jose Alencar, which was considered by many to be influenced by conservative evangelicals. The system of complicated coalitions extended further in 2006 when the PMDB, the old classical party of the bourgeois elite, joined in, headed by former president, Jose Sarney, whose family literally commands the regional state of Maranhão in the North of Brazil. In 2010, the coalition with the PSDB continued, and encompassed beyond the leftist PSB and PCdoB a number of smaller proxy parties representing either evangelical churches or clientelist elites, getting 311 seats in Congress. This meant, with the PT holding only 88 seats in Congress, that it only commanded a little over 20 per cent in the coalition itself, and 137 seats, below 50 per cent, if the seats of the left-leaning parties, PT, PCdoB and PSB were combined. This arithmetic exercise explains why the PT and its more progressive allies had little say in the governments in which the PT participated. Although the presidential candidate came from the PT, the widespread use of the term 'PT governments' is rather misleading. In these coalitions, in order to stay in power, the PT aligned with, amongst others, clientelist elites in the regional states, like Ciro Gomes in Ceará, whose family has run the Northeastern state for more than 50 years. These practices bypassed the local or regional PT in a number of cases.

The alliance with the PMDB, one of the two big parties that remained the strongholds of the old elite in the 2000s, also had the strong effect of pushing the once social democratic PSDB more to the neoliberal right – ideological flexibility once again. In 2014, the coalition of the PT with eight other parties gained 304 seats in Congress, a bit less than in 2010, but once the PSB chose to leave the coalition, only 80 seats in the coalition were held by left parties (70 by the PT and 10 by the PCdoB) – the remaining 224 went to conservative parties, again many newly founded parties that were linked to evangelical churches.

Until 2006, the electorate of the PT came, paradoxically, more from the middle class than from the poor. That means that the majority of the poor voted for conservative parties until 2006, another indicator of the strong grip of clientelism that also goes with jobs and certain favours. Since voting is obligatory in Brazil, and illiteracy was still quite significant in the 1980s and 1990s, fraud might have played a considerable role. Beginning in 2006, there was a trend that remained relevant during the elections in 2010 and 2014: the majority of the votes for the PT started to come from the poor, and the section of the middle classes that had supported the PT earlier increasingly deserted them.

In households earning more than 10 times the minimum wage (roughly, the 'middle class'), PT support fell from 32 per cent in 2002, to 17 per cent in 2006 ... In 1997, the PT had 5.5 million 'high income' and 3.1 million 'low income' supporters, and only 17 per cent of PT supporters earned less than the minimum wage. In 2006, the PT had only 3.3 million 'high income' supporters but 17.6 million 'low income' ones, and 47 per cent of its supporters earned less than twice the minimum wage. (Saad-Filho and Morais, 2013: 230; see also Singer, 2012)

This change in the profile of their electorate reflected the effects of the government from 2003 to the end of 2005: the Mensalão scandal in 2005, related to illegal payments from top PT officials to other deputies, damaged the image of Lula in the perception of the middle classes, while the stepping up of cash transfers for poor people and a higher minimum wage was welcomed by poorer voters. These material changes had an impact on the lifestyle of the middle classes. Domestic servants had to be paid more, and poor people began to move into social spaces that had been the exclusive domain of relatively better off parts of the population.

ECONOMIC AND SOCIAL POLICY OF THE TWO LULA AND DILMA GOVERNMENTS

The Lula governments

The prelude to the first Lula government was the electoral campaign in 2002. This period was marked by a fear that there would be capital flight if Lula were elected as president, or even before the elections. In order to prevent this, Lula wrote his famous 'Carta ao povo brasileiro', a letter to the Brazilian people, in which he promised not to attack the current economic and political system once in power, primarily focusing on the repayment of debt to the IMF. It was also a period in which Lula began to design his own strategies and campaign independently from his PT party – recycling the Latin American tradition of caudillismo (strong leader) in a left variant. The first Lula government kept all neoliberal policies in place and formed an alliance with big capital, facilitated by the entry of the conservative owner of a textile company, José Alencar, into the government as vice-president. Alencar was not a member of a party, but joined the Partido Liberal (PL) at the beginning of his term, and changed to another party in 2005. Despite its small number of seats, members of the PT joined 21 of 31 ministries (Xavier de Holanda, 2013: 109).

The continuation of neoliberal macroeconomic policy (Morais and Saad-Filho, 2005; Paulani, 2008: 15ff; Xavier de Holanda, 2013: 61ff) was accompanied by an extension of the Bolsa Familia and Hunger Zero programmes. Due to the previous absence of encompassing cash transfer programmes in Brazil, these programmes allowed the Lula government to maintain and extend its popular support despite the huge Mensalão corruption scandal that unfolded in 2005, in which both Lula and the PT did not demonstrate a willingness to contribute to the investigations (Xavier de Holanda, 2013: 86ff). Francisco Uribam Xavier de Holanda wrote that Lula did not really take command of national politics in this first period, which is why the national leadership of the PT acted as if it was the national government (2013: 85). Nonetheless, the growth rates that could be sold as a success story, the extension of the social programmes and a moderate rise of the minimum wage (11.7 per cent between 2003 and 2005; Xavier de Holanda, 2013: 107) contributed to the decisive shift in the electorate that kept Lula in power. In 2006, 45 million people in Brazil received transfers from the Bolsa Familia programme. It was directed to families with a per capita income of less than 140 Real, and was only granted if the children of a family attended school and were being vaccinated, thus combining basic health and education provisions with the transfer. The cash transfer varied between 22 and 200 Real per month, people with a per capita income below 70 Real could receive the basic benefit of 70 Real (up from 20 Real). Other programmes included the extension of the provision of electric energy to 617,000 families, credits of $720 million to small farmers, 20,000 new jobs for health workers and child care for 881,000 children (Xavier de Holanda, 2013: 80).

These expenses were possible due to a favourable global economic environment after the burst of the dot.com bubble in 2001 – the huge liquidity generated by the US Federal treasury after the burst of the bubble was increasingly invested in emerging economies (King, 2010). In March 2006, 33 per cent of the gross domestic product (GDP) of Brazil was generated by commodity exports, a large contribution of which came from agricultural exports.

The second Lula government extended the Bolsa Familia programme even further. As of February 2011, the programme covered 52 million people. And right after taking office again, Lula announced something new: the Programa de Aceleração do Crescimento (PAC), which consisted of an investment programme for traffic infrastructure, hydroelectric plants and petrochemical industrial complexes. The first programme totalled 500 billion Real, the bulk of which was financed by the Brazilian development bank, Banco Nacional de Desenvolvimento

Social (BNDES) and state companies. It created profits for the large construction companies and the state oil company Petrobras, but also for a large number of small and medium companies – and it created a huge number of jobs in a short period, primarily in construction.

Some of the critical accounts of this period underlined that agrarian reform, one of the old demands of the PT, was not really moving forward, a participatory budget was far from being implemented at the national level, and more extended taxation of national and international large companies and rich individuals had not moved forward either. And, while cash transfers were extended, an extensive public system of health and education was not systematically installed. Even so, Lula's popularity moved steadily upwards from 53 per cent in April 2006 to 87 per cent in December 2010 (Saad-Filho and Morais, 2013: 233) – a previously unseen record to close a presidential term.

In these two terms, the Lula governments acted in the traditional social democratic vein of 'normalizing' the Brazilian model of capitalism, i.e. establishing a basic system of social security and increasing public investments in traffic and energy infrastructure. After the neoliberal phase in the 1990s, the country lacked investments in basic infrastructure and could not really catch up to international standards of infrastructure investment, but the Lula governments were able to fill in some gaps. This 'normalization' of Brazilian capitalism reproduced the already existing patterns of uneven development. Industrialization of the North and Northeast of the country was intended to close the income gap between the advanced and backward regions (medium income in the states of Rio de Janeiro and São Paulo was threefold that in the North and Northeast). 'In the 2000s, 22 million new jobs were created, in contrast to 11 million in the 1990s, and around 80 per cent of them were in the formal sector. Significantly, around 90 per cent of jobs created in the 2000s paid less than 1.5 times the minimum wage (51 per cent in the 1990s)' (Saad-Filho and Morais, 2013: 232). This meant that the income of the bottom decile was rising enormously (91 per cent between 2001 and 2009), and faster in the Northeast.

But an overwhelmingly large number of workers remained within the 70 per cent of the population that earned something below the minimum wage (IBOPE, 2013). At the same time, their wage share rose 'from 38 per cent in 2000 to less than 50 per cent' in 2013 (Saad-Filho and Morais, 2013: 233). It was an alliance of the PT, as the representative of the working classes, with big Brazilian and international capital that allowed for some redistribution – but along very limited lines. This redistribution did not touch the privileges of the elite to evade taxes, practice large-scale corruption using public funds and continue with a model of super-exploitation. The significant change was the development of a more professional government, which brought more workers into formal employment, but also exposed them to super-exploitation due to the persistence of low wages.

The first Dilma government: strikes and social protests

Dilma Rousseff, who had been Minister of Mining and Energy before becoming a presidential candidate, had a harder time winning the elections. She won the presidential elections in the second round in 2010, with 56 per cent of the votes. As a candidate she lacked the working-class background of Lula and did not have a strong linkage to the PT, since she was a member of Brizola's PDT until the late 1990s. Lula was lucky to leave the presidency in late 2010. Until this point in time, although crisis had hit Brazil like many other countries around the globe, 2010 was a year of economic recovery and growth numbers remained steady in the North and Northeast, due to the large investment programmes of the PAC. The problems started right in the first months of 2011, when inflation soared and the enormous strike wave in the construction sector began.

The first Dilma government was characterized by strikes and social protests, that is, a radicalization of the working class that started to demand what the PT had promised but had only fulfilled to a certain extent. The growth of the construction sector in 2010 saw its biggest jump since 1986 increasing to 11.6 per cent. In 2011, it grew only 3.6 per cent, and only 1.4 per cent in 2012, when total national growth rates were at 2.7 per cent and 0.9 per cent, respectively (DIEESE, 2013: 7). Thus, it was not accidental that labour unrest exploded in the construction sector in February and March 2011. In these two months, 180,000 workers went on strike, primarily on big construction sites such as Pecém (6000 workers), San Antonio (15,000), Jirau (25,000) and Abreu e Lima (35,000). The traditional protest rituals of construction workers, that is, large-scale destruction of housing and transport facilities, accompanied the strike. The *Força Nacional*, the National Public Security Force created in 2004, was used then for the first time to repress strikers (Nowak, 2016b; Véras, 2013, 2014).

The entire year of 2011 saw 580,000 construction workers on strike, and 500,000 in 2012. The strike wave was a response from the working class to the continuation of uneven development. While the big infrastructure projects had been funded with public money, the big Brazilian construction companies stuck to the same conditions of work they had used in the past 40 or 50 years: poor transport and accommodation facilities; poor quality of food leading to the intoxication of hundreds of workers; no compliance with legal security standards at work; and a lack of basic infrastructure (medical assistance, financial services, restaurants) at the new industrial sites. The government showed a quick response to the strikes and called for a summit of trade unions, employers and the government. At the summit, the *Mesa Nacional da Construção* was designed to implement minimum standards at the big public construction sites, but it was implemented almost nowhere and remained just a showcase instrument.

While the strikes in construction kept up momentum in 2012, with bigger revolts at the construction sites of petrochemical complexes in Abreu e Lima close to Recife in August and at the Belo Monte dam in Pará in Amazonia in November, the summer of 2012 also saw a month-long national public sector strike that strained relations between the trade union confederation CUT and the government. One of the driving forces were the teachers at grammar schools and universities who were threatened with wage cuts, but also strikes of police officers had a huge impact, causing the breakdown of public order (a steep increase of violent criminal assaults) in some cities. Inflation went up to 7.1 per cent in August 2011, dropped after that, but went up again to 6.7 per cent in May/June 2013. The inflation was seen to be an outcome of sluggish growth accompanied by wage increases and low unemployment both in 2012 and 2013, and seemed to be a trigger both for the strikes in 2011 and the protest wave in summer 2013.

But the government came under attack from the corporate elites, too, after it encountered stiff resistance from the working classes. The Dilma government intervened in 2012 in the energy sector, keeping electricity and gasoline prices low. This was seen as contributing to a lack of business confidence, creating subsequent hesitations for new investment (Rapoza, 2013). The low unemployment of 5 to 6 per cent allowed workers to raise demands, and did not allow employers to lower wages. A third factor for the diminishing confidence of economic elites in the government's policies was the lower growth and lower demand for commodities all around the world, which included China, the main motor driving exports from Brazil (Saad-Filho and Morais, 2013: 235).

In the early months of 2013, the media, which was predominantly controlled by the old right-wing elite, started a campaign about the failure of the government that signalled the uneasiness of the corporate sector with the policies of the Dilma government. It was in this climate, and after their protests were attacked by the police, that the small anarchist movement against fare hikes in the public transportation system gained some momentum. A new kind of alliance came into being when the right-wing mainstream media started to support and amplify the protests, using them as an instrument to create discontent with a government that right-wing elites were eager to remove. After the mainstream media publicized the protests, they spread to all major and smaller cities in Brazil. In the early phase of the protests in June 2013, the demands resembled the classical demands of the Brazilian left for better and cheaper public transportation, and more effective and qualified public health and education systems. Dilma Rousseff was quick to respond positively to the demands, and the fare hikes in São Paulo and Rio de Janeiro were taken back (only to be introduced somewhat later in the early days of January 2015; Nowak, 2016a). But in the second phase of the protests, when the profile of the participants became dominated by the middle class, a focus on corruption, security issues and an anti-left-wing stance gained hold, and right-wing issues rose to prominence (Estanque, 2014). All in all, the protests evaporated as quickly as they started, and observers stated that their characteristics had been a lack of common identity and a fragmentation of demands (Estanque, 2014; Gohn, 2014).

At the same time, the Dilma government wanted to approve a law, PL 4330, that allowed for an encompassing flexibilization and casualization of labour that was already a strong tendency in state-owned enterprises and the service sector. In the aftermath of the protests in June, the trade union movement was able to block the law, but like the fare hikes in public transportation, this law was approved in the second Dilma term in spring 2015. The hot summer of protests was followed by a number of strikes in the urban areas that were joined by some of the young and newly mobilized protesters, like the strike of teachers in Rio de Janeiro, and oil platform workers at Petrobras against privatization of oil fields (both in autumn 2013), strikes of bus drivers in most of the major cities and a strike of street sweepers in Rio de Janeiro during carnival in February 2014. Many of these strikes had been led against trade union leaderships that struck unfavourable accords with employers or with considerable tensions between workers and their trade unions; this was the case also for the strikes of construction workers.

Thus, the first Dilma government was plagued both by the effects of an adverse global economic context that reinforced the effects of Brazil´s dependency on exports and the effects of Lula's successful policies. The massive investment in industrialization projects backfired in the form of strikes of construction workers, the increase in car production backfired in the form of strikes about the lack of public transport and overcrowded car traffic, and the increase in the minimum wages and formal employment created new demands for a more encompassing welfare state. At the same time, the traditional elite and part of the middle classes, already troubled by the upsurge of strikes and popular demands, supported and merged with street protests that had started with left-wing demands, thereby creating an atmosphere of revolt with unclear political orientation. Policies that favoured the working classes, like a ban on energy price hikes, combined with low unemployment led to sluggish investment by corporate elites, and growth remained low to non-existent. The third way social democratic project started by Lula got stuck in its own contradictions and Dilma Rousseff's government could not find an easy way out.

The second Dilma government: the return of conservatism and austerity

The election campaign in 2014 reflected the new mood. Considerable parts of both the working class and the middle class deserted the PT and Dilma Rousseff. The PT lost about 3 million votes and Rousseff lost more than 4 million votes in the first round, while the size of the electorate grew by about 4 million due to population growth. Marina Silva, a former minister in the Lula government, and former social movement activist turned conservative ecologist with a background as a poor rubber tapper, was perceived to be Rousseff's main rival during the campaign leading up to the first round. The profile of Silva's electorate coincided exactly with the social composition of the protesters in June 2013 – people with higher education were grossly overrepresented – and Silva made ample reference to the protests in her speeches, promising free fares for students. But due to Silva's unclear economic programme, Aécio Neves of the PSDB, representing a neoliberal programme, won almost 35 million votes in the first round (almost 2 million more than his forerunner José Serra in 2010), and Silva made only third position with 22 million votes, still 2.5 million more than in 2010. Also, the Partido Socialismo e Liberdade (PSOL) candidate, a split from the left sections of the PT, doubled its votes from around 900,000 in 2010 to 1.6 million in 2014. All in all, Rousseff's three main oppositional candidates from the right, centre and left collected 5 million additional votes, while Rousseff lost votes. In the end, Rousseff won the presidency with a narrow margin of 1.64 per cent (or about 3 million votes), only achieving 4 million additional votes in the second round, while Neves collected 14 million additional votes.

The new government coalition also reflected a new internal balance. The centre-left PSB left the coalition and lent itself to Marina Silva in the 2014 elections. Since the coalition supporting the Dilma government still had a comfortable majority of 304 out of 513 seats in the lower house, and 53 out of 81 in the upper house, the internal composition in the coalition was a significant factor. In 2010, 165 seats in the lower house in the coalition had been held by the four leftist parties, the PT, PSB, PCdoB and PDT, 123 by conservative-liberal parties and 67 by parties with links to evangelical churches. In the new coalition in 2014, the balance shifted to the liberal-conservative parties that held 150 seats, the left parties went down to 89 and the parties with evangelical background held 55 seats. Although the left-leaning parties could never form a majority in any of the Lula or Dilma coalitions, in 2014 the influence of these parties was dwarfed because of their low number of seats. This was reflected in some of the decisions regarding the delegation of ministers to the government: the key post of the Ministry of Agriculture was given to the former head of the association of big farmers, Katia Abreu, and only eight of 24 ministries went to members of the PT. In the face of meagre growth that continued through 2014, the second Dilma government embarked on an austerity programme in 2015.

The announcement in early January 2015 of the price hikes for public transportation proved to be symbolic of the new government term. This time the protests remained small. Throughout 2015, several carmakers like Volkswagen, General Motors and Volvo announced dismissals of large numbers of workers, but could not succeed against striking workers. The Volkswagen workers struck for ten days in January, resulting in 2000 workers being taken back, and similar things happened in other automobile plants. These strikes showed that the workers had a combative stance. Then the government introduced new plans to cut spending for public services, and PL 4330 allowing for casualization of labour was passed in April 2015, amid trade union protests. But the trade unions were divided, the second biggest union, Força Sindical, aligned with the opposition and spoke in favour of the law. CUT and other trade unions called for a one-day general strike at the end of May that saw a huge turnout, and a national teachers strike had been sweeping the country for more than six weeks. This was immediately followed by a strike of half the federal universities that took off at the end of May. But these strikes did not achieve the hoped for results. The promise to spend more on the public education system, one of the responses of Dilma Rousseff after the street protests in 2013, was still not kept. In fact, part of the austerity package has been a cut to the education budget of 10 billion Real in the year 2015 alone. Overall, the austerity move of the second Dilma government saw some resistance, but it was not a storm, only a low wind with some occasional sudden flares.

The PT project turned into its opposite, and Dilma Rousseff became a prisoner of the alliances formed with conservative forces as soon as the economic and political context changed. But this is not the whole story. The right-wing opposition started smaller protests demanding the impeachment of Dilma immediately after her slight victory in 2014, and when the Petrobas corruption scandal unfolded in the following weeks and months, the opposition took the chance to revive the street protests of 2013 in its own fashion. In March 2015, somewhere between 500,000 and 2 million protesters took to the streets to protest against corruption and the Dilma government, mounting pressure from outside it. While the strikes and protests during the first Dilma government had been undoubtedly dominated by the left, despite partly successful efforts by right-wing forces to make themselves heard, these protests were clearly dominated by the right-wing, though not in an absolute manner. Thus, the new political and economic context was used successfully by the neoliberal and conservative forces to mount a simultaneous attack from inside the Dilma government, approving harsh austerity and anti-labour laws, and from outside the government, attacking the so-called 'left' in power and its corruption. The corruption charges against Petrobras were highly relevant for the government since Dilma Rousseff had always engaged closely with Petrobras and had installed political friends in key posts of the company. The more volatile public opinion during the Dilma terms was reflected in the levels of public approval. In early 2011, 47 per cent approved of the Dilma government as 'good or very good' (Portuguese: *otímo, bom*), going up to 65 per cent in spring 2013. Then, due to inflation and the protests in June 2013, the approval fell rapidly to 30 per cent, went back up to 40 per cent in late 2013, remained there until late 2014, only to embark on a steep fall after the second election of Dilma to 23 per cent in June 2015.

As of this writing (June 2015), it seems inevitable that the efforts of the traditional elite to regain full power in Brazil will be successful, at least in the next elections in 2018.

CONCLUSION

The social democratic modernization of Brazilian capitalism had contradictory effects. It facilitated higher expectations in the masses of low paid workers, who finally turned against the Dilma government in the form of strikes and street protests against a lack of left alternatives and the inability of the second Dilma government to address the expectations of the poor. The right-wing middle class then picked up these protests, successfully reappropriating the workers' discontent. As in many other countries, the global crisis has led the Brazilian variant of social democracy into a deadlock, but with specific consequences related to a system of domination rooted in regional clientelism and an electoral system that effectively blocks the development of parties with stable ideological orientations.

It proved difficult for the social democratic episode in Brazil to rupture the model of uneven development (Smith, 1984) that the country had inherited from the military dictatorship and the neoliberal era that followed suit. The focus was set too narrowly on cooperation with big Brazilian capital, which proved to be the key to success during the Lula governments, but limited the Dilma governments.

Governance that is independent from big Brazilian capital is all the more difficult to achieve since the five major construction companies in Brazil not only finance the electoral campaigns of all major parties but are also involved in the construction of major industrial districts. In addition, they are associated with petrochemical companies that are closely cooperating with the state company Petrobras. Thus, the practical and organizational proximity of state companies and the government to big Brazilian capital is a serious impediment to any sustainable progressive development, given the practices of labour relations, corruption and land grabbing entrenched in the business models of such companies.

These models of neodevelopmentalism grapple with intrinsic contradictions, due to the fact that they are based on the existence of an internal periphery in Brazil, and an external periphery in the states, like Mozambique, that see major Brazilian investment. What has been repeatedly praised as the 'soft power' of Brazil (Fontes and Garcia, 2013) is a new reconfiguration of its sub-imperialism within and beyond the borders of the Brazilian state (Maurini, 1973) since many of the projects of Brazilian multinationals have been financed by the state-led development bank BNDES. The industrial projects both in the North of the Brazil – the Belo Monte dam and the Carajás areas are the most well-known examples – have seen increasing resistance from local traditional and Indigenous communities, as well as different industrial projects of Brazilian multinationals in Mozambique and other African countries.

Therefore, the long-term effects of the old and new developmentalism are finally coming home to the centre of sub-imperialism. The water crisis in São Paulo, escalated by the lack of rainfall since 2014, and resulting in the first uprisings of middle-class constituencies due to water shortages, is an effect of the deforestation of the Amazon rainforest, the very thing that provided the humidity supplying the São Paulo areas with sufficient water from rainfalls. One can conclude that the social democratic episode in Brazil, which effectively ended with the second Dilma term, was faced with both (a) the inherited (or 'path-dependent') contradictions of the Brazilian model rooted in its history as a slave colony and the power structure established during the military dictatorship; and (b) the new contradictions that emerged from the successes of the social democratic normalization of Brazilian capitalism, that is, the facilitation of the end of extreme poverty for millions of people enabled these millions to demand less degrading working conditions, a well-equipped transportation system and better public services in general. The Dilma governments failed to deliver on these demands despite the quick and positive government response in the summer of 2013, and the inability to deliver on these demands stems to a large extent from the hesitation to cut into the profits and private wealth of the Brazilian elite – which would harm the alliance of the PT with big capital on which the whole social democratic project was based. Suffice it to say that a considerable part of the Brazilian bourgeoisie never made its peace with the social democratic episode, resorted to resentment against the social democratic governments even before the protests of 2013 and contributed to strengthen the protests via the bourgeois mass media. But one also has to underline that the Brazilian social democratic episode does seem to be a political rupture from the perspective of the earlier, very much conservative and 'Prussian' path of Brazilian capitalism (Nelson Coutinho, 2011). But from the perspective of 'classical' social democracy, the Brazilian episode of social democracy was a very light version as it did not include a consistent model of progressive taxation and redistribution that included the whole population. To sum up, the PT in government represented a deviation from the Prussian path of Brazil's capitalism on the political level and in the realm of social policies, but the main pillars of the economic strategy of PT-led governments did not alter significantly the existing model of development, these governments rather modernized it, made it more effective and applied larger sums of public investment. Older elements were strengthened like the sub-imperialist aspect of the Brazilian social formation, like the investments of Brazilian capital in Mozambique and other African countries that were supported with public funds – and the internal colonization of the Amazon area into a reservoir for extractivist enterprises.

The recent developments in Brazil allow us to conclude that more immediate and unmediated confrontations between the main classes are unfolding. This development resembles similar tendencies that other left-leaning governments in Latin America that were elected in six other countries since 1998 are facing. With regard to Brazil, two questions are important. First, what will happen to the PT in the course of the second Dilma government and after a possible exit from presidency in 2018? Will it be able to recover as a legitimate representative of the poor majority or will the damages suffered by manifold compromises transform the PT into another variant of a clientelist distribution of positions and public revenues? And second, will the other leftist governments in Latin America succeed in remaining in power in the coming years, and how will a restoration of a considerably less restricted elite power in Brazil affect the other variants of left governments on the continent?

BIBLIOGRAPHY

Antunes, R. (1988). *A rebeldia no trabalho. O confronto operário no Abc Paulista: As greves de 1978/80.* São Paulo Campinas: Editora Ensaio/Editora da UNICAMP.

Branford, S. and Kucinski, B. (2003). *Politics Transformed – Lula and the Workers' Party in Brazil.* London: Latin American Bureau.

DIEESE (2013). 'Balanço das Greves em 2012'. Estudos pesquisas No. 66. DIEESE, São Paulo.

Do Monte, P.A., Rodrigues da Silva, J.A. and Ferreira Gonçalves, M. (2012). 'A Dinâmica do Emprego na Região Nordeste no Período 2000 a 2009'. In I. Targino and R. Véras de Oliveira (eds), *Cenários da Crise e do Trabalho no Brasil.* Joao Pessoa: Editora Universitária da UFPB: 321–57.

Estanque, E. (2014). 'Rebeliões de classe média? Precariedade e movimentos sociais em Portugal e no Brasil (2011–2013)'. *Revista Crítica de Ciências Sociais,* 103 (May): 53–80.

Gohn, M. da Glória (2014). 'A Sociedade Brasileira em Movimento: vozes das ruas e seus ecos políticos e sociais'. *Caderno CRH,* 27 (71): 431–41.

IBOPE (Instituto Brasileiro de Opinião e Estatística)(2013). www.ibope.com.br/pt-br/noticias/Paginas/89-dos-manifestantes-nao-se--sentem-representados-por-partidos.aspx (accessed 12 March 2014).

King, S.D. (2010). *Losing Control. The Emerging Threats to Western Prosperity.* New Haven and London: Yale University Press.

Krein, J.D. and Baltar, P.E. (2013). 'A retomada do desenvolvimento e a regulação do mercado do trabalho no Brasil'. *Cadernos CRH,* 26 (68): 273–92.

Maurini, R.M. (1973). *Dialéctica de la dependencia.* México DF: Ediciones Era.

Morais, L. and Saad-Filho, A. (2005). 'Lula and the Continuity of Neoliberalism in Brazil: Strategic Choice, Economic Imperative or Political Schizophrenia?'. *Historical Materialism,* 13 (1): 3–32.

Nelson Coutinho, C. (2011). *Cultura e Sociedade no Brasil: Ensaios sobre idéias e formas* (4th edn). São Paulo: Expressão Popular.

Nowak, J. (2016a, forthcoming). 'Class Coalitions or Class Struggles Within the Working Class? Middle Class and Working Class Mobilisations in India and Brazil During the Global Crisis'. *Workers of the World,* No. 8 (June).

—— (2016b, forthcoming). 'Mass Strikes in Brazilian Construction After 2011'. In M. Dutta, P. Birke and J. Nowak (eds), *Strikes and Workers Movements in the 21st Century.*

Paulani, L. (2008). *Brasil Delivery.* São Paulo: Boitempo.

Rapoza, K. (2013). 'Is Brazil a Fail?'. *Forbes Magazine*, 11 October. Available at www.forbes.com/sites/kenrapoza/2013/11/10/is-brazil-a-fail/ (accessed 24 July 2015).

Saad-Filho, A. and Morais, L. (2013). 'Mass Protests: Brazilian Spring or Brazilian Malaise?'. In L. Panitch, G. Albo and V. Chibber (eds), *Registering Class*, Socialist Register 2013. London: Merlin: 227–46.

Sader, E. (2011). *The New Mole. Paths of the Latin American Left*. London: Verso.

Singer, A. (2012). *Os Sentidos do Lulismo – Reforma gradual e pacto conservador*. São Paulo: Companhia das Letras.

Smith, N. (1984). *Uneven Development, Nature, Capital and the Production of Space*. New York: Basil Blackwell.

Véras, R. (2013). 'Suape em Construção, peões em luta: o novo desenvolvimento e os conflitos do trabalho'. *Cadernos CRH*, 26 (68): 233–52.

—— (2014). 'Brasil em obras, peões em luta, sindicatos surpreendidos'. *Revista Crítica de Ciências Sociais*, 103: 111–36. DOI: 10.4000/rccs.5559.

Xavier de Holanda, F.U. (2013). *O PT e a Lenda do Boto Cor de Rosa*. Fortaleza: Expressão Gráfica e Editora.

11

Politics of Social Democracy in a Communist-ruled State in India

Arup Kumar Sen

The very idea of social democracy is contested terrain. It has been suggested that every social democrat has his or her own personal answer to the question of what social democracy stands for. But, in fact, social democracy 'has a tradition of ideas shaped by more than a hundred years of theoretical debate and practical politics'.[1] Social democracy as a political force has a long tradition linked to the emergence of the workers' movement.[2]

In the European context, the dichotomy between communism and social democracy dominated the debate within the left in the twentieth century. The main point of discussion centred around the question of whether capitalism had to be transformed (communism) or could instead be reformed (social democracy). The social democrats were keen to point out the absence of basic democratic rights under communism. But the widespread belief among West European social democrats that the capture of state power through the ballot box would inevitably lead to socialism contributed to the endorsement of an uncritical statism by the stalwarts of the Second International. Kautskyanism, Bernsteinian revisionism, Fabianism and most variants of continental Marxist thought were united in this belief in statism. Unfortunately, statism of both the communist and social democratic variants neglected the problem of social power and did not actively seek to empower working people in their everyday lives.[3]

The dominant communist parties in India practised the politics of social democracy after they came to power through participation in elections. In other words, the electoral rise of the communist parties is organically connected with the politics of social democracy in India. So, the dichotomy of communism and social democracy witnessed in the European countries does not hold true in India. It may be mentioned in this connection that the provincial government formed by the communists in the Indian state of Kerala in 1957 was toppled by the central (national) government of the Congress Party in 1959 on the plea of a breakdown of law and order. When the communist parties came to power in West Bengal in later years, they eschewed the path of radical politics for staying in power. It is quite natural that when the Indian government started following the neo-liberal paradigm of governance from the 1990s, the Left Front government in power in West Bengal did not follow any radical agenda and started following the same paradigm in course of time.

EARLY POLITICS OF SOCIAL DEMOCRACY IN INDIA

Indian society underwent a most fundamental transformation under British colonial rule. From the middle of the nineteenth century the role of the colonial state has been absolutely central in the social transformation of India. The rule of the colonial state ended in 1947, but the new British way of organizing social life through 'politics', making society state-centric, has not merely continued but expanded its jurisdiction over all aspects of social life. In fact, the Indian nation-state after 1947 was a successor to both the British colonial state and the movement of Indian nationalism. The legal institutions and coercive apparatuses of the state remained broadly similar to those of the last phase of colonial rule. On the other hand, the ideological discourse of nationalism created vast popular expectations of the state once it was taken over by the Congress Party,[4] which represented the dominant tradition of nationalism during colonial rule in India.

Jawaharlal Nehru, the first prime minister of post-colonial India, argued in 1953: 'In India, most progressive groups, and certainly the Congress, have talked of socialism in more or less precise terms for the last thirty years or more. We have thought of it more in terms of social democracy, keeping in view the special characteristics and outlook of India.'[5]

In fact, the Congress Party represented the politics of social democracy in the early years of post-colonial India. Nehru was India's nearly unchallenged ruler for some 15 years after independence. He and his associates in the Congress Party earned their legitimacy in the public life of India as the prominent leaders of the national movement. The foundations of a state-guided industrializing economy were laid during the Nehru period and the Indian state consolidated its power under the leadership of Nehru. The Congress Party played a hegemonic role in Indian politics by incorporating diverse interests and identities. Atul Kohli has characterized the post-colonial Indian state as the 'fragmented-multiclass' state. By the 1970s, the Congress Party started losing its hegemonic position under the strain of a variety of distributive conflicts.

Over time the state in India has shifted its position from a reluctant pro-capitalist state with a socialist ideology to an enthusiastic pro-capitalistic state with a neo-liberal ideology.[6]

The challenge to the Congress hegemony came from different classes and interest groups. In the Indian state of West Bengal, the left under the leadership of communist parties started posing challenges to the Congress Party in the 1960s, both on the electoral front and other fronts. Ultimately, the Left Front government came to power in West Bengal in 1977 and ruled the state for more than three decades under the leadership of the Communist Party of India (Marxist) – CPI(M). The present chapter is concerned with exploring the diverse aspects of the politics of social democracy practised by the CPI(M)-led government while in power.

EARLY POLITICS OF COMMUNIST PARTIES IN WEST BENGAL

West Bengal witnessed strikes, *hartals* (suspension of normal life) and mammoth political rallies in the mid 1950s, organized by the Communist Party of India (CPI). The politics of protest eroded the basis of the politics of order represented by the Congress Party. The momentum of this kind of radical politics led to the victory of the United Front in 1967, the first non-Congress government in West Bengal. This testified to the popular perception that the Congress was no longer the party of the people but of the propertied.[7]

Trade union membership rates doubled in West Bengal between the mid 1950s and mid 1960s. The majority of West Bengal's communists and its trade unionists and rank-and-file militants sided with the 'left' faction that would form the Communist Party of India (Marxist) – CPI(M) – at its Kolkata conference when the CPI split in 1964. One major reason for the split was the India-China border dispute in 1962. While some leaders of the CPI had campaigned against Nehru and opposed the war, others on the Central Committee of the party supported Congress' 'patriotic war'. The anti-Congress faction formed the CPI(M). In the West Bengal state assembly elections in 1967, the CPI(M) won 43 seats out of 280 and joined the United Front (UF) coalition government led by the Bangla Congress, a breakaway group of the Congress Party, as a junior partner. The CPI(M) leader, Jyoti Basu, became the deputy chief minister and Harekrishna Konar, also of the CPI(M), was the Minister for Land and Land Revenue.[8]

After joining the UF government in March 1967, the West Bengal State Committee of the CPI(M) made the following declaration: 'the Ministry is formed on the basis of a conglomeration of fourteen parties with different politics and ideologies and they are united with the aim of serving the people's interests. It has to function on the basis of a non-class outlook.'[9] The CPI(M) realized very soon that it was not possible to serve people's interests from a 'non-class outlook'. Soon after his swearing in, Harekrishna Konar announced that the government had decided to distribute land among the landless and poor peasants and stop eviction of *bargadars* (share-croppers) by the *jotedars* (landlords). He also invited militant initiatives from the peasantry. He probably did not realize then that 'popular initiative, once unleashed, could go far beyond the expectations of the leaders'.[10]

In May 1967, a peasant rebellion erupted in a village of Naxalbari in the Darjeeling district of West Bengal, led by the CPI(M)'s peasant front. Harekrishna Konar, the minister and the veteran peasant leader, tried to convince the peasants to put down their arms, to no avail. The chief minister sent police forces to repress the rebellion and it was crushed with extreme brutality. The first serious encounter between the peasants and the state machinery took place on 23 May, when a police inspector was killed by the armed tribal peasants after police had gone to a village to arrest some rebel leaders. On 25 May, the police retaliated and fired upon a crowd of villagers, killing nine, including six women and two children. Later, several peasants were arrested and subjected to persistent police interrogation.[11]

The incident described above created tensions both within and outside the UF. The West Bengal State Secretariat of the CPI(M) initially condemned the police firing and demanded a judicial inquiry into the incident. It also accused Chief Minister Ajoy Mukherjee of the Bangla Congress for the police brutality. Meanwhile, reports of clashes between the rebel peasants and landlords kept pouring in from Naxalbari. By the end of June, the CPI(M) leadership was coming out openly against the Naxalbari rebels. On 12 July, a major police action was launched at Naxalbari to round up the rebels and their leaders. Although the chief minister claimed that the CPI(M) was also party to the cabinet decision to launch the action, the West Bengal State Secretariat of the CPI(M) in a statement sought to dissociate itself from the action.[12] However, the fact that the CPI(M) leaders were dissociating themselves from militant class politics is evident in the statements of its two prominent leaders in October 1967. 'We do not want strikes and lock-out. We seek an amicable settlement of labour disputes', commented the Deputy Chief Minister Jyoti Basu after a cabinet meeting. Harekrishna Konar, the Minister for Land and Land Revenue, told reporters informally after the meeting that in the struggle between *jotedars* (landlords) and *bargadars* (share-croppers), there would in future be much less of the 'impatience and childishness' displayed by certain sections of the peasantry from time to time in the past.[13] It may be mentioned in this connection that the peasant uprising in Naxalbari spread its wings very quickly. It led to revolts within the CPI(M), and to the birth of the Communist Party of India (Marxist-Leninist) – CPI(ML) – in 1969. The movement led by the CPI(ML) in India in the late 1960s and early 1970s is popularly known as the *Naxalite* movement.

The above background of the early participation of the CPI(M) in electoral politics is important for an understanding of the politics of social democracy practised by it in West Bengal for more than three decades (1977–2011).

LEFT FRONT GOVERNMENT AND ITS RURAL POLITICS

The year 1975 was a turning point in the political history of India. Indira Gandhi, daughter of the late Jawaharlal Nehru, central figure in the Congress Party and the prime minister of India, declared a national Emergency on 25 June on the grounds of 'internal threat' to the security of India, arrested hundreds of opposition leaders and party workers and removed the democratic rights of the people of India during the emergency period (1975–77). In the parliamentary elections in 1977, the Congress Party was ousted by the Janata Party and the first non-Congress central government was formed in India.

The Left Front won 243 seats in the West Bengal state assembly elections in 1977 and the CPI(M) emerged as the largest party in the West Bengal legislative assembly, winning 178 seats out of 294. The first Left Front (LF) government was formed with Jyoti Basu as the chief minister. The other constituents of the LF government were the CPI, the Revolutionary Socialist Party (RSP), the Forward Bloc, the Marxist Forward Bloc, the Revolutionary Communist Party of India (RCPI) and the Biplabi Bangla Congress. West Bengal had witnessed more than three decades of LF rule. Atul Kohli characterized this rule as 'the rise of reform communism'. It should be noted in this context that the CPI(M) dictated the mode of functioning of the LF. The dynamics of the LF rule should therefore be studied in the context of the politics of the CPI(M).

After coming to power, the LF government avoided the path of open violence in social transformation and concentrated on winning the confidence of the rural voters. To put it in the words of Atul Kohli:

The success of the Naxalites among the peasantry forced the CPM to take peasant support seriously. The result was that over the last two decades the CPM increasingly became a rural party with the bulk of its seats being won in the rural constituencies and its programme being concentrated in the villages.[14]

A report of the World Bank (2007) noted in this context that 'attention to land reform is widely seen as one of the key reasons for the remarkable political stability in West Bengal'.[15]

The recording/registration of share-croppers (*bargadars*) under Operation Barga and giving them some legal rights and security of cultivation was an important measure incorporated in the agrarian programme of the LF at the time of its election in 1977. The implementation of this programme in the early years of its rule helped the LF to strengthen its support in rural West Bengal. In quantitative terms, over 1.6 million share-croppers were recorded and given hereditary rights of cultivation. They were also promised a fair deal in crop-sharing with the land-owners. Moreover, about a million acres of vested land were distributed among 2.5 million landless and land-poor peasants. Thus, the land reform measures of the government directly benefited a little over 4 million rural households in West Bengal, a significant proportion of the rural population.[16]

Immediately after coming to power the LF government started reforming the mode of local governance in rural West Bengal. The institutions of local governance collectively known as panchayat raj include gram panchayat, panchayat samity and zilla parisad for the village, block (cluster of adjoining villages) and the district, respectively. The first three-tier panchayat elections were held under the new regime in 1978. Since then elections to panchayats have been held on a regular basis in the state and contested along party/political lines. The success of the LF candidates in these elections had been overwhelming until the panchayat elections in 2008, when the hegemony of the LF in the institutions of local governance came to an end. The LF candidates were defeated in many districts. In 2003, 71 per cent of gram panchayats, 86 per cent of panchayat samitis and 88 per cent of zilla parishads were controlled by the LF. In 2008, these proportions were reduced to 49 per cent for gram panchayats, 69 per cent for panchayat samitis and 76 per cent for zilla parishads.[17]

In a report prepared for the government of West Bengal in the early 1990s on the mode of functioning of panchayat institutions, it was found that the panchayats brought a middle category of society into key positions, and many of them were school teachers. The firm control of the rural middle class over the panchayats did not change in the coming years. The largest occupational group elected at the highest level of panchayat administration, zilla parishad, in 1993 was that of teachers (32.5 per cent).[18] It should be noted here that school teachers as a key component of the rural middle class played an important role in legitimizing the rule of the CPI(M). In fact, they acted as a crucial link between the party and the peasants by placing themselves in various committees.[19]

Under the LF regime, the panchayat institutions came to represent an alternative structure of authority to the police, civil service officers and other official departments in the rural areas. In the early period of panchayat rule, the local activists of the CPI(M) often resorted to political tactics to challenge the administrative officers, and the Block Development Officers (BDOs) were the frequent targets for such actions at the local level. Party activists would mobilize village supporters and the BDO would be *gheraoed* (detained) in his office. Over time, the civil servants accepted the fact that the political opposition to the LF government was unlikely to defeat it in the near future and a general willingness to compromise was shown on their part.[20]

While recalling his field experiences in some villages of the Bardhaman district in the early 1990s, Neil Webster noted:

> Twelve years ago, when first conducting research in the area, reference was often made to the village 'babus', those who had wealth and a strong political presence in the village, the village leaders … When poor Scheduled Caste men were asked why they do not speak, the most frequent reply was 'What would I have to say? I just sit and listen to the others'. When asked who is speaking at these meetings – it is the 'babus'. The difference between twelve years ago and today is that the babus are now CPI (M) members or activists.[21]

The voiceless conditions of marginal people in the villages found in Webster's study may not be true for villages in West Bengal in general. Pranab Bardhan and Dilip Mookherjee jointly conducted a study involving a sample of 80 villages in West Bengal and collected data concerning the operation of panchayats between 1978 and 1998. It was found that landless agricultural workers, women and Scheduled Caste (SC)/Scheduled Tribe (ST) members could stand up in public meetings and pose critical questions regarding public services to village leaders. But many serious limitations of the panchayat administration in West Bengal were revealed in the study. The village households owning more than 5 acres of land were vastly overrepresented in the gram panchayats – a group of less than 4 per cent of the households in the village held approximately one third of gram panchayat seats throughout the period of study (1978–98). The underrepresentation was greatest for the landless persons. Villages with greater landlessness or low caste status among the poor received substantially less resources as a whole. Moreover, allocation of benefits followed political party lines – those who did not belong to the local party in power were severely discriminated against.[22]

A field study of two villages in the Bardhaman district showed that in certain cases the marginal people in rural West Bengal had been able to raise their voices by affiliating themselves with the CPI(M).[23] In a CPI(M)-dominated village of the same district, one agricultural worker communicated to the field researcher the bare truth – actually comrades, not panchayats, rule the village and decide the names of beneficiaries.[24] This is not an isolated case. The village narratives in West Bengal substantiate the fact that the panchayat institutions have frequently come to be perceived by a growing section of people to have played a narrow, instrumental and bureaucratic role, due to excessive party control during the LF regime.[25] The fact that the panchayat institutions lost their credibility among the people over the years was noted in a report published by the LF government:

> Average attendance at Gram Sansad and Gram Sabha meetings has been relatively low and declining in recent years. Official data indicate that average attendance at Gram Sansad meetings declined from around 16 per cent in 1997 to around 12 per cent in 2001, while for Gram Sabha meetings, where attendance was 30 per cent in 1997, the decline has been even sharper.[26]

The above experiences show the decay of institutions through which the LF government promised to deliver welfare to the rural population after they came to power. They also testify to the failure of this social mechanism of delivering justice to the people.

LEFT FRONT AND INDUSTRIAL LABOUR

Radical trade unionism and workers' militancy in the 1960s scared away new private investment in West Bengal. But then large-scale entrepreneurs started farming out production to the small-scale units in the unorganized sector. Thus, they could avoid the trouble of militant trade unionism while simultaneously grabbing the incentives enjoyed by the small firms. By the end of the 1980s, as a result of the decline in the traditional industries, such as jute, cotton and engineering, a large number of workers had lost their jobs. Consequently, the working class in West Bengal became vulnerable, and the trade unions agreed to terms of settlements in the 1980s that would have been unthinkable in the past. In fact, West Bengal witnessed a significant decline in the number of strikes and a spectacular rise in the number of lockouts after the LF government assumed office in 1977. In a field report on the plight of workers published in 2005, it was found that of the total number of cases where factories stopped production in West Bengal, 92 per cent were due to lockouts declared by the management. The land belonging to many of the locked-out factories was then used for the construction of shopping malls and multi-storied buildings for the elites.[27] The use of factory land for the construction of shopping malls and multi-storied apartments for the elites has transformed the urban landscape of Kolkata and its surrounding areas, which contributed to the vulnerability and reduction in militancy of the workers. The LF allowed this to happen by their choice of anti-worker policies.

Since the assumption of office, the LF followed 'pragmatic policies' and avoided the path of militant politics of the working class. This put the workers in a weakened position. In the moments of industrial disputes, the CPI(M) and its trade union front, the Centre of Indian Trade Unions (CITU), often took anti-worker positions. This was evident in the major capital-labour conflicts in the 1990s.

Victoria Jute Mill in the Hooghly district of West Bengal was one of the units of Titagarh Private Limited Company (TPLC), which owned four jute textile mills in West Bengal. R.J. Brealey, a British citizen, was the chairman of the TPLC's Board of Directors and resided in London. He took over the ownership and management in 1988, and came to Kolkata and met the leaders of the LF government including the chief minister, Jyoti Basu, and the labour minister. However, the mill was actually run by R.K. Jain, a speculator in raw jute, whom the workers knew to be the real decision-maker. In fact, Jain was the financier and supplier of other materials to the mill. The mill manager, the trade unions and the administration all depended on him for payment of wages, bonuses and other dues of the workers and for running the mill.[28]

A major conflict cropped up in the Victoria mill in the early 1990s. A tripartite meeting took place on 7 October 1993, with the Labour commissioner and representatives of the management and the trade unions. It was decided that the weekly wages, and an arrears bonus for 1988–89, would be paid to the workers on 17 October. But no payment was made and the speculator, R.K. Jain absconded. The long accumulated anger of the workers found violent expressions. The wrath of the workers was directed not so much against the management as the trade unions. The workers attacked the houses of the union leaders and assaulted some of them on 20 October. Some unions lodged a First Information Report (FIR) – a written document prepared by the police when they receive information about the commission of a cognizable offence – against the workers and seven workers were arrested. On the following morning, about 1000 workers assembled at the police station and demanded release of their colleagues. It was a spontaneous protest by the workers, who did not carry any party flag and did not seek the leadership of any trade union leader. As the police did not release the arrested workers, there was a scuffle between the workers and the police. The police fired at the workers and the workers threw brickbats – pieces of brick used as weapons or missiles – at the police, leading to injury of several workers and death of a police constable. The workers smashed the offices of all the unions situated at the mill gate, including that of the CITU and Indian National Trade Union Congress (INTUC), trade union wing of the Congress Party. The police then went on a rampage in the workers' slums situated near the mill gate and arrested many more workers. Work-suspension was declared in the mill and Section 144 of the Criminal Procedure Code (CrPC) was clamped in the mill area, empowering the District Magistrate to prohibit an assembly of five or more persons in the area. According to the workers' testimonies, a worker named Bhikhari Paswan was picked up by the police force from his slum and he remained untraced. It was suspected that he was killed in police custody.[29]

The Victoria Jute Mill case is not an isolated example of the plight of workers brought on by LF policies. Many such developments took place during the LF regime. Hindustan Lever, a reputed soap and detergent manufacturer, had one of its largest factories located in the Garden Reach area in the southern part of Kolkata. It employed about 1800 workers. The CITU won the elections for workers' representatives in the factory in the early 1980s and remained in power, postponing elections (which were constitutionally mandatory every two years) under one pretext or another. The workers' unions in the different factories of West Bengal are usually affiliated to one political party or the other, and they usually carry the party decisions imposed from outside, often sacrificing the interests of the workers. In 1986, the CITU leadership signed a settlement agreement with the management, and this was deeply resented by the workers. In a secret ballot election, which the management was forced to conduct in 1987, an independent group contested the elections and its members won the seats of workers' representatives in the factory. The management decided to close down one of its manufacturing departments in the same year and laid off 300 contract workers. The new independent union opposed the closing down of the department, and the workers went on a wildcat strike. The management immediately suspended all the executive committee members of the independent union. The workers followed a 'go slow' policy for six months, and the management retaliated by not treating the independent union as the representative body of workers. In its place, the management formed a *yukhta* (joint) committee comprised of the leaders of the CITU and INTUC groups. In the meantime, the management laid off 100 more workers in the same department. This was followed by a massive offensive by the management on the workers. The police raided the houses of workers in the nearby slum, and 300–400 policemen were posted inside the factory to intimidate the workers.[30]

There are many more examples that we could cite. The point of our argument is that the LF government either failed to protect the interest of the workers or actively supported the management through the use of coercive arms of the state and through the collaborationist gestures of their trade union wing, the CITU. There are instances where the CITU members threatened the workers who opposed them. In the late 1980s, an independent union, Majdoor Samithi (MS), was formed in the Hanuman Jute Mill, which employed about 4000 workers, when the workers lost faith in the recognized party unions representing them. By the early 1990s, the MS earned the trust of the workers and won most of the important posts in the elected bodies of the workers. The leaders of the MS faced constant threats and pressures from the CITU people in the mid 1990s.[31]

The LF government adopted a policy of peaceful settlement of industrial conflicts. In 1983, Jyoti Basu, then chief minister, in his speech delivered at the eastern regional conference of the All India Organisation of Employees, said, 'both the industrialists and workers are required to adopt a realistic and reasonable attitude to resolve problems'. In the same speech, Basu advised the workers to desist from the path of confrontation.[32] But the industries, particularly the jute industry, in West Bengal experienced bitter labour management conflicts on a number of occasions. When the situation got out of control, the government did not hesitate to use the police force and its party functionaries against the militant workers and their leaders.

There was a clear policy shift towards large-scale industrialization in the state of West Bengal in the 1990s. This change of stance was manifested in the industrial policy announced by the LF government in September 1994. It was proclaimed in the policy document: 'The Government of WB has formulated a liberal and investor-friendly industrial policy to change the industrial scenario in the state.' Welcoming foreign technology and investment, and assigning a key role to the private sector in accelerating industrial growth were the salient features of the new industrial policy. However, not much improvement could be discerned in the performance of the manufacturing sector in the state.[33] On the other hand, due to the closure of traditional industries in the state, many workers had to resort to odd occupations for their survival and entered into the category of 'footloose labour'.

LEFT'S NEO-LIBERAL TURN AND POPULAR RESISTANCE

In spite of the announcement of its neo-liberal policy of industrialization in the mid 1990s, the LF government did not make the full-fledged neo-liberal journey during the tenure of Jyoti Basu, who served as the chief minister of West Bengal up to November 2000. His successor was Buddhadeb Bhattacharya, who opted for an aggressive land acquisition strategy for industrialization in West Bengal after the landslide victory of the LF in the state assembly elections, winning 235 seats out of 294, in 2006. The CPI(M) itself won 176 seats in the same elections. The government acquired, by coercive methods, a little less than 1000 acres of fertile multi-crop agricultural land in Singur in the Hooghly district for Tata Motors, the big Indian multinational company, for the manufacture of low-cost Nano cars. The villagers learned about the land acquisition for the Tata factory from the media, there being no panchayat meeting or party spokesman who informed them. Many of the small land-owners refused to accept compensation money from the government to protest against the forced surrender of their land. The unregistered share-croppers and landless agricultural labourers were not offered any compensation. There was ruthless violence by the police force against the villagers who demonstrated against land acquisition with peaceful methods, especially on 25 September and 2 December 2006. Women were beaten up by male policemen, and villagers and protesters were brutally lathi-charged (beaten with wooden sticks), resulting in severe injuries. A young girl active in the movement, Tapasi Malik, was found brutally murdered on 18 December.[34] Ultimately, before starting production, Tata Motors was forced to shift the factory site from West Bengal to Gujarat due to the popular protests.

The 'success story' of land acquisition in Singur was followed by ruthless state violence in Nandigram in the district of East Medinipur in connection with land acquisition for a Special Economic Zone (SEZ) chemical hub project of the Salim group, an Indonesian conglomerate. Several villagers were killed in different phases. The state terror in Nandigram during 14–16 March 2007 filled one 'with a sense of cold horror'. Fourteen people were shot dead and many severely injured on 14 March. A significant number of bullet wounds seemed to have been caused by firing from the back while the protesting villagers were running away. A fact-finding report categorically gave the verdict that the West

Bengal government, particularly the district administration, engaged police forces along with armed ruling party tough men to 'teach a lesson' to the poor villagers for their resistance. A disturbingly large number of cases of sexual violence by both police and armed CPI(M) cadre against women were noted in the report. Many villagers who participated in the movement had previously been CPI(M) cadres. To put it in the words of a woman participant, 'We were all CPM but now we only have our movement.' In fact, the area earmarked for land acquisition was inhabited mostly by Muslims and lower caste Hindus. The CPI(M) controlled five out of six panchayats in the affected area. However, the panchayat bodies had not been consulted for the decision on land acquisition. It should be mentioned that the CPI(M) was completely ousted from both Singur and Nandigram in the panchayat elections in 2008.[35]

The popular movements in Singur and Nandigram put a big question mark against the legitimacy of the more-than-three-decade-long LF regime in West Bengal. Trinamool Congress, a breakaway group of the Congress Party, who aggressively fought the CPI(M) on the floor of the state assembly and in many street battles, appropriated the popular dissent and came to power in West Bengal in 2011 after winning the state assembly elections with an absolute majority (184 seats). Scheduled castes, scheduled tribes and marginal and small farmers had constituted the major 'vote bank' of the LF since the inception of its rule. But only 48 per cent of this vote bank voted for the LF in 2011, and more than half of the committed voters switched their allegiance.[36]

THEORIZING LEFT FRONT POLITICS

The fact that the CPI(M) is a disciplined Leninist political party should be kept in mind in understanding the dynamics of its social democratic politics. Party discipline facilitated a strong link between the party leadership and the cadres. This enabled the leadership to effectively translate organizational goals into grassroots actions.[37] Some of the local committee offices had telex links with party headquarters in Kolkata. Others maintained contact with the headquarters by telephone. Especially in the rural areas, a large number of the CPI(M)'s cadres were engaged on an everyday basis in political work in connection with the running of the panchayats. The party could, without much difficulty, set up an effective machinery for a door-to-door campaign in almost every constituency in West Bengal. In the urban sector, the electoral success of the LF was limited. However, the CPI(M)-led government in West Bengal had been more or less successful in winning the confidence of many eminent Bengali intellectuals. This was an important factor in legitimizing its rule.[38] After noting this mode of operation of the CPI(M), some political theorists argued, 'It is the normative principles of the "modern regime of power" which the CPI(M) seeks to reproduce in its own organizational practice.'[39]

In fact, the CPI(M) extended its influence and control over the state, civil society and community through a network of mass organizations affiliated and subordinated to the party. The LF rule in West Bengal had almost realized the Foucauldian conception of discipline and governmentality.[40] The major outcome of the LF rule was the death of the relative autonomy of civil society in West Bengal. The government had successfully incorporated the multiple institutions of civil society – educational and cultural institutions – in its rule. The CPI(M) often used the coercive power of the state to maintain its control over the 'civil society'. This strategy could be termed in the language of Ranajit Guha, the eminent theorist of *Subaltern Studies*, a strategy of 'dominance without hegemony'.[41]

The Foucauldian reading of the LF regime helps us to understand the nuances of its exercise of power. A Gramscian reading of the same gives us insights for unearthing its class dimensions. What actually happened in West Bengal under LF rule was a 'passive revolution' in the Gramscian sense.[42] In spite of such a long period of CPI(M) rule, no fundamental change took place in the class positions of rural and urban subalterns. Popular grassroots leaders of the party were either appropriated into the dominant power structure controlled mostly by the *babus* (upper caste Hindu middle-class Bengalis) or marginalized. Under the leadership of the *babus*, the party pursued the neo-liberal policy of industrialization with the support of coercive state power. This led to revolts from its core constituency, the rural subalterns including its own cadres. The CPI(M) maintained centralized control over the institutions of local governance, the panchayat institutions, and did not give them any autonomy. So the party failed to read the dissenting minds of the people before its demise in the state assembly elections in West Bengal in 2011, in which it bagged only 40 seats. The trajectory of CPI(M) politics in West Bengal shows how the politics of social democracy merged with the Leninist concept of the vanguard party dictating the masses. This dictatorship of the party in West Bengal led to, in the words of Rosa Luxemburg, the 'brutalization of public life'.

NOTES

1. I. Carlsson and A.-M. Lindgren (2007). *What is Social Democracy*, Stockholm, Sweden: Arbetarrorelsens Tankesmedja: 3.

2. J. Blasius, T. Gombert, C. Krell and M. Timpe (eds) (2009). *Social Democracy Reader 1*. Berlin: Friedrich-Ebert-Stiftung: 68.

3. For the above arguments, see S. Berger (2002). *Communism, Social Democracy and the Democracy Gap*. ARAB: 1–14. Available at www.arbark.se/pdf_wrd/berger_int.pdf (accessed 15 May 2016).

4. S. Kaviraj (2009). 'The Post-colonial State: The Special Case of India'. *Critical Encounters* (a forum of critical thought from the Global South), 19 January: 1–16.

5. See M. Khosla (ed.) (2014). *Letters for a Nation: From Jawaharlal Nehru to His Chief Ministers (1947–1963)*. New Delhi: Allen Lane: 173–4.

6. See A. Kohli (2010). 'Politics and Redistribution'. In N.G. Jayal and P.B. Mehta (eds), *The Oxford Companion to Politics in India*. New York: Oxford University Press: 499, 502. A. Kohli (2012). *Poverty Amid Plenty in the New India*. New York: Cambridge University Press: 21–4. A. Kohli (2009). 'States and Economic Development'. *Brazilian Journal of Political Economy*, April–June: 215.

7. R. Mukherjee (2015). 'Bengal: Success of Failure'. *Telegraph*, 7 January.

8. K. Bag (2011). 'Red Bengal's Rise and Fall'. *New Left Review*, July–August: 73–4.

9. Quoted in 'U F Government and the Role of 'Marxists' (1967). *Liberation*, 1 (1) (November). Available at www.bannedthought.net/India/CPI(ML)-Orig/index.htm (accessed 15 May 2016).

10. S. Banerjee (1980). *In the Wake of Naxalbari*. Calcutta: Subarnarekha: 104–5.

11. Ibid., p. 112–14; Bag, 'Red Bengal's Rise and Fall': 74–5.

12. Banerjee, *In the Wake of Naxalbari*: 113–15.

13. See *Liberation*, 1 (1), 1967 for the statements of Basu and Konar.

14. A. Kohli (1990). 'From Elite Activism to Democratic Consolidation: The Rise of Reform Communism in West Bengal. In F.R. Frankel and M.S.A. Rao (eds), *Dominance and State Power in Modern India*. Volume II. Delhi: Oxford University Press: 371.

15. The World Bank (2007). *India: Land Policies for Growth and Poverty Reduction*. New Delhi: Oxford University Press: 58.

16. D. Bandyopadhyay (2007). *Land, Labour and Governance*. Kolkata: Worldview: 80.

17. P. Bardhan, S. Mitra, D. Mookherjee and A. Sarkar (2009). 'Local Democracy and Clientelism: Implications for Political Stability in Rural West Bengal'. *Economic and Political Weekly (EPW)*, 28 February: 46.

18. N. Mukherji and D. Bandyopadhyay (1993). *New Horizons for West Bengal's Panchayats: A Report for the Government of West Bengal*. Calcutta: 38–9. Also *West Bengal Human Development Report (WBHDR) 2004*. Government of West Bengal, May.

19. See D. Bhattacharyya (1999). 'Politics of Middleness: The Changing Character of the Communist Party of India (Marxist) in Rural West Bengal (1977–90)'. In B. Rogaly, B. Hariss-White and S. Bose (eds), *Sonar Bangla? Agricultural Growth and Agrarian Change in West Bengal and Bangladesh*. New Delhi: Sage: 293.

20. N. Webster (1992). *Panchayati Raj and the Decentralization of Development Planning in West Bengal.* Calcutta: K.P. Bagchi: 114–15.

21. Ibid.: 98–9.

22. See P. Bardhan and D. Mookherjee (2006). 'Decentralisation in West Bengal: Origins, Functioning and Impact'. In D. Mookherjee (ed.), *Collected Essays: Market Institutions, Governance and Development.* New Delhi: Oxford University Press: 361–9.

23. A.E. Rudd (1999). 'From Untouchable to Communist: Wealth, Power and Status Among Supporters of the Communist Party-Marxist in Rural West Bengal'. In B. Rogaly, B. Hariss-White and S. Bose (eds), *Sonar Bangla? Agricultural Growth and Agrarian Change in West Bengal and Bangladesh.* New Delhi: Sage: 253–78.

24. H. Bhattacharyya (1998). *Micro Foundations of Bengal Communism.* Delhi: Ajanta: 121.

25. See R. Dasgupta (2009). 'The CPI (M) "Machinery" in West Bengal: Two Village Narratives from Kochbihar and Malda'. *Economic and Political Weekly (EPW),* 28 February: 80.

26. *WBHDR 2004:* 67.

27. See D. Chakravarty and I. Bose (2010). 'Industrializing West Bengal?: The Case of Institutional Sickness'. Working Paper No. 83, February. Centre for Economic and Social Studies, Hyderabad: 8–9. Also *A Report on Locked-out Factories, Plight of Workers and Urban Space* (2005). January–August. Nagarik Mancha: Kolkata.

28. A Special Correspondent, 'Trade Unions Abdicate' (1994). *Economic and Political Weekly (EPW),* 1–8 January: 20.

29. Ibid.: 20–1.

30. See S. Davala (1996). 'Independent Trade Unionism in West Bengal'. *Economic and Political Weekly (EPW),* 28 December: L44–5.

31. Ibid.: L47.

32. See *Jyoti Basu Speaks: A Collection of Selected Speeches of Jyoti Basu* (1991). Department of Information and Cultural Affairs, Government of West Bengal: 23.

33. Chakravarty and Bose, 'Industrializing West Bengal?'.

34. Interim Report of the Citizens' Committee on Singur and Nandigram (2007). *Mainstream,* 9–15 February: 13.

35. Ibid.: 11–12. Also All India Citizens Initiative, *Nandigram: What Really Happened?* (2007) (based on the Report of the People's Tribunal in Nandigram). Delhi: Danish Books. Also A.K. Sen (2008). 'Nandigram: A Tale of Developmental Violence'. *Economic and Political Weekly (EPW),* 13 September: 31–2.

36. P. Bardhan, S. Mitra, D. Mookherjee and A. Nath (2014). 'Changing Voting Patterns in Rural West Bengal: Role of Clientelism and Local Public Goods'. *Economic and Political Weekly (EPW),* 15 March: 56.

37. Kohli, 'From Elite Activism to Democratic Consolidation': 369, 372.

38. P. Chatterjee, P.K. Bose and R. Samaddar (1998). 'Discipline and Development'. In P. Chatterjee (ed.), *The Present History of West Bengal: Essays in Political Criticism*. Delhi: Oxford University Press: 149, 151, 153.
39. Ibid.: 153.
40. S. Mukherjee (2007). 'The Use and Abuse of Democracy in West Bengal'. *Economic and Political Weekly (EPW)*, 3 November: 104–5.
41. A. Gupta (2001). 'Left Front Rule in West Bengal: Domination without Hegemony'. *Economic and Political Weekly (EPW)*, 10 November: 4320.
42. See R. Samaddar (2013). *Passive Revolution in West Bengal: 1977–2011*. Los Angeles: Sage. Also A.K. Sen (2009). 'Politics of Governance in Rural West Bengal'. *The Calcutta Journal of Political Studies*, April 2007–March 2009: 28.

12

South Africa's Pseudo Social Democracy: Tokenistic Nuances Within Neoliberal Nationalism

Patrick Bond

SOCIAL DEMOCRATIC RHETORIC IN A MOST UNEQUAL SOCIETY

The exceptionally high-profile visit to South Africa by Thomas Piketty in October 2015 was instructive. At the initial event at the University of Cape Town on 30 September, his talk (broadcast on a malfunctioning video feed) was disrupted by RhodesMustFall activists who expressed their powerful class and race critique of the host institution (Stanwix, 2015). But even more dramatic was the attention given to Piketty's two main speeches (at the Universities of Johannesburg and the Witwatersrand) the following two days applying his *Capital in the 21st Century* study of world inequality to South Africa. Both the political and business-intellectual elite were captivated. The idea of social democracy imposed from above was suddenly back on the agenda, after a hiatus since the 1994 liberation of black people from apartheid had turned into the liberation of business from a variety of prior statist constraints.

Among the hot ideological wars South Africans wage, especially after a viable left began rising in the trade unions and parliament in 2014, perhaps none is as vibrant as inequality. For example, the rejigging of the Gini coefficient by the World Bank in November 2014 drew wide attention. (This number is zero if everyone shares income perfectly equally and one if only a sole person gets it all.) Calculated as the distribution of formal income prior to any form of state redistribution, South Africa's Gini – as measured by the World Bank (2014) – was then 0.77, the highest of any major country. But the Bank's Pretoria staff claimed that after a rethink on what constitutes *effective* income, the Gini is reduced from 0.77 to 0.59, thanks to South African state social spending on social grants, education, health, municipal services and other state functions. This finding was reiterated a year later (Woolard et al., 2015) and repeatedly endorsed by a leading business newspaper editor, Hilary Joffe (2014, 2015):

> Though both progressive income taxes and a progressive wealth tax are central to the Piketty programme for addressing inequality, the World Bank study argued that you have to look at both the taxing and the spending sides of government policy – and, on that basis, *SA can claim to have one of the world's most redistributive public purses.* Fiscal policy in SA reduces the Gini coefficient – the globally accepted measure of income inequality – by almost a quarter, the multilateral institution found. Even if the government had the money, there's a big question about how much more it is worth doing in the way of taxing for redistribution and whether that would do any more to cut inequality. (Joffe, 2015, emphasis added)

The argument was fairly typical of responses by South Africa's elites. Instead of directly opposing Piketty's social democratic agenda, the strategy was co-optation, in a make-believe story about South African income and state services redistribution. It is not hard to pick apart Joffe's and the Bank's exaggerations, for although the child support grant was provided to 11.9 million recipients at the time, it was only $0.75/day (using a R15/$1 exchange). This was just 40 per cent of the level that the World Bank considered the poverty line: $1.88/day in October 2015 (an estimate similar to what Statistics South Africa used). But most importantly from the standpoint of rebutting the view that 'SA can claim to have one of the world's most redistributive public purses', the Bank research was fatally flawed insofar as vast state-funded benefits enjoyed by corporations and the rich (crony capitalism) simply evaporate from the analysis (Bond, 2015a).

No matter how biased this rejigged Gini, the Bank's optimism triggered applause from commentators, economists and politicians heralding how well redistribution was going, and how little more could be done given fiscal constraints:

- Brand South Africa manager Simon Barber (2014) in the journal *Foreign Policy*: 'The World Bank recently compared 12 middle income economies and found SA had performed the best in reducing poverty and inequality. That said … "the fiscal space to spend more to achieve even greater redistribution is extremely limited"… choices will have to be made between expanding the politically important safety net which now protects 16 million plus South Africans and making the investments needed to clear blockages to the one thing that's required above all, growth.'

- Investec Bank chief economist Brian Kantor (2014): 'The World Bank shows, in a recent study, that SA does more to redistribute income in cash and kind to the poor than its developing economy peers ... The imposition of higher tax rates on the high income earners would achieve little by way of extra collections; more important it would undermine the incentives of high income earners to deliver more taxable income.'

- Neoliberal commentator Jonathan Katzenellenbogen (2014) at PoliticsWeb: 'a World Bank report warned last week that government no longer has the cash to expand the grant system ... "due to the high fiscal deficit and debt." According to the Bank report, transfers have caused the poverty rate to fall from 46.2 percent to 39 percent ... This reduction in inequality through tax and spending is larger than in any other country.'

- Rothschilds banker (and former finance and planning minister) Trevor Manuel (2014): 'The World Bank study released last week confirms that fiscal policy is significantly redistributive, on both the tax and spending sides ...'.

The cacophony culminated on Budget Day 2015 with the country's highest-profile economist, Iraj Abedian, warning of imminent credit rating agency downgrades, and making a prominent call for social grants to be cut 'way below inflation' (Ensor, 2015). Finance Minister Nhlanhla Nene then reduced the already tokenistic survival funds given to South Africa's poorest by more than 4 per cent. He simultaneously deregulated exchange controls, allowing rich South Africans to increase their offshore wealth expatriation from $267,000 to $667,000 per person per year (Bond, 2015b).

'DILUTING RADICALISM'

Piketty would be aghast at this interim outcome of the recent inequality debate. Yet, he put up no objection to the neoliberal attempt to co-opt his message in late 2015. The most extreme case of promoting Piketty for the sake of status quo policy was Raymond Parsons (2015), who for more than 40 years was South Africa's highest-profile white business spokesperson. At the peak of South Africa's revolutionary anti-apartheid drive, *New York Times* correspondent Alan Cowell (1986) was grateful that Parsons divulged 'correspondence dating to 1960 between [the SA Chamber of Business, which he ran] and Hendrik F. Verwoerd, at that time the Prime Minister'. Parsons communicated how 'business in South Africa responds more to crisis in its quest for reform than to the years of economic growth and of black quiescence'. Furthermore, Parsons indicated, 'By embracing the ANC, the idea seems to be, its radicalism might be diluted.'

Within 15 years, as Nelson Mandela's 1994–99 government gave way to Thabo Mbeki's 1999–2008 reign, the 'Faustian Pact' dilution of the African National Congress' (ANC) commitment to its radical 1955 Freedom Charter was conclusively accomplished. There were at least ten steps along the route:

- repay $25 billion of inherited apartheid-era foreign debt (October 1993)
- give the South Africa Reserve Bank 'independence' in the country's 1993 interim constitution and 1996 final constitution (November 1993)
- borrow $850 million from the International Monetary Fund (IMF) with tough conditions (December 1993)
- reappoint apartheid's finance minister Derek Keys and South Africa Reserve Bank governor Chris Stals (May 1994)
- join the World Trade Organization on adverse terms as a 'transitional' (not 'developing') economy (August 1994)
- lower primary corporate taxes from 48 per cent to 29 per cent and maintain countless privileges enjoyed by white people and corporations (1994–99)
- privatize parts of the state and demutualize mega-insurance firms (1995–99)
- relax exchange controls (the 'finrand') and raise interest rates (March 1995)
- adopt the neoliberal Growth, Employment and Redistribution ('Gear') macroeconomic policy (June 1996)
- approve South Africa's biggest companies moving their financial headquarters and primary stock market listings to London (1999) (Saul and Bond, 2014).

But when Jacob Zuma took power in 2009 thanks partly to manoeuvres by the South Africa Communist Party and trade unions, Parsons (2009: 7) again turned to co-optation, this time in his edited collection *Zumanomics*, which pronounced, 'the unavoidable reality that narrowed options will have been dictated by world-wide economic events'. After budget deficits of 2008–09, he insisted, the government 'will need to return to its normal fiscal flight path'. Fast forward to the Piketty visit and Parsons' (2015) *Business Day* column, in which he revealed a similar agenda. But instead of Mandela or Zuma turning radical, the fear in 2015 was more general renewal redistribution rhetoric. Parsons' tactic, once again, was to embrace and enthusiastically co-opt the French economist: 'The extent to which several of Piketty's points for reducing inequality resonate with the overall thrust of the National Development Plan (NDP) is striking.'

In reality, the state's 2012–30 National Development Plan is severely wanting for ambition when it comes to inequality, projecting that its strategies will reduce the Gini only from 0.69 (in 2012 measured slightly differently from the Bank) to 0.60, that is, that the income share earned by the poorest 40 per cent will rise from 6 to just 10 per cent. As trade union official Neil Coleman (2013) argued, '0.6 would still make our levels of inequality higher than any other major country in the world! This long-term target (which Brazil has surpassed by far in less than 10 years) is an embarrassment for a country claiming to be serious about combating inequality.'

Parsons' desired neoliberal strategy faced resistance from a working class that the World Economic Forum considered to be the most militant on earth, amongst 140 major countries in its 2012–15 polling (rising from seventh most militant in 2011). As a result, argued Parsons (2015), an

important reason for decision makers to tackle the inequality gap is to get it [class resistance] out of the way. For as long as income distribution in SA is seen as too far from what is 'socially desirable', necessary policies for allocative efficiency are constantly suspect, such as the appropriate role of user charges, the need for fiscal discipline or making SA more globally competitive.

The latter three goals represent the unfinished neoliberal agenda. To make the case for fiscal discipline (budget cuts), Parsons (2015) intoned, 'A 2014 World Bank report outlined the progress SA has made in reducing poverty and inequality through fiscal policy, but concluded that there was now minimum scope for further redistribution through the budget.' In reality, there was enormous scope for domestic borrowing to pay for higher levels of immediate social spending: in 2011 (the latest available data) South Africa ranked fifth from the bottom of 40 major countries in this category (as a share of gross domestic product (GDP)) according to the Organisation for Economic Co-operation and Development (2011), and in the last public debt and deficit analysis by Barclays

Capital (Weisenthal, 2012), the state was considered substantially under-borrowed (in local terms, not foreign debt) compared to peers.

In this context, a classical social democratic policy of growth-through-redistribution is certainly desirable, as argued by University of the Witwatersrand political economists Imraan Valodia (2015) and Vishnu Padayachee (2015), who hoped that Piketty's influence could revive this tradition. Valodia concluded, 'the question the country needs to answer is: what political forces are needed to generate more equality in the opportunities available to South Africans?'. But aside from co-optative rhetoric of the sort Parsons offered, and hostility of the sort Joffe (2015) and bank economists provided in his wake, there was no shift in power. In October 2015, Nene continued with real budget cuts to poor people's grants and, as a major student revolt began to converge on national targets including his medium-term budget speech, he simply termed their protests 'unconstructive' (though within two subsequent days of national protest they had won their short-term demand of a 5 per cent real cut in 2016 fees).

Indeed, Nene was considered so fiscally tight-fisted that in December 2015, he was replaced after two specific conflicts: over an expensive airplane purchase and lease arrangement for the national carrier and over the acquisition of nuclear energy reactors from Russia and China, both of which he opposed. Nene's replacement (a yes-man) was considered so potentially amenable to Zuma's fiscal irresponsibility and patronage instincts, that massive turmoil roiled the financial markets, and after four days he was replaced by a trusted neoliberal, Pravin Gordhan, who was formerly a Marxist revolutionary strategist in Zuma's Durban networks during apartheid, but later made crucial reversals, signing the 1993 IMF agreement and serving Mbeki as tax commissioner and then Zuma as finance minister from 2009–14 before being shifted to local government minister. Zuma's flip-flop decision to rehire Gordhan appeared to be mainly the result of pressure from the local leadership of three powerful banks – Barclays (in South Africa called ABSA), Goldman Sachs and Investec – behind whom sat three even more powerful international credit rating agencies that were openly threatening to lower the country's rating to junk status, as Brazil also experienced at that time. In his first week in office, Gordhan's decisions were ambiguous: he backed Nene's critique of South African Airways but then failed to use fiscal discipline to halt the nuclear reactor acquisition programme. In opening the latter route, potentially spending tens of billions of dollars, he would in future foreclose many other options ranging from renewable energy subsidies to higher levels of social spending. The era of pseudo social democracy appeared to come to an end, replaced by more open austerity.

SOCIAL DEMOCRACY OR CLASS WAR?

The immediate post-apartheid era should have been the period to most decisively establish a generous welfare state. The adoption of the ten Faustian Pacts and other socio-economic policies had the opposite effect, rendering social democratic policies *tokenistic* (Bond, 2014a). That word implies that the extension of the apartheid-era social policy – which had been limited to white, 'Indian' and 'coloured' South Africans – was pursued in a manner that stressed 'width not depth' and that fell far short of potential resource allocation. Social policy and state services suffered cutbacks in financial ambition – for example, the Lund Commission's 26 per cent reduction in the main child support grant in 1996 (from $37 to $27/month) – even while many more people gained access. The number of South Africans receiving monthly grants soared from fewer than 3 million in 1994 to 17 million two decades later (out of 55 million residents). Measured in late 2015 exchange rates (following substantial currency depreciation), monthly grants were just $22/month for supporting each poor child under age 18. In addition, there was an $83/month pension for retirees over 60 years old and the disabled.

In all cases, these were means-tested, although the Treasury promised to shift to universal access for old-age pensions, as a strategy to avoid distorting savings incentives for elderly people (that move was repeatedly delayed). Ironically, however, social grants spending was less progressive – i.e. less directed to the poorest South Africans – in 2006 than in 1995, by quite substantial amounts, according to Servaas Van der Berg's (2009) modelling. Using a −1 value as the most progressive outcome in which all spending benefits the poorest, and +1 the most regressive, Van der Berg found a progressivity shift for social grants worsening from −0.371 in 2000 to −0.359 in 2006 (Van der Berg, 2009: 12).

As a result, after the first decade of liberation – from 1995 to 2005 – the slight positive impact of these grants and other social policies were unable to offset the general income deterioration that accompanied neoliberal economic policies. University of Cape Town researchers found that African households lost 1.8 per cent of their overall income (including wages, salaries and unearned income), whereas white households gained 40.5 per cent (Bhorat et al., 2009: 8). A 2010 report of the Organisation for Economic Co-operation and Development by a team led by Murray Leibbrandt concluded that since 1994, 'poverty incidence barely changed in rural areas, while it increased in urban areas' (Leibbrandt et al., 2010: 37). In 2012, those under the $43 'national poverty line' numbered 47 per cent, up from an inflation-adjusted 1994 level in which 45.6 per cent were poor, according to Haroon Bhorat (2013). An update of the poverty line by Statistics South Africa (2015), drawing on 2011 data and with a line of $52/month in late 2015, estimated the poverty rate to be 53 per cent. During the same period, the ratio of surplus in the economy given to labour versus that taken by business (i.e. wages to profits) shrunk by 5 per cent, so not just the poor but the formal working class were victims of the neoliberal era (Forslund, 2012). In contrast, by all accounts, market income inequality rose (to what the World Bank in 2014 measured as a Gini coefficient of 0.77) and so did unemployment: the official rate soared from 16 to 25 per cent from 1994–2015, and adding those who gave up looking for jobs brought the rate to 35 per cent (Bond, 2014b).

At the same time, extremely high increases in fees for consuming basic state services began to kick in by the late 1990s. As a result of rising social protest and the 2000 municipal election campaign, the early 2000s witnessed a municipal Free Basic Services programme. But this too was tokenistic, insofar as cities such as Durban (the pilot municipality) doubled the overall price of water from 1997–2004 while offering a meagre 6 kilolitres per month per household free. With the second bloc of consumption soaring in price, the results were higher non-payment rates, higher disconnection levels and a third less consumption of water by Durban's poorest million residents (Bond, 2010: 456–7).

The irony is that during this era, there were vast surpluses that were allowed to escape social control. The country's 'natural capital' rose, as the commodity price index soared from 2002–11, leaving South Africa with the world's greatest mineral resource endowment, valued at peak by Citi Group at $2.5 trillion (Mala, 2012). But because of lax regulation, the mainly foreign-owned mines and smelters were stripped, with the Washington non-governmental organization Global Financial Integrity naming South Africa the country seventh most prone to Illicit Financial Flows in 2015, with an average of nearly $21 billion in annual losses over the prior decade.

This propensity to misinvoice, transfer price or simply evade taxes was one reason that Johannesburg's commercial elite was in 2014 considered the most corrupt corporate class on earth according to the business consultancy PricewaterhouseCoopers. Drawing on its survey, *The Sunday Times* labelled South African management: 'the world leader in money-laundering, bribery and corruption, procurement fraud, asset misappropriation, and cybercrime', with 77 per cent of all internal fraud committed by senior and middle management (FM Fox, 2014; Hosken, 2014). All this may help explain South Africa's 2013 rating as the third most profitable country for corporations among major economies, according to the IMF (2013).[1] The permission the South African capitalist class needed to wage class war was given by the state, including a 2012 massacre of platinum mining workers at Marikana by Lonmin's allies in the police force, and took precedence over any residual social democratic instincts left in the liberation movement.

IN DEFENCE OF SOUTH AFRICAN 'SOCIAL DEMOCRACY'

With such little progress – and often regress – on social indicators and with enormous surpluses allowed to escape, it is a stretch to label South Africa a social democracy, or even a welfare regime moving in that direction. Yet many do, including one of the presidency's chief strategists during the Mbeki era, Alan Hirsch (2005: 3):

> [A]t the centre is a social democratic approach to social reform – it is the state's job to underwrite the improvement in the quality of life of the poor and to reduce inequalities, but with a firmly entrenched fear of the risks of personal dependency on the state and of the emergence of entitlement attitudes ... The ANC's approach is sometimes summarised as elements of a northern European approach to social development combined with elements of Asian approaches to economic growth, within conservative macroeconomic parameters. This remains the intellectual paradigm within which the ANC operates.

Other intellectuals have made the same points. Stephen Devereux (2011: 414) considered South Africa social protection 'exceptional not only because of the extensive coverage, relative generosity and efficient delivery of its social grants, but because these grants are underpinned by political commitment and legislated rights'. Jeremy Seekings (2005: 50) termed the grant system 'exceptionally generous', and with Nicoli Nattrass more recently argued:

> We accept that, if 'neoliberalism' is defined rather more precisely in terms of market-strengthening policies and practices of commodifica-tion, and especially recommodification, then large parts of the critique of South African neoliberalism is warranted ... Where we differ fun-damentally with critics of neoliberalism is ... what the critics *omit* to argue. The critique of neoliberalism largely ignores the various ways in which public policy under the ANC has been very different to – and perhaps even the antithesis of – 'neoliberalism.' Processes of commod-ification and recommodification have been matched by processes of decommodification. (Seekings and Nattrass, 2015: 12, emphasis in the original)

Using categories developed by Richard Sandbrook and his colleagues, Seekings and Nattrass (2015: 18) conclude that

> post-apartheid South Africa should clearly be categorised as social democratic. It rendered public education and health care more accessible and allocated public funding in pro-poor ways. Housing, infrastructural development and municipal services were directed towards the poor. Pensions and other grants were financed out of taxation, and social insurance was expanded (with promises of further major reforms). Labor market and developmental policies were geared towards promoting better-paid, 'decent' work. Most redistribution to the poor was programmatic, not channelled through patronage networks ...

But there are devils-in-the-detail problems when it comes to assessing not only whether services and infrastructure were delivered at one point, but whether they are sustained. Here the claims are sometimes even bolder. Just prior to the 2004 election, for example, the government's communications director, Joel Netshitenzhe (2004), claimed in the leading Sunday newspaper, '10 million people connected to water [from 1994–2004] cannot by any stretch of the imagination be compared with the *few households occasionally cut off*' (emphasis added). (As noted below, more than 10 million had been at least briefly disconnected, due to inability to pay their bills by then.) Likewise, the South Africa Institute of Race Relations – self-described as 'South Africa's Leading Research and Policy Organisation' – argued in 2012:

> A myth has taken hold in South Africa that service delivery was a failure. However research we have published over the past several years suggests that this is not the case ... The number of households with access to piped water increased from 7.2 million to 12.7 million or by 76.6 percent [between 1996 and 2010]. The proportion with access to piped water increased from 80 percent to 89 percent. Increases of a similar magnitude are true for all 15 service delivery indicators tracked by the Institute. (Cronje, 2012a)

I asked the institute's main research official, Frans Cronje, 'Do you have data on service delivery not just in terms of the capital investment and services *installation*, but also *service standards* (e.g. flush toilet in contrast to pit latrine) and the *operations and maintenance* of services, e.g. pricing, breakdowns, disconnections and other service disruptions?' The reply: 'All good questions. Truth is few answers exist in SA. Would have to do the field work to establish the answer' (Cronje, 2012b). His institute never did, and instead, drawing on these statistics, the neoliberal newspaper *Business Day* (2012) quickly applauded the government, as did a communist leader within the government, Higher Education Minister Blade Nzimande (2012).

DEFINING STATE FINANCES AND SOCIAL DEMOCRACY

To judge these claims requires an assessment of whether in each case, the policies and programmes are indeed oriented to the classic ideas of social democratic decommodification, or are merely tokenistic, or indeed actually support the existing maldistribution of wealth. Taking Gosta Esping-Andersen's 'three worlds of welfare capitalism' seriously requires detailed consideration beyond the scope of this chapter. But several indicative conclusions can be offered, especially in relation to the welfare grants (as already discussed), housing, infrastructure and municipal services (water and electricity). A counter-factual case of non-tokenistic state policy – free anti-retroviral (ARV) medicines to combat AIDS – is considered in the concluding section.

The specific claims by Seekings and Nattrass that state-financed infrastructure is 'directed towards the poor' or that public funding is allocated 'in pro-poor ways' must be assessed in full context. After all, the main roles for a state in modern society are not only the minimal necessary functions for reproducing capitalism – maintaining a monopoly of violence, assuring legal contracts are honoured and facilitating exchange through a well-functioning monetary system. As David Harvey's (1985) diagrammatic representation of 'three circuits of capital' shows (Figure 12.1), there are also a wide variety of other activities that ensure the market system generates surpluses at the point of production, in the primary circuit of capital. States also typically provide financing and regulation of the secondary circuit: managing the built environment and lubricating financial markets. It is in the tertiary circuit that state regulation is most obvious: levels of taxation are established, science and technology are subsidized, the security forces are funded and the labour force is renewed by judicious spending on the quantities and capacities of workers available for the market in large part through education, health, welfare and ideological inputs.

If we add all the functions of the state to the analysis, including those that directly benefit capital – such as the US/European/Japanese Quantitative Easing and other post-2008 bail-out strategies – then it is evident that only a relatively small fraction of any state's spending and financing (including loan guarantees) is directed towards social welfare. It is the failure to

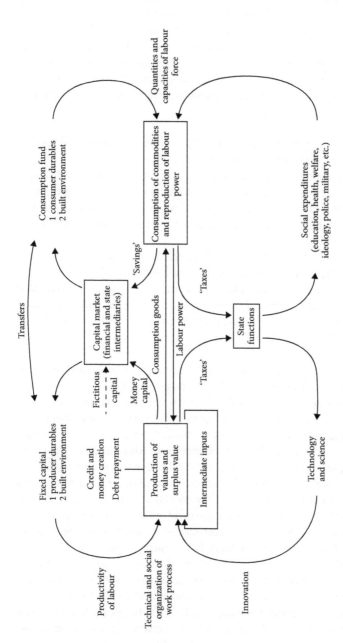

Figure 12.1   The State Within Modern Capitalism's Three Circuits

Source: David Harvey (1985).

incorporate a comprehensive view of the bias in state fiscal, monetary, security and social policy that fatally undermines the World Bank (2014: v) study that so strongly praised South Africa's 'sizable reduction in poverty and inequality through its fiscal tools'. The components of the state's role in society above were so glaring that upon omitting these other fiscal tools from an analysis claiming a reduction in Gini from 0.77 to 0.59, the Bank's staff and consultants were compelled to admit data and methodological 'limitations':

- the analysis does not take into account the quality of services delivered by the government;
- the analysis excludes some important taxes and spending such as corporate income, international trade, and property taxes, and spending such as infrastructure investments due to the lack of an established methodology for assigning these outlays across households;
- it does not capture the growing debate on how asset accumulation and returns to capital affect income inequality;
- turning to the data used in the analysis ... there are questions about the ability of a survey of this type to collect adequate information on households at the top of the distribution. (World Bank, 2014: 26)

Without these kinds of corrections to the Bank's analysis, it is impossible to declare that public funding reduces the Gini coefficient so dramatically (Woolard et al., 2015; World Bank, 2014) or is allocated in pro-poor ways (Seekings and Nattrass, 2015: 18). As one reflection of how dubious the alleged benefits are for recipients, the country's single largest budgetary spending commitment is to education. Yet, like access to most municipal services (e.g. rubbish collection that occurs regularly in mainly white neighbourhoods, but rarely if at all in the shack settlements that house a third of a typical city's residents), extreme quality differentiation results not only from racial apartheid but from ongoing segregatory processes associated with market-related residential locations. Most public schools produce an extremely low-quality education. The World Economic Forum's (2015) *Global Competitiveness Report 2015–16* rated South African schools the worst of 140 countries in terms of science and mathematics training, and 138th in overall quality. If education spending is meant to be a proxy for human capital investment (in terms of Bank logic), in many cases the result is better considered *dis*investment. As Nicholas Spaull (2013) remarked after studying 1994–2011 outcomes:

with the exception of a wealthy minority, most South African pupils cannot read, write and compute at grade-appropriate levels, with large proportions being functionally illiterate and innumerate. As far as educational outcomes, South Africa has the worst education system of all middle-income countries that participate in cross-national assessments of educational achievement.

The wealthy minority's public schools are sufficiently funded and produce extremely good education in part because of top-up systems in which parents contribute further funds. So, it could just as easily be argued that inequality is amplified (not mitigated) by the tokenistic manner in which public education is provided to the low-income majority.

This story is fairly typical of maldistributed state resources. Many of the largest spending categories – such as infrastructure mega-projects – are even more biased to supporting corporations (in this case by adding to their asset valuation through geographic advantage), which in turn adds to the explicit capital of shareholders, a form of deferred income that Bank staff should attempt to quantify, just as they do the deferred income that they assume is the outcome of education spending. In 2015, I asked the Bank's main equity consultant, Nora Lustig, why more accurate assessments of state pro-corporate spending were not attempted, so as to offset the extreme bias generated by only incorporating social spending. Her reply: 'Your questions are very valid. Regretfully, we have yet to figure out a solid methodological approach to allocate the burden/benefit to households of the list of interventions you list.'

As the October 2015 medium-term budget indicated, from $89 billion in the next year's (2016) anticipated spending, after $13.2 billion (15 per cent) allocated to public education subsidies (where differential quality is the main caveat), the next largest spending categories include $12.2 billion for 'Economic affairs' (especially economic infrastructure), $11.5 billion for housing and municipal infrastructure (including local-level facilities that support businesses and wealthier residents), $11.1 billion for 'Defence, public order and safety' (with their strong upward class biases), $10.2 billion for public health (whose merit-good disease control benefits are vital to wealthier citizens) and $8.2 billion for debt servicing. In the latter category, financiers and other bondholders are the main beneficiaries of South Africa's ever higher interest rates, resulting in projected debt payments rising faster than any other spending outlay (10.9 per cent annually) over the coming three years. When World Bank researchers consider such a budget, the biases above are impossible to contemplate: a class-analytic approach to crony capitalism, to state corporatist policies and to outright corruption of the public purse on

Table 12.1   South Africa's State Spending, 2014–19*

	2014/15 Outcome	2015/16 Revised	2016/17	2017/18	2018/19	Average annual growth 2015/16–2018/19
			Medium-term estimates			
R billion						
Basic education	**197.4**	**213.9**	**228.6**	**249.8**	**270.0**	**8.1%**
Basic education	189.2	204.5	219.2	239.6	259.3	8.2%
Arts, sport, recreation and culture	8.2	9.4	9.5	10.2	10.7	4.5%
Health	**144.6**	**157.7**	**169.7**	**184.7**	**200.6**	**8.3%**
Defence, public order and safety	**162.6**	**172.0**	**183.7**	**198.9**	**211.8**	**7.2%**
Defence and state security	47.5	50.0	53.0	57.2	60.8	6.7%
Police services	78.3	83.1	88.7	96.0	102.5	7.3%
Law courts and prisons	36.9	38.9	42.0	45.7	48.5	7.6%
Post-school education and training	**54.4**	**63.7**	**66.2**	**71.0**	**76.6**	**6.3%**
Economic affairs	**168.8**	**187.6**	**202.3**	**208.5**	**222.5**	**5.9%**
Industrial development and trade	26.4	30.4	32.2	32.6	34.9	4.7%
Employment, labour affairs and social security funds	52.3	65.7	73.1	75.4	77.8	5.8%
Economic infrastructure and network regulation	71.9	71.1	76.0	78.8	86.0	6.5%
Science, technology, innovation and the environment	18.1	20.5	20.9	21.7	23.8	5.2%
Human settlements and municipal infrastructure	**156.4**	**178.7**	**189.9**	**204.2**	**222.6**	**7.6%**
Agriculture, rural development and land reform	**24.2**	**25.6**	**26.5**	**28.3**	**30.0**	**5.4%**
General public services	**62.2**	**72.5**	**71.8**	**75.8**	**79.8**	**3.3%**
Executive and legislative organs	10.2	12.6	13.1	14.0	14.9	5.7%
General public administration and fiscal affairs	37.5	44.9	44.0	46.5	47.1	1.6%
Home affairs	7.0	7.2	7.2	7.4	9.3	8.8%
External affairs and foreign aid	7.4	7.7	7.5	7.9	8.5	3.5%
Social protection	**143.4**	**154.0**	**168.0**	**181.3**	**195.7**	**8.3%**
Allocated by function	**1114.0**	**1225.7**	**1306.6**	**1402.6**	**1509.5**	**7.2%**
Special appropriations: Eskom and New Development Bank	–	25.0	–	–	–	–
Debt-service costs	114.8	127.9	142.6	157.2	174.6	10.9%
Contingency reserve	–	–	2.5	9.0	15.0	–
Consolidated expenditure	**1228.8**	**1378.7**	**1451.7**	**1568.8**	**1699.1**	**7.2%**

Note: * Consisting of national, provincial, social security and public entities.

Source: National Treasury.

behalf of wealthy beneficiaries is apparently beyond its researchers' comprehension. Thus, in spite of Lustig's 'very valid' doubts regarding her work's value neutrality, Bank claims about South Africa's 'highly redistributive' state spending continued a year after being hotly contested (Bond, 2015a; Woolard et al., 2015).

TOKENISTIC SOCIAL POLICY IN POLITICS AND PHILOSOPHY

Setting aside all the fiscal components omitted from Bank analysis, we are assisted in judging how social democratic South Africa is by utilizing the categories of commodification and stratification, for which there are both political and philosophical underpinnings. According to Esping-Andersen (1990), three types of welfare state regimes – social democratic (Scandinavia and some other Northern European countries); corporatist (middle-Europe); and neoliberal (Anglo-Saxon countries) – reflect some of the institutional characteristics associated with the nature of the societies in which they arise (e.g. open/closed, early/late democracy and nature of state-society bargaining systems).

From the standpoint of politics, class power is usually the determinant factor: the interests of workers are to 'decommodify' their own labour power, by assuring benefits that allow them to leave the job market and to 'destratify' access to welfare services through universal (not means-tested) access. In the process, the workers' interests are to insist upon redistribution within contribution systems such as unemployment insurance, health schemes and pensions. To these ends, class coalitions are crucial to understanding how a numerically important but minority class (workers) can forge alliances with, for example (in Scandinavia), rural people, to establish social democratic systems, and conversely, why close relations between capital and the state often lead to more neoliberal welfare systems that commodify labour and generate less generous, means-tested benefits.

In South Africa during the early 1990s, class divisions suddenly opened between the mass of poor people and employed working-class members of trade unions who were formerly resident in the same slums as the poor but then became geographically mobile after racial restrictions in suburbs were lifted. The latter forged a formal Alliance with the ANC and Communist Party during the early 1990s, and then became corporatist insiders whose leaders were assimilated into the power structure (many labour elites were given the tasks of state services commercialization, for example), until in late 2013 a break was initiated by the largest trade union (the National Union of Metalworkers of South Africa), in part because of the political contradictions represented by this malfunctioning class coalition.

Philosophically, the South African ruling party is schizophrenic. It regularly talks left, and walks right – indeed oftentimes politicians talk left in order to walk right. The 'conservative macroeconomic' policy Hirsch remarked upon never changed, in spite of a 2008–10 budget deficit – one that could be blamed not on welfare expansion but instead on the 2010 World Cup's (white elephant) infrastructure financing. When it came to social policy, Franco Barchiesi (2005: 382) concluded, 'The priority on individual self-activation, under the guise of "empowerment" discourse, was combined with a view of social security and social services as "investments which lead to tangible economic gains". There was always a view, at the top levels of the ANC, that beneficiaries would change their behaviour. In the most extreme case, the 1996–2009 finance minister, Trevor Manuel, claimed at an IMF (2005) press conference:

> We have a peculiar problem in South Africa where people are entitled to a disability grant while they are receiving medication for tuberculosis. So when they heal, presumably, their disability grant, it's about US$150 a month, ends. So people have no incentive to get well. And so, they tend to come off treatment.

But three studies conducted at the same time, according to Human Sciences Research Council (HSRC) researchers, showed

> no evidence to suggest that grants, particularly the Disability Grant, act as a perverse incentive to influence individuals to deliberately neglect their health in order to access the welfare system. While this research does not exclude the possibility that such abuses may occur, it highlights the fact cases are rare and should not serve as an argument against the introduction of a necessary and constitutionally guaranteed social service. (Makiwane and Hamnca, 2010: 9)

For James Ferguson (2013: 223), the ANC's expressed fear of 'dependency' is not simply a 'lamentable manifestation of a reactionary and retrograde yearning for paternalism and inequality', it is instead 'an entirely contemporary response to the historically novel emergence of a social world where people, long understood (under both pre-capitalist and early capitalist social systems) as scarce and valuable, have instead become seen as lacking value, and in surplus'. In this context, social grant provision remains a logical component of a neoliberal state's policy repertoire, as Susan Booysen (2011: 15) argues, because it is a part of the ruling party's 'political regeneration ... the ANC-in-government is the dispenser, the patron that ensures social grants and other benefits. This is recognised as the "ANC doing good". Indeed, Moeletsi Mbeki (2011) even projects a South African 'Tunisia Day' in 2020 when, due to austerity following declining Chinese imports of minerals, 'the African National Congress government will have to cut back on social grants, which it uses to placate the black poor and to get their votes' (he was off by five years on those two pre-conditions). But more than patronage, there is also the political importance of appearing to be a generous social welfare state, especially when tokenistic expansion of social policies stands in contrast to the deeper, genuinely 'Northern European' approach based on decommodfication and destratification that Hirsch so erroneously claims.

Barchiesi (2009) concludes that South African social policy 'is characterised by a high degree of commodification, intended, borrowing from Esping-Andersen, as the dependence of social provisions and living standards on individual labour market positions and waged employment, rather than on subsidization from either employers or the state'. In describing 'the art of neoliberalism' in South Africa, Nicolas Pons-Vignon and Aurelia Segatti (2013: 507) agree that 'direct transfers can alleviate poverty, but they do little to address inequality; furthermore, they act to entrench neoliberalism if they are associated, as has been the case in South Africa, with encouraging private provision of services to the poor'. Such private provision regularly results in scandals, including an apparently corrupt $1 billion outsourcing of benefits payments, as Jane Duncan (2014) observes:

> the very act of placing public functions in private hands means that social security inevitably becomes debased by the profit motive. South Africa's social security-dependent poor are a massive captive market for profit-seeking companies. In the name of efficiency, the SA Social Security Agency has entrusted the administration of millions of South Africans' livelihoods to a private sector that appears to be more concerned about lining its own pockets than serving the poor and vulnerable.

There are caveats to South African applications of Esping-Andersen's three regime types and of his categories commodification and stratification (Sampie Terreblanche, 2002 has offered its most sophisticated expression so far), not least traditional concerns that gendered aspects of social reproduction and service provision are downplayed. But the inability of poor people to rely upon welfare as an escape from the wage labour market – since there is only a six-month unemployment grant for those who are not children, disabled or aged – leaves the typical South African worker highly commodified. The standard African (continental) response to weak employment markets is home-based agriculture, but the extent of displacement of South Africans to poorly irrigated, inhospitable farming areas makes this form of decommodifying labour very difficult.

Moreover, means-testing is applied in most areas of social policy. South Africa's 1996 Constitution locked in the principle of the means test: 'Everyone has the right to have access to social security including, *if they are unable to support themselves and their dependents*, appropriate social assistance' (emphasis added). For the Child Support Grant, as Jimi Adesina (2007: 21) complained, 'The onerous procedure for accessing the grant (documentation, forms to fill and means-testing) by applicants in mostly rural provinces, and for those who are less able to navigate the bureaucracy, is without doubt the primary source of the low take-up rate.'

Another philosophical feature of South African social policy is decentralization, which means the transfer of responsibilities to lower levels of government without the requisite financial resources to deliver services, also known as 'unfunded mandates'. By 2002, the result of these unfunded mandates meant that service charges on water and electricity were raised to cross-subsidize other municipal functions, although by then such charges consumed 30 per cent of the income of those households earning less than $70 per month (Bond, 2002). This is just one of the ways that the commodification of services led to social unrest in the form of 'service delivery protests', by some measures reaching thousands per year (Bond, 2014b).

TOKENISTIC SOCIAL POLICY IN PRACTICE:
SERVICE DISCONNECTIONS AND PRICING

By 2003, the country's leading water official, Mike Muller (2004), admitted that '275,000 of all households attributed [water supply] interruptions to cut-offs for non-payment', which extrapolates to in excess of 1.5 million people affected that year alone. The Municipal Services Project estimated that 10 million people lost services from 1994–2001 (McDonald and Pape, 2002: 22). Of these, 60 per cent were not reconnected within six weeks, according to municipalities' 'Project Viability' reports during the late 1990s (Bond, 2000: 359), indicating that poverty was primarily to blame and not the so-called 'culture of non-payment' that those now in power alleged as a negative legacy from the days of effective anti-apartheid activism (Bond, 2002). The worst disconnection rate was for fixed telephone lines, where, of 13 million people connected for the first time, 10 million were cut by 2000, as prices per call soared. This was due to the partial privatization of state phone company Telkom that resulted in the demise of internal cross-subsidies, as the new Texan and Malaysian investors attempted to maximize profits at the expense of poor customer retention during the late 1990s (Bond, 2014b).

As another reflection of commercialization and commodification processes, the 1998 national electricity policy called for the parastatal agency Eskom to apply 'cost-reflective' pricing policies, which meant much higher charges for poor people, especially those who during the 1980s and early 1990s had fought successfully for a nominal township service fee: then a $3 'fixed charge'. But the fee rose drastically by the early 2010s when much higher prices and volumetric metering applied (Bond, 2012: 188). In contrast, recognizing how vital it was to provide cheap electricity and water, the 1994 Reconstruction and Development Programme (the ANC's campaign platform) had endorsed the progressive principle of cross-subsidization, which imposed a block tariff that was meant to increase substantially for higher-volume consumers. This redistributive approach would have consciously distorted the relationship of cost to price and hence sent economically 'inefficient' pricing signals to consumers. Such signals should have meant that poor people could consume more essential services (for the sake of gender equity, health and economic side benefits), while rich people and big businesses would embrace conservation (and hence environmental protection) by cutting back on their hedonistic consumption levels, thanks to much higher prices.

Neoliberal critics of progressive block tariffs insisted that such distortions of market logic would introduce a disincentive to supply low-volume users; their assumption is that the whole point of public utility supply is to make profits or at least to break even in narrow cost-recovery terms. In advocating against the proposal for a free lifeline and a rising block tariff, a leading World Bank expert (Roome, 1995: 51) advised the first democratic water minister, Kader Asmal, that privatization contracts 'would be much harder to establish' if poor consumers had the expectation of getting something for nothing. If consumers weren't paying, the advisor argued, South African authorities required a 'credible threat of cutting service'. To that end, new technologies for disciplining poor people also emerged in this period, as Greg Ruiters (2007: 195) found: 'The prepaid system in telephones, electricity and increasingly water has clearly become a state "civilising" tool for the marketised political "management" of the ungovernable poor.'

These approaches foiled a genuinely redistributive strategy. Not even the next water minister, the vocal communist revolutionary Ronnie

Kasrils, could fulfil his (heartfelt) commitment to implement a free basic water policy. Indeed, Kasrils' high-profile promise in early 2000 led the authors of the World Bank's (2000: Annex 2, 3) *Sourcebook on Community Driven Development in the Africa Region* to recommend a typical neoliberal policy for pricing water: 'Work is still needed with political leaders in some national governments to move away from the concept of free water for all.' In 1999, the Bank had claimed that the water advisor's 1995 pricing recommendations were 'instrumental in facilitating a radical revision in South Africa's approach to bulk water management' (World Bank, 1999: Annex C, 5), and also to Asmal's revision away from the 1994 Recon-struction and Development Programme 'lifeline' water supply mandate (Bond and Khosa, 1999).

By the time that mandate was finally honoured by Kasrils, the commercialization instinct was already thoroughly accepted by munici-palities. As a result, the right to water ended up either being sabotaged or delivered in a tokenistic way, that is, free for merely the first 6 kilolitres/ household/month (kl/hh/m). To illustrate, in Durban – the main site of Free Basic Water pilot-exploration starting in 1998 – the overall cost of water ended up doubling for poor households because of a huge price increase in the second bloc (the city soon had the second-highest price amongst its South African peers for 6–10 kl/hh/m). For poor people, this led to consumption cuts by a third in the subsequent six years, from 22 kl/hh/m to 15 (Bond, 2010: 456). Matters were even worse in rural areas, where extremely serious problems arose in the community water supply projects, and the main reasons for unsustainability of a water system invariably included genuine affordability constraints (Hemson, 2003).

FUNDING CONSTRAINTS TO SOUTH AFRICAN SOCIAL DEMOCRACY?

Could South Africa's Treasury spend more? After all, state spending in relation to GDP has stayed in the 22–29 per cent range since 1994, far lower than typical European social democracies. In relative terms, Pretoria's capacity to serve its citizenry steadily shrunk in comparison to the size of the economy, for across the terrain of social and public policy, government's 'general services' role in GDP rose from 16.2 per cent in 1994 to 17.3 per cent in 1998, but fell back to 15.8 per cent by 2002 and 13.7 per cent in 2012. Reflecting the cost-recovery approach to service delivery and hence the inability of the state to properly roll out and maintain these functions, the category of GDP components termed 'electricity, gas and water' declined steadily from 3.5 per cent to 2.4 per cent to 1.8 per cent of GDP from 1994 to 2002 to 2012. The cutbacks were not due to the elimination of fraud and waste; instead, the state was underspending in general, compared to peers. The 2010 internal gross public debt of South Africa was less than 40 per cent of GDP, well below high-performance countries Malaysia, Brazil, Argentina and Thailand, and was rising relatively slowly (Figure 12.2).

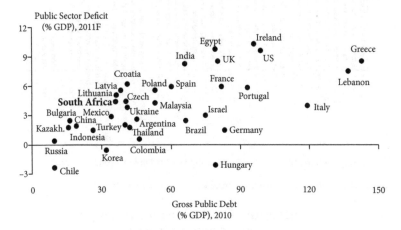

Figure 12.2 Annual Public Deficit and Public Debt in Comparative Terms, 2011

Source: Barclays Capital (2012).

So, on the one hand, with political will (not the cynical stinginess exhibited by a succession of finance ministers), state fiscal support for the social wage was not terribly difficult to raise in absolute and relative terms. This was partially attempted, but in a tokenistic way, by broadening the inherited, formerly racially delineated social programmes, like the child grant and pension, to include all South Africans. The expansion entailed a fiscal commitment that was actually quite limited, with state social spending never exceeding a 3 per cent increase in GDP beyond 1994 levels. As the Financial and Fiscal Commission (2011: 14) reported, even dating to 1983, social transfers rose from just 1.8 to 4.5 per cent of GDP through 2007 and, as a result, 'Post-1994 expansion of the grants system has not threatened fiscal sustainability.' From an inherited budget deficit of –7.3 per cent in 1993, the Treasury shrunk the deficit and even achieved a primary budget surplus of more than 1 per cent by 2008, before the subsequent economic meltdown forced a renewal of (moderate) deficit spending. However, the sum of state social spending by the South African government was so limited that in relation to GDP, only four out of the world's 40 largest economies had a lower ratio (South Korea, Mexico, China and India – all of which had much lower Gini coefficients) (Figure 12.3).

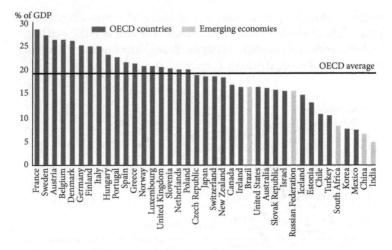

Figure 12.3 Public Social Expenditure in the World's Largest Economies, 2011

Source: Organisation for Economic Co-operation and Development (2011).

CONCLUSION: BOTTOM-UP *COMMONING* NOT TOP-DOWN *TOKENISM*

South Africa's welfare state is terribly unsatisfactory, given the society's wealth, world-leading inequality and record of social mobilization against injustice. The repeated claim that South African welfare grants lift people from poverty needs to be considered critically. Barchiesi (2009) rebuts, 'More useful would be rather to see social grants as a specific biopolitical intervention. Taken individually, they are in fact so meagre that even receiving more than one in a single household is no guarantee of a life out of poverty.' Overall, the size and orientation of social grants is inadequate, and a summary more than a decade ago by Nina Hunter, Julian May and Vishnu Padayachee (2003: 21) still applies: 'The grants do not provide comprehensive coverage for those in need. Unless they are able to access the disability grant, [pre-retiree] adults are largely excluded from this framework of assistance.'

Other problems were legion: means-testing was utilized with the inevitable stigmatization that comes with a state demanding proof of poor people's income; cost-recovery strategies were still being imposed, by stealth, on recipients of state services; the state's potentially vast job-creating capacity was never utilized aside from a few short-term public works activities; and land and housing were not delivered at appropriate rates. State housing, for instance, is tokenistic because it is supplied:

- in forms usually half as large, built with flimsier materials than during apartheid
- typically with over-priced water and electricity via self-disconnecting meters
- with lower-grade state services including rare rubbish collection, inhumane sanitation, dirt roads, no street lights, no sidewalks and inadequate storm-water drainage
- even away further from jobs and amenities than under apartheid (Bond, 2000, 2014b).

What can we conclude about the ANC government's commitment to South Africa's increasingly angry poor and working-class majority? While Barchiesi (2011) makes a compelling, detailed case to link state policy and practices to the changing nature of the labour market using the phrase 'precarious liberation' (emphasizing as he does the imperative of wage labour for the majority of people), I prefer *tokenistic* to describe how neoliberal nationalism treats its poorer constituencies, who in 2014 voted for the same party whose policies and practices drove them to what is quite possibly the world's highest per capita rate of social protest. To be sure, the share of eligible voters who supported the ANC fell from 53 per cent in 1994 to 42 per cent in 1999 to 39 per cent in 2004 and 2009, to 36 per cent in 2014, what with the steady rise in stay-away voters (McKinley, 2014). It may take quite a while before that figure falls to the point that leftist electoral alternatives can become a threat, including the Economic Freedom Fighters (who campaigned to double the size of grants and won more than 6 per cent of the vote in 2014) or a potential new workers' party led by the metalworkers' union.

The practical alternative to tokenistic welfare in South Africa is a policy based on *commoning* of social resources, funded by more progressively applied state tax and fee revenues, and won through bottom-up struggle in which policy is shaped by activists. To conclude, two examples are illustrative: AIDS medicines and water. The first relates to the world's most important breakthrough in commoning activism: knowledge production, especially the various facets of the internet that decommodify and destratify information. The most vital gain to South African society came thanks to a specific attack on intellectual property in the period 1999–2004 by the Treatment Action Campaign (TAC), made up mainly of black HIV+ South Africans.

An individual's access to ARV medicines cost $15,000 per year in the early 2000s, restricting the ability to buy decades worth of longer life to a tiny, wealthy (and mainly white) minority. As a result of strong lobbying by progressive new bureaucrats and the courage of Health Minister

Nkosazana Dlamini-Zuma, the South African government's 1997 Medicines Act made provision for compulsory licensing of patented drugs, especially ARVs for the country's 5 million HIV+ population. That law was immediately confronted by the US State Department's 'full court press' (the formal description given to the US Congress), in large part to protect intellectual property rights generally, and specifically to prevent the emergence of a parallel inexpensive supply of AIDS medicines that would undermine lucrative Western markets (Bond, 2014b; Nattrass, 2003).

US Vice President Al Gore directly intervened with South African government leaders in 1998–99 to revoke the law's implementation. But in July 1999, Gore launched his 2000 presidential election bid, a campaign generously funded by big pharmaceutical corporations (which in a prior election cycle provided \$2.3 million to the Democratic Party) and as an explicit counterweight, the TAC's allies in the AIDS Coalition to Unleash Power (ACTUP) began to protest at his campaign events. The protests ultimately threatened to cost Gore far more in adverse publicity than he was raising in Big Pharma contributions, so he withdrew opposition to the Medicines Act, as did Bill Clinton a few weeks later at the World Trade Organization's aborted Seattle summit. By late 2001, the Doha Agenda of the World Trade Organization adopted explicit language permitting violation of Trade Related Intellectual Property Rights for medical emergencies (Bond, 2003).

The South African government remained reluctant to provide medicines, however, for a variety of dubious reasons, in part related to Mbeki's 'denialism' that HIV causes AIDS (Geffen, 2010; Mbali, 2013). As a result, the TAC was compelled to file a Constitutional Court case that succeeded in at least gaining access to Nevirapine for pregnant, HIV+ women in public hospitals. The TAC then won a ferocious battle within the ANC government, and by late 2003 managed to have the ANC policy reversed by the party's National Executive Committee, although implementation took several more years. Local generics-medicines manufacturers Aspen and Adcock Ingram then managed to lower costs substantially through voluntary licensing of the major AIDS drugs. It is in this sense that not only decommodification but also deglobalization of capital was considered vital to expanding access, as was likewise the globalization of solidarity a critical factor in weakening global capital's power. The resulting gain in South African average life expectancy was from 52 in 2004 to 62 by 2015, as 3 million people were brought into state ARV treatment, people who would not before have had a chance.

A similar programme of decommodification occurred in grassroots social movements and amongst sophisticated community groups that learned how to illegally reconnect water piping and electricity wiring in the anti-apartheid struggle era, and applied those skills during the era of water commercialization, from the 1990s through the present. Initially, some were inspired by the 1996 South African Constitution's promises that 'Everyone has the right to have access to sufficient food and water ... [and] to an environment that is not harmful to their health or well-being.' Water activists insisted upon a social entitlement to an acceptable supply of clean water, amounting to at least 50 litres each day, delivered via a metering system based on credit, not 'prepayment'. As noted in the pages above, however, the system chosen was tokenistic, with just 25 litres per capita per day and via prepayment meters, with water provided by the Paris company Suez that had commercialized Johannesburg's supply.

The Soweto activists took their case to court, but also engaged in popular resistance tactics: informal, illegal reconnections to official water supplies and destruction of prepayment meters in public protests. These represent grassroots communing strategies, as teams of electricians and plumbers fanned out regularly from groups like the Soweto Electricity Crisis Committee to not only vigorously protest services commodification but act concretely to solve the problem. And their orientation was not just of a practical day-to-day nature but also firmly ideological, aiming towards a community-empowered socialism that, in its finest hours, delivers the basic necessities of life to residents free, using their popular mobilizing capacities (Bond and Ngwane, 2010).

The Soweto activists' Constitutional Court challenge to water services failed in late 2009, but in the process, a broader conception of rights emerged that entailed making water primarily an 'eco-social' rather than a commercial good (Bond, 2013a). Including eco-systemic processes in discussions of water rights potentially links consumption processes (including over-consumption by firms, golf courses, commercial agriculture and wealthy households) to environmental sustainability; in other words, the broader hydropolitical systems in which water extraction, production, distribution, financing, consumption and disposal occurs. This necessarily leads to a vision of commoning, far different and more expansive than welfarist politics generally allow.

All too briefly we have seen how South Africa's progressive forces established the difference between 'reformist reforms' and reforms that advanced a 'non-reformist' agenda, to borrow the terminology of Gorz (1967). The latter attempts were to win gains that did not strengthen the internal logic of the system, but that instead empowered the system's opponents. Hence, unlike reformist reforms, non-reformist reforms would not have a co-optive character. Neither would they lessen the momentum of reformers (as did many successful reformist reforms). Rather, they heightened the level of meaningful confrontation by opening up new terrains of struggle. For accessing AIDS medicines and water – and many other decommodification agendas – the South African commoning cases are both inspiring and useful.

Finally, there is a raft of complementary macroeconomic policies that should be considered for adoption, if ever a social democratic (or socialist) ruling party replaces the ANC neoliberal nationalists. These would reverse the tendency of the post-apartheid government to adopt policies generally favourable to financial institutions and the Minerals Energy Complex (Bond, 2013b). Such alternative policies would in turn make financing a generous welfare state feasible:

- reimpose exchange controls, lower interest rates, audit South Africa's 'Odious Debt', control illicit capital flows and trade
- adopt industrial policy aimed at import substitution, sectoral rebalancing, social needs, eco-sustainability
- increase state social spending, paid for by higher corporate taxes, cross-subsidization and more domestic borrowing (and loose-money 'Quantitative Easing' too, if necessary, aimed not at bank bail-outs but at raising domestic demand)
- reorient infrastructure finance away from high-carbon export-oriented mega-projects to instead meet unmet basic needs, and expand/maintain/improve energy grid, sanitation, public transport, clinics, schools, recreational facilities and the internet and
- adopt 'Million Climate Jobs' strategies to generate employment for a genuinely green 'Just Transition'.

It will be a heroic feat to establish the political basis for social democracy, much less socialism, even though a 'United Front' of labour, community, women, youth, the elderly, environmentalists, the gay rights movement and other progressives was initiated by the National Union of Metalworkers of South Africa – Africa's largest trade union with 380,000 members in 2015 – to do just that (Bond, 2014b). Under construction at the time of writing, the Front had many teething pains, and major fissures began opening up between labour and others in civil society by late 2015. A socialist party was mooted by the metalworkers, to bring demands to fruition in state policy, but its failure to achieve the anticipated launch in 2015 allowed leftist political space in the 2016 municipal elections to again be taken by the Economic Freedom Fighters.

However, no matter the success of various alliances that appeared logical (though by no means assured) in the period leading up to South

Africa's next national election in 2019, non-reformist reform initiatives could still be undertaken in civil society, in the spirit of TAC's extraordinary victory. Campaigning for non-tokenistic welfare policies could at least point South Africa towards a broader liberatory politics so urgently needed in so many spheres of society, even if genuine social democracy remained on the horizon for many years to come.

NOTE

1. By 2015 the national profit rate had plummeted, along with the price of commodities. Several major firms with strong South African operations – Anglo American, Glencore, Lonmin and others – were devalued by London investors to levels as low (in Lonmin's case) as 5 per cent of prior recent peaks. Once Africa's largest corporation and the biggest company on the Johannesburg Stock Exchange until its delisting in 2000, Anglo American announced in late 2015 that it would fire more than 60 per cent of its global workforce; its peak to trough share value decline was 95 per cent. The South African state's purchase of failing mining houses – 'lemon socialism' – began to occur by stealth, via the civil service pension fund. The decline in state revenues that followed logically from such systematic corporate corruption and the fiscally austere context means that even the mere extension (not transformation) of apartheid's inherited social policies will be truncated. Potentially transformative strategies such as National Health Insurance have been put on hold. As 2016 brought more explicit austerity, including 2016–17 real budget cuts in social welfare grants, municipal subsidies and housing, the claim that South Africa is social democratic looked ever more outlandish.

BIBLIOGRAPHY

Websites were last accessed 16 December 2015.

Adesina, J. (2007). 'Social Policy and the Quest for Inclusive Development: Research Findings from Sub-Saharan Africa'. United Nations Research Institute for Social Development Social Policy and Development Programme Paper No. 33, Geneva, May.

Barber, S. (2014). 'South Africa's ANC Moves from Detente to Entente with a Dynamic Private Sector'. *Foreign Policy*, 18 November. Available at www.foreignpolicy.com/sponsored/southafricaat20/in-south-africa-a-new-plan-for-private-sector-growth.

Barchiesi, F. (2005). 'Social Citizenship and the Transformations of Wage in the Making of Post-apartheid South Africa, 1994–2001'. Doctoral thesis, University of the Witwatersrand, Johannesburg.

—— (2009). 'That Melancholic Object of Desire'. Johannesburg Workshop on Theory and Criticism, University of the Witwatersrand, Johannesburg. Available at http://jwtc.org.za/the_salon/volume_1/franco_barchiesi.htm.

—— (2011). *Precarious Liberation*. Albany: State University of New York Press.

Barclays Capital (2012). 'Global Portfolio Manager's Digest'. 4 March, London.

Bhorat, H. (2013). 'Economic Inequality is a Major Obstacle'. *New York Times*, 28 July.

Bhorat, H., Van der Westhuizen, C. and Jacobs, T. (2009). 'Income and Non-income Inequality in Post-apartheid South Africa: What are the Drivers and Possible Policy Interventions?'. University of Cape Town. Available at www.researchgate. net/publication/228269383_Income_and_Non-Income_Inequality_in_Post-Apartheid_South_Africa_What_are_the_Drivers_and_Possible_Policy_Interventions.

Bond, P. (2000). *Cities of Gold, Townships of Coal*. Trenton: Africa World Press.

——(2002). *Unsustainable South Africa*. London: Merlin.

——(2003). *Against Global Apartheid*. London: Zed Books.

——(2010). 'Water, Health and the Commodification Debate'. *Review of Radical Political Economics*, 42 (3): 445–64.

—— (2012). *Politics of Climate Justice: Paralysis Above, Movement Below*. Pietermaritzburg: University of KwaZulu-Natal Press.

——(2013a). 'Water Rights, Commons and Advocacy Narratives'. *South African Journal of Human Rights*, 29: 1.

——(2013b). 'Historical Varieties of Space, Scale and Speculation in South Africa: The Uneven and Combined Geographical Development of Financialised Capitalism'. *Transformation*, 81/82: 179–207.

——(2014a). 'Tokenistic Social Policy in South Africa'. *Transformation*, 86: 48–77.

——(2014b). *Elite Transition: From Apartheid to Neoliberalism in South Africa*. London: Pluto Press.

—— (2015a). 'Bretton Woods Institution Narratives About Inequality and Economic Vulnerability on the Eve of South African Austerity'. *International Journal of Health Services*, 45 (3): 415–42. DOI: 10.1177/0020731415584561.

——(2015b). 'Nene Falls in with Big Business'. *Mail&Guardian*, 6 March. Available at http://mg.co.za/article/2015-03-06-nene-falls-in-with-big-business.

Bond, P. and Khosa, M. (1999). *An RDP Policy Audit*. Pretoria: Human Sciences Research Council Press.

Bond, P. and Ngwane, T. (2010). 'Community Resistance to Energy Privatisation in South Africa'. In K. Abramsky (ed.), *Sparking a Worldwide Energy Revolution: Social Struggles in the Transition to a Post-petrol World*. Oakland, AK Press: 197–208.

Booysen, S. (2011). 'The ANC and the Regeneration of Political Power, 1994–2011'. Paper presented at the conference, One Hundred Years of the ANC: Debating Liberation Histories and Democracy Today, Johannesburg, 20–24 September.

Coleman, N. (2013). 'The National Development Plan: The Devil is in the Economic Detail'. *Daily Maverick*. Available at www.dailymaverick.co.za/opinionista/2013-04-03-national-development-plan-the-devil-is-in-the-economic-detail/#.Vn9o4FIpV4M.

Cowell, A. (1986). 'South Africa Without Apartheid'. *New York Times*, 22 June. Available at www.nytimes.com/1986/06/22/business/south-africa-without-apartheid.html.

Cronje, F. (2012a). 'SA Service Delivery "No Failure": SAIRR'. Press statement, Johannesburg, 11 September. Available at http://nepadwatercoe.org/south-africa-sa-service-delivery-no-failure-sairr/.

——(2012b). Private correspondence with Patrick Bond, 13 September. Available upon request from pbond@mail.ngo.za.

Devereux, S. (2011). 'Social Protection in South Africa: Exceptional or Exceptionalism?'. *Canadian Journal of Development Studies*, 32 (4): 414–25.

Duncan, J. (2014). 'Social Security Debased by the Profit Motive'. *Mail&Guardian*, 3 January. Available at http://mg.co.za/article/2014-01-02-social-security-debased-by-the-profit-motive.

Ensor, L. (2015). 'Nene Urged to Make Real Commitment to Fiscal Discipline'. 24 February. Available at www.bdlive.co.za/economy/2015/02/24/nene-urged-to-make-real-commitment-to-fiscal-discipline.

Esping-Andersen, G. (1990). *The Three Worlds of Welfare Capitalism*. Princeton: Princeton University Press.

Ferguson, J. (2013). 'Declarations of Dependence: Labor, Personhood, and Welfare in Southern Africa'. *Journal of the Royal Anthropological Institute*, 19 (2): 223–42.

Financial and Fiscal Commission (2011). 'Submission for the Division of Revenue 2011/12'. Midrand, 6 September. Available at http://pmg-assets.s3-website-eu-west-1.amazonaws.com/docs/100602FFC_0.ppt.

FM Fox (2014). '8 Out of 10 Managers Commit Economic Crime in SA, PwC Survey'. *Financial Mail*, 20 February. Available at www.financialmail.co.za/fmfox/2014/02/20/8-out-of-10-managers-commit-economic-crime-in-sa-pwc-survey.

Forslund, D. (2012). 'Wages, Profits and Labor Productivity in South Africa'. *Amandla!*, 24 January.

Geffen, N. (2010). *Debunking Delusions*. Johannesburg: Jacana Media.

Gorz, A. (1967). *Strategy for Labor*. Boston: Beacon Press.

Harvey, D. (1985). *The Urbanization of Capital*. Baltimore: Johns Hopkins University Press.

Hemson, D. (2003). 'Rural Poor Play a Role in Water Projects'. *Business Day*, 1 July.

Hirsch, A. (2005). *Season of Hope: Economic Reform under Mbeki and Mandela*. Ottawa: International Development Research Centre.

Hosken, G. (2014). 'World Fraud Champs'. *The Times*, 19 February. Available at http://m.timeslive.co.za/thetimes/?articleId=11053736.

Hunter, N., May, J. and Padayachee, V. (2003). 'Lessons for PRSP from Poverty Reduction Strategies in South Africa'. University of KwaZulu-Natal School of Development Studies, Durban. Available at http://sds.ukzn.ac.za/files/wp39.pdf.

IMF (International Monetary Fund) (2005). Transcript of a Joint IMF/World Bank Town Hall with Civil Society. Washington, DC. Available at www.imf.org/external/np/tr/2005/tr050922a.html.

—— (2013). 'South Africa: 2013 Article IV Consultation'. Washington, DC. Available at www.imf.org/external/pubs/cat/longres.aspx?sk=40971.0.

Joffe, H. (2014). 'World Bank Tax Study Holds Important Lessons for SA'. *Business Day*, 12 November. Available at www.bdlive.co.za/opinion/columnists/2014/11/12/world-bank-tax-study-holds-important-lessons-for-sa.

——(2015). 'Piketty's Wealth Tax Fails to Solve SA's Inequality Riddle'. 7 October. Available at www.bdlive.co.za/opinion/columnists/2015/10/07/pikettys-wealth-tax-fails-to-solve-sas-inequality-riddle.

Kantor, B. (2014). 'Address Poverty in SA and Let Inequality Look After Itself'. *ZAeconomist*, 20 November. Available at www.zaeconomist.com/sa-economy/address-poverty-in-sa-and-let-inequality-look-after-itself/.

Katzenellenbogen, J. (2014). 'SA's Choice: Crisis or Reform?'. *PoliticsWeb*, 11 November. Available at www.politicsweb.co.za/politicsweb/view/politicsweb/en/page71619?oid=797617&sn=Detail&pid=71616.

Leibbrandt, M., Woolard, I., McEwen, H. and Koep, C. (2010). *Employment and Inequality Outcomes in Southern Africa*. Report for the Organisation for Economic Co-operation and Development by the Southern Africa Labor and Development Research Unit and School of Economics, University of Cape Town.

Makiwane, M. and Hamnca, M. (2010). 'A Proposal for the Establishment of a Chronic Diseases Grant'. Human Sciences Research Council, Pretoria.

Mala, J. (2012). 'Economic Overview'. Industrial Development Corporation, *Access Newsletter*, April. Available at www.idc.co.za/access/economicoverview-april-2012.

Manuel, T. (2014). 'Confronting the Challenge of Poverty and Inequality'. Helen Suzman Memorial Lecture, Gibson Institute for Business Studies, University of Pretoria, 7 November. Available at www.politicsweb.co.za/politicsweb/view/politicsweb/en/page71656?oid=798431&sn=Detail&pid=71616.

Mbali, M. (2013). *South African Aids Activism and Global Health Politics*. London: Palgrave Macmillan.

Mbeki, M. (2011). 'Only a Matter of Time Before the Bomb Explodes'. *ThoughtLeader*, 12 February. Available at www.leader.co.za/article.aspx?s=23&f=1&a=2571.

McDonald, D. and Pape, J. (eds) (2002). *Cost Recovery and the Crisis of Service Delivery in South Africa*. London: Zed Books.

McKinley, D. (2014). 'The Real Story of South Africa's National Election'. *Links*, 11 May. Available at http://links.org.au/node/3845.

Muller, M. (2004). 'Keeping the Taps Open'. *Mail&Guardian*. Available at http://mg.co.za/article/2004-06-30-keeping-the-taps-open.

Nattrass, N. (2003). *The Moral Economy of AIDS*. Cambridge: Cambridge University Press.

Netshitenzhe, J. (2004). 'A Social Partnership is Required for Growth in the Next 10 Years'. *The Sunday Times*, 4 April.

Nzimande, B. (2012). 'Transforming University and Society'. *Politicsweb*, 2 October. Available at www.politicsweb.co.za/politicsweb/view/politicsweb/en/page72308?oid=32 9837&sn=Marketingweb+detail&pid=90389.

Organisation for Economic Co-operation and Development (2011). 'Public Social Expenditures in OECD Countries and Emerging Economies'.

Paris. Available at www.keepeek.com/Digital-Asset-Management/oecd/social-issues-migration-health/divided-we-stand/public-social-expenditure-in-oecd-countries-and-emerging-economies_9789264119536-graph23-en#page1.

Padayachee, V. (2015). 'Piketty's Contribution to Unpacking Inequality'. *The Conversation*, 29 September. Available at https://theconversation.com/pikettys-contribution-to-unpacking-inequality-timely-and-relevant-48070.

Parsons, R. (ed.) (2009). *Zumanomics*. Johannesburg: Jacana Media.

——(2015). 'Piketty's Fix for Inequality in Sync with Development Plan'. *Business Day*, 28 September. Available at www.bdlive.co.za/opinion/2015/09/28/pikettys-fix-for-inequality-in-sync-with-development-plan.

Pons-Vignon, N. and Segatti, A. (2013). '"The Art of Neoliberalism": Accumulation, Institutional Change and Social Order since the End of Apartheid'. *Review of African Political Economy*, 40 (138): 507–18.

Roome, J. (1995). 'Water Pricing and Management: World Bank Presentation to the SA Water Conservation Conference'. Unpublished paper, Johannesburg, 2 October.

Ruiters, G. (2007). 'Disciplinary Commodification and Self-disconnections: Contradictions in Municipal Services in Contemporary South Africa'. *Critical Social Policy*, 27: 487–508.

Saul, J. and Bond, B. (2014). *South Africa – Present as History*. London: James Currey Press.

Seekings, J. (2005). 'Visions, Hopes and Views About the Future: The Radical Moment of South African Welfare Reform'. In S. Dubow and A. Jeeves (eds), *South Africa's 1940s: Worlds of Possibilities*. Cape Town: Double Storey Books.

Seekings, J. and Nattrass, N. (2015). *Policy, Politics and Poverty in South Africa*. Geneva: United Nations Research Institute on Social Development.

Spaull, N. (2013). 'South Africa's Education Crisis: The Quality of Education in South Africa 1994–2011'. Centre for Development and Enterprise Working Paper, Johannesburg, October.

Stanwix, B. (2015). 'Rhodes Must Fall Replaces Piketty', *GroundUp*, 30 September. Available at http://groundup.org.za/article/rhodes-must-fall-replaces-piketty-uct_3349.

Terreblanche, S. (2002). *A History of Inequality in South Africa, 1652–2000*. Pietermaritzburg: University of Natal Press.

Valodia, I. (2015). 'What South Africa Can Learn from Piketty About Addressing Inequality'. *The Conversation*, 20 September. Available at https://theconversation.com/what-south-africa-can-learn-from-piketty-about-addressing-inequality-47658.

Van der Berg, S. (2009). 'Fiscal Incidence of Social Spending in South Africa. 2006'. Working Papers 10/2009. Department of Economics, Stellenbosch University.

Weisenthal, J. (2012). 'This Country Defaulted, and Now it has One of the Healthiest Public Sectors in the World'. *Business Insider*, 5 March. Available at www.businessinsider.com/chart-of-the-day-this-country-defaulted-and-now-it-has-one-of-the-healthiest-public-sectors-in-the-world-2012-3.

Woolward, I., Metz, R., Inchauste, G., Lustig, N., Maboshe, M. and Purfield, C. (2015). 'How Much is Inequality Reduced by Progressive Taxation and Government Spending?'. *Econ3x3*. Available at www.econ3x3.org/article/how-much-inequality-reduced-progressive-taxation-and-government-spending#sthash.nuwTTm2n.dpuf.

World Bank (1999). *Country Assistance Strategy: South Africa.* Washington, DC: World Bank, Annex C.

——(2000). *Sourcebook on Community Driven Development in the Africa Region: Community Action Programs.* Washington, DC, 17 March.

——(2014). *Fiscal Policy and Redistribution in an Unequal Society.* South Africa Economic Update No. 6. Washington, DC: World Bank Group, 1 November. Available at http://documents.worldbank.org/curated/en/2014/11/20339043/south-africa-economic-update-fiscal-policy-redistribution-unequal-society.

World Economic Forum (2015). *Global Competitiveness Report 2015–16.* Davos. Available at www.weforum.org/reports/global-competitiveness-report-2015-2016/.

13

Conclusion: Limits to Social Democracy, Populist Moments and Left Alternatives

Ingo Schmidt

Social democracy is at a dead end, but by no means dead. The idea of providing legal protections against the inequalities produced by unfettered market competition used to be of prime importance to social democratic parties, now this potential equalizer has been downgraded to just one among other issues. For most of the twentieth century, this idea gripped the masses more than anything else coming from the left. Ruling elites and bourgeois parties felt compelled to strike deals with social democrats and unions who represented a large portion of these masses. Yet, when the elites felt the deal was turning into a threat to their property and profits, they found ways to appeal to those same masses. Masses who, around the same time, felt increasingly alienated from party and union bosses that made decisions on their behalf in increasingly bureaucratic and arcane institutions of the welfare state. Capitalists, keen to restore their class power, stepped into the breach between the toiling masses and their representatives, a breach that had opened because of increasing distrust, with a call for market liberties as opposed to state regulations. They terminated the truce between labour and capital, on which the Keynesian welfare state was built, and began rebranding the state as a tax absorbing machine feeding unproductive rent-seekers, sucking the life-blood out of the productive elements of society.

Marxist notions of capitalist exploitation of the working class were effectively transformed into charges against the state as the exploiter of both workers and their employers. By doing so, the assault on the Keynesian welfare state, a system that provided workers certain protections against unfettered capitalist rule, was disguised as state assault on workers and capitalists alike. This masterpiece in ideological warfare picked up widespread discontent within existing welfare states and, by doing so, offered an alternative to the divisive articulations of discontent coming from the left. Rather than agitating for class struggle, as much of the left did, the neoliberal right successfully appealed to notions of 'the people' against state-protected privilege, notions deeply entrenched in Western political imagination since the English and French revolutions. At the same time that neoliberal populism articulated the resentments felt by many of the people who benefited from the welfare state, because of the bureaucratic and patronizing ways in which it was managed, the message increasingly lost its appeal as social standards were reduced by neoliberal practice.

Once the neoliberal class struggle from above began, many of the same people who had fallen for neoliberalism's populist message recognized that they weren't on the receiving end of the new policies. They also realized that, for them, a bureaucratic welfare state was better than no welfare state. At a time when capitalists were celebrating the collapse of Soviet communism and busy elevating neoliberalism to a global level, social democratic parties had a comeback in their Western European heartlands. But the parties that were voted back into office in the 1990s weren't the same as those who had been unseated in the 1970s or early 1980s. The resurgence in voter support in the 1990s did not indicate that the same social basis that had supported social democracy and its welfare state project from the 1950s to the 1970s was back in power after a period of electoral estrangement between working class core con- stituencies and their representatives in the political system (Rennwald and Evans, 2014). The parties were still there, but the working classes that once supported them were no longer connected by networks of the ideas and identities that had tied individuals together, not despite but because of the fact that they were hotly debated at various times. Without this ideological cement, the institutions that had been built to run the welfare state became porous and open to the infusion of neoliberal ideas (Schmidt, 2014a). Also, the reorganization of labour processes with their relocations, outsourcings and implementation of labour-saving technologies had significantly undermined workers' bargaining power (Silver, 2003). Unions that were used to representing workers within the institutional framework of the welfare state had no capacity to stage an effective fightback against neoliberal restructuring.

With the ideological cement of labour movements crumbling and its bargaining power fading, social democrats loosened their ties to labour. To get their share in the electoral market, they thought it was time to diversify their political offerings. Consequently, party strategists downgraded the welfare state agenda, added allegedly post-materialist values such as gender equality and ecological concerns and wrapped the new policy mix into civil society discourse (Kitschelt, 1994; Meyer, 2008). This discourse became popular in intellectual circles who were disappointed by the defeat of 1970s radicalism and were unable to imagine socialism after the collapse of the Soviet Union. This new policy mix was good to convert scattered discontent into occasional election victories, but it never gripped the masses in a way that would have turned them into a material force capable of weathering economic crises and class struggle from above. Without such a force, though, social democratic parties, once elected into office, were captive to capitalist demands to slash social standards, spending and corporate taxes. Social democratic parties proved incapable of representing social democratic ideas. While the latter gained popularity with the advance of neoliberalism, the former could gain nothing more than the occasional election victory.

There simply wasn't the social force necessary to re-establish the social democratic hegemony comparable to that of the post-World War II (WWII) period, when even conservative and liberal parties had to integrate welfare state expansion into their political platforms. The 1980s saw the retreat of not only labour movements but also the new social movements. In the 1970s, new social movements were a fresh force establishing gender and ecology as items on agendas across the political spectrum. However, they were not as deeply grounded in the class politics of the left, and less institutionalized than the welfare state, and thus more open to neoliberal cooptation (Fraser, 2009; Wolf, 2007). This was particularly so because new social movements and neoliberalism, even though originally coming from entirely different angles, rallied support around the critique of welfare states and their bureaucracies. The new social movements and the welfare state left were unable to turn the critique coming from the former into a fruitful coalition to build more inclusive and less bureaucratic welfare states, and the new social movements were also too weak to establish themselves as an independent force of the left. Consequently, the agenda they had launched was up for grabs by the emerging neoliberal bloc (Schmidt, 2011). By the time social democrats eventually added ecology and gender to their platforms, the movements behind these issues had been pushed to the radical margins. As party strategists were trying to modernize the fuddy-duddy image of social democracy, it was precisely the welfare state agenda associated with this image that became popular again. Unfortunately, social democratic parties would only cater to this resurgence of welfare state popularity in very small portions.

As a result, social democratic ideas increasingly lost their representation in the political system and were thus open for redefinition and rearticulation in different terms. More and more, the rather specific social democratic idea of using the state as a countervailing power to unfettered markets was replaced by populist notions of 'us' against 'them'.

Neoliberal populism was the trailblazer of this tactic when it articulated discontent with the Keynesian welfare state as a conflict between an all usurping state and a mass of hard working individuals, no matter whether they sold their ability to work or were the ones buying this ability (Bray, 2015; Weyland, 1999). Once neoliberal practice produced its own discontent, 'us' and 'them' was redefined to articulate these new discontents. Populisms from the right, such as 'us domestics' versus 'them immigrants', or the left, such as 'the 99% versus the 1%', caught the fading hegemony of neoliberalism, and social democrats who created their own civil society version of it, in the middle. The inability of social democratic parties to articulate discontent in their own terms and forge a new social bloc to advance social democratic policies contributed to this rise of populism.

In other parts of the world, the discrepancy between the demand for social protections and the social democrats' ability to deliver these protections was even bigger. One of the reasons for this was that the communist parties in the East, and also a number of radical organizations in the South, embraced social democracy at a time when its glory days in the West were already over. Moreover, this belated embrace occurred on the ruins of these communist and developmentalist regimes. More specifically, the alienation between workers and party leadership was much more profound in the East, where party leaders claimed to speak for the workers, than in the West, where leaders had assumed the role of welfare state managers. In the South, working classes existed only in embryonic forms. They were never at the core of developmentalism to the same degree that they were in Western welfare states. Moreover, the imperial rents that had softened the neoliberal onslaught on workers and the welfare state in the West were extracted from the working classes of the South who, therefore, had to carry the double burden of capitalist and imperialist exploitation. This double burden had already curtailed the room for class compromise during the post-WWII prosperity. Even though the turn from developmentalism to export-oriented integration into the world market since the 1980s accelerated economic growth in some Southern countries, the room for redistribution that domestic and foreign capitalists could tolerate remained extremely narrow. The same was true for the East once previously communist countries became peripheries of the capitalist world system. Thus, while neoliberal capitalism produces inequalities around the world, social democracy's ability to contain these inequalities is limited.

Capitalists are much less willing to give in to workers' demands now than during the long boom that followed WWII. At that time, exceptional growth rates of labour productivity and economies at large allowed concessions that wouldn't produce a profit squeeze. Moreover, working classes were better organized and the Cold War competition with the Soviet Union also worked in favour of workers in the capitalist parts of the world. The turn to slower growth in the 1970s, accompanied by neoliberal efforts to bypass organized workers and unmake then existing working classes altogether, destroyed much of social democracy's ability to negotiate class compromises. Nowadays, social democracy is caught in a cycle of hopes and disappointments. The hopes of the many who are tired of waiting for capitalist wealth to trickle down, looking for and wanting the social democrats to offer some level of social protection instead. Disappointment following suit when it becomes clear that, once in office, social democrats defer such protections to balanced budgets and investor confidence. This deferral might indicate the betrayal of voters, in the case of some party careerists, but for the most part it is due to the lack of a social force strong enough to hold the social democrats accountable to their election platforms in the face of the capitalists' threat of an investment strike (Schmidt, 2012).

Chances of a new prosperity making it easier for social democrats to negotiate a new class compromise are bleak. In fact, hopes for prosperity, dubbed the New Economy at the time, underpinned social democratic efforts to consolidate their electoral comeback in the 1990s. However, these hopes were dashed when the dot.com bubble burst in 2001. Since the Great Recession of 2008/9 even mainstream economists assume that the capitalist centres have entered an era of secular stagnation (Teulings and Baldwin, 2014). Some point at the petering out of the productivity effects that the diffusion of information technology had produced in the 1980s and 1990s, others stress the increasing gross domestic product (GDP) share taken up by service industries that have limited potential for productivity growth, and a third group of economists point at the private and public debt hangovers from the crisis. This latter group also stresses the difficulties of reducing debts, avoiding asset bubbles and stimulating the economy at the same time. To sustain profits in times of sluggish growth, capitalists will keep up pressure on wages and public spending. Under conditions where capitalists plainly reject even modest social reforms and demand austerity measures instead, it is impossible to negotiate a new class compromise (Wright, 2012).

At the depth of the Great Recession, ruling circles in the West speculated that emerging economies might take the lead in pulling the world economy out of recession. It didn't happen that way. China was clearly key to the emerging market boom Western rulers were banking on. This is where, beginning in the 1990s, a combination of original accumulation and rapid build-up of production capacity enabled exactly the kind of export-oriented growth that neoliberal ideologues had praised, from the 1980s onwards, as the way forward for the entire Global South. Migration from rural areas to the mushrooming export production zones created an almost unlimited supply of cheap labour that allowed manufacturing industries in China to conquer significant shares of world exports in manufactured goods. By the same token, the pressure on wages, originating from economic crises in the 1970s and the neoliberal turn in the 1980s, increased even further after Chinese rulers shifted gears from moderate market reform to capitalist accumulation in the early 1990s (Li, 2008). These pressures further decoupled wages from productivity growth in the countries that lost market share to Chinese exports and thus created an increasing gap in aggregate demand (International Labour Organization, 2014). At the same time, though, strong investments and a rapidly growing middle class in China produced internal demand for machinery and upscale consumer goods from the old industrial countries in the West and for resources from places around the world. This demand for resources led to the massively rising prices for minerals, energy and agricultural products that were key to economic growth in large countries such as Argentina, Brazil and South Africa.

However, since the Great Recession the investment share in GDP, partially due to government stimulus during the recession, increased even beyond the high levels it had reached prior to the recession. As a result, the young Chinese capitalism is increasingly squeezed between a rising capital-output ratio, weighing down on profit rates, and the build-up of overcapacities, cumulative debt, impeding sales (Li, 2016). Compared to other countries, and even to the post-WWII prosperity, capital accumulation in China is still strong but it is slowing down and nobody expects it to rebound to the exceptional levels it had reached during the previous two decades. The most recent slowdown in China has already been too much for the resource exporters among the emerging economies. Argentina, Brazil, South Africa, but also Russia, are caught in recession. The Indian economy, despite its size and continued growth, is still too small to compensate for the growth shortfall in China and the recession in other emerging economies. The peripheries of global capitalism, whether it's the new peripheries in Eastern Europe or the more numerous old peripheries of the South, are, of course, in no position to stimulate capital accumulation on a global scale. In fact, the working classes in these countries feel the pinch of crises and stagnation in the centres and emerging economies more than anyone else.

Neoliberalism is a project of the world's propertied classes against the working classes (Harvey, 2005; Schmidt, 2008). Crises and stagnation work to their advantage as unemployment, and the revenue shortfalls that come with them, are effective levers for cuts in wages, social spending and legal standards, all in the name of restoring profitability and inducing capitalists to invest. However, the neoliberal class struggle from above advances at different speeds and strategies. In the capitalist centres, where the workers' bargaining power had been institutionalized to a considerable degree during the welfare state era, neoliberalism relies mostly on gradual counter-reforms embedded in a permanent war of position. Developmental states in the South have always been weaker than Western welfare states because economic possibilities to integrate the working classes were more limited and the social blocs supporting them were also more fragile and fragmented. Therefore, the domestic and international forces of capital that rallied around neoliberalism could wage a war of manoeuvre, mixing political intervention, counterinsurgency and economic blackmail, against developmental states. The least expected but most radical turn to neoliberalism occurred in Eastern Europe though (Andor and Summers, 1998). The collapse of Soviet communism allowed a social counter-revolution that dismantled the social protections granted by the old regime faster and to a larger extent than anywhere else in the world.

The different trajectories of neoliberalism in different parts of the worlds shaped, along with different economic conditions in the centres, peripheries and emerging economies, the three worlds in which social democracy is responding to the discontent produced by neoliberalism. Yet, none of these worlds is bound for the prosperity that would allow a return to social democracy's post-WWII successes in welfare state building. Social democratic policies are in strong demand as a remedy for at least some of the inequalities and insecurities that are hallmarks of neoliberal capitalism. The ability of social democratic parties, or other organizations that have adopted social democratic ideas, to deliver such remedies are constrained by capitalists' continued assertiveness in times when capital accumulation is weak and unstable, but also by the defeats that workers' and other social movements have suffered since the neoliberal offensive began. These defeats translate into the continued weakness of social democracy, no matter how popular its ideas, and also lead the discontented to look for other alternatives to neoliberalism. Such alternatives exist on the left, but also on the political right. They are ideologically vague and lack a social basis capable of overcoming capitalist opposition just as much as social democracy does. For the most part, they can be described as populist (Kriesi, 2014; Priester, 2012).

POPULIST MOMENTS

In the past, populist ideas and movements gained ground when capitalist expansion or restructuring led to massive inequalities and thus a clash between the moral economies of the popular classes, which granted them some autonomous space despite their subordination and exploitation, and the conspicuous consumption of society's upper echelons. These populisms were either passing outbursts of discontent or precursors of class-based movements with greater ideological and strategic coherence (Thompson, 1963 [1991]). This was the case with the Levellers and Diggers in seventeenth-century England and the American and Russian populists in the nineteenth century. Working class movements of one kind or another succeeded these three populisms in the nineteenth and twentieth centuries, respectively. In many countries, though, the making of working classes and working class movements was heavily mixed with, if not entirely subordinated to, national oppression and imperial exploitation. Populist movements could last for decades and, organized around charismatic leaders, even establish themselves as political regimes. This was the case with Peron in Argentina and Vargas in Brazil, two prime examples of populism, but also with India's Mahatma and Indira Ghandi (Ayyangar, 2007).

The social coherence of populist regimes in the capitalist peripheries was much weaker than that of countries in the centre where classes, or different factions of them, had consolidated into historical blocs. That's why the social forces that galvanized into a transnational neoliberal bloc from the 1970s onwards found it much easier to unmake developmental states in the peripheries than to unmake welfare states in the core countries of capitalism. To this effect, the working classes that had been integrated into these states had to be undone, no matter how far class formation had gone in different countries. On a material level, the unmaking of classes formed by the historical blocs was achieved by spatial, organizational and technological changes of labour processes. These changes hollowed out or even destroyed social networks of the popular classes that were important for the reproduction of moral economies and workers' organizations. Even where the latter survived, they were severely weakened by declining memberships (Williamson and Sano, 2008). On an ideational level, neoliberal populism effectively undermined self-confidence amongst the working classes. However, it could only do so because both welfare and developmental states had produced a rift between the grassroots of these classes and their representatives in burgeoning state apparatuses. Alienation and powerlessness that were increasingly felt amongst the grassroots vis-à-vis their well-dressed and well-spoken representatives were the point of departure for the neoliberal message that it was time for the former to abandon the latter.

The individualism that distinguishes neoliberal populism from any other form of populism resonated with widespread feelings of isolation and alienation. The forces of capital advocated this individualism to disperse the still existing forces of labour whose strength had always been in their numbers. Yet, the more successful the neoliberal practice was in this regard, and the more working classes felt that the new riches of the upper classes would never trickle down to them, the more neoliberal populism lost its appeal. When this happened, nostalgia for the good old days and the protections they had provided, however limited and often in alienating ways, began spreading.

While this was happening, it also became clear that social democrats would neither be willing nor able to bring back those good old days. The unmaking of working classes and their identities had been too effective to commit social democratic parties to social democratic policies. The parties had gone too far towards adopting parts of the neoliberal agenda to return to Keynes at the flick of a switch. It is true that social democrats had abandoned the rhetoric of working classes and socialist reformism, which had distinguished them from revolutionary socialists on the left during the welfare state era. Arguably, negotiating a class compromise wouldn't have been possible without social democratic parties rebranding themselves as catch-all parties open to all citizens regardless of their class background. Ironically, though, the denial of the continuing relevance of class during the welfare state era was only possible on the basis of well-organized class interests and identities on both sides of the labour-capital accords that underpinned the welfare state.

When bourgeoisies turned from accepting a Keynesian deal to aggressively pushing a Hayekian agenda, thereby transforming and strengthening their coherence and confidence as a class, they successfully undermined the working class identities on which social democracy's political bargaining power was relying even at a time when the language of class had been largely replaced by the technocratic idioms of welfare state managers (Marcuse, 1964). Workers who originally had signed on to the neoliberal promise of liberation from patronizing politicians, union bosses and state bureaucrats soon found out that the isolation and powerlessness they felt vis-à-vis the welfare state was transformed into even greater subordination to the newly acquired powers of organized capital and its neoliberal state. The neoliberal credo of individual choice and self-realization that needed to be liberated from red tape just didn't apply to them. The dismantling of the welfare state opened more investment choices to capitalists but left workers with little other choice than trying to somehow get by. If they had felt powerless in the welfare state because there was always a party or union boss claiming to fix their problems, they really were powerless and alone in the neoliberal era when even the party and union bosses, who once presented themselves as workers' reliable problem solvers, had little more to offer than to hope for good economic conditions.

Nostalgia for the welfare state wasn't the only response to the awakening from the neoliberal dream in which everybody could make it in a market place of equals. The other response was a growing taste for collective identities and the protections they might offer (Amin, 2014; Langenbacher and Schellenberg, 2011). Right-wing appeals of belonging to an allegedly superior nation or race cater to this taste. Underlying the mystifications in which these appeals are articulated is a cold-heartedly calculated, though not necessarily serious, offer: if the undeserving belonging to inferior nations or races are excluded, even cash-strapped remnants of the old welfare state would be able to look after the needy belonging to the chosen nation or race. On an international level, such right-wing appeals are supplemented by promises to keep out unwanted competition from emerging economies and secure access to cheap resources in whichever part of the world. Neoliberalism couched its global vision in an updated version of capitalism's civilizing mission that had served nineteenth-century imperialists so well in dressing up colonial conquests at the time. Right-wing populists, thriving on neoliberalism's crisis of legitimacy, drop the ideological veil of humanitarian intervention and advocate a naked imperialism, possibly dressed up as a clash of civilizations in which a beleaguered West has to stand its ground in the face of, allegedly, inferior but assertive civilizations in other parts of the world (Huntington, 1993).

In the South, nationalism played an entirely different, if not exactly opposite, role as in the West. Originally the rallying cry of the Third Estate against the *ancien régime*, 'the common people forming a complete nation in opposition to the nobility and the clergy', Western ruling classes would later invoke their respective nations to rally support for imperial expansion and rivalry. Although the suffering and slaughter of the working classes during the two world wars outweighed the imperialist spoils from imperialist exploitation, today's right-wing populists successfully appeal to nostalgic images of imperial greatness, imagined pasts when one's economic wellbeing was not under threat from emerging economies and desperately poor immigrants. In the peripheries of the South, including countries now labelled as emerging economies, cross-class coalitions were formed under the banner of the Third World, an imagined community of the wretched of the earth that drew some of its inspiration from eighteenth-century struggles of the Third Estate against the *ancien régime* and updated this to the anti-colonial struggles of the twentieth century (Prashad, 2007). Progressive nationalism became part of the ideological cement of developmental states. As already mentioned, the social coherence of developmental states was much weaker than that of welfare states in the West, their unmaking was therefore much easier. Yet, even after capitalist and middle classes in the South had aligned with foreign capital, effectively transforming themselves into outposts of the emerging transnational neoliberal bloc, they retained some of the nationalist rhetoric to garner support. The ideological appeal to Southern nations having to stand their ground against imperialist domination still resonated because the South really was, and still is, dominated by the imperialist centres of the West.

However, the defeat of developmentalism, including the hopes to overcome this domination, also led to a transformation of nationalist ideology. The same social forces that helped the capitalist classes of the West to regain their global dominance after the developmentalist challenge accused the adherents of developmentalism of not fully breaking with Western influences. Third Worldist references to the Third Estate, revolution and enlightenment thinking, right-wing populists in the South declared, were alien to the true nature of Southern nations or religions. This nature, they said, was located in some distant past long before free trade and colonial conquest had begun to draw the entire world as one capitalist system. The resurrection of such a mystical past required ideological warfare against progressive nationalism and the dismantling of the developmental state (Amin, 1989, Chapter 4: The Culturalist Evasion: Provincialism and Fundamentalism).

In some cases, for example, India's Hindu-nationalists or Turkey's Islamists, the transformation of national liberation into religiously charged nationalism allowed capitalist and middle classes to attract a certain following from the working classes (Ahmad, 2015; Saad-Filho and Boito, 2015: Subramanian, 2007; Yates, 2007). In economically weaker countries, ranging from Afghanistan to Libya, religious fundamentalism won the support of those who didn't have any hope of improving their real world existence. In Eastern Europe, a less religiously loaded but even more aggressive nationalism began attracting mass support when their desire to liberate themselves from the rule of communist politburos was thwarted by the all too apparent subordination of Eastern European economies to the dictates of Western corporations and European Union (EU) institutions (Tamás, 2015). Whatever forms right-wing populism takes in the South or former East, the claim to represent political projects that are home-grown and distinctly non-Western feeds into

Western-grown notions about a clash of civilizations. Without a doubt, second-hand dealers in religious creeds and in national and racial pride are busy carving out regional, but partially also transnational, shares in the world market of ideologies. However, the desperate and discontented who subscribe to any of these right-wing populisms are nothing more than the foot soldiers of elite projects, in which Western ruling classes seek to sustain their leading position in the face of emerging economies whose rulers are seeking a seat at the masters' table while the ruling classes, not to speak of the warlords ravaging the failed states of the South, compete for the spoils of the masters' table.

Professing the uniqueness of one's own brand of civilization is an indispensible part of ideology of sellers' marketing, of course. And so is their alleged incompatibility with any other civilization. What all of these populisms have in common, though, is that they thrive on the discontent that neoliberal capitalism produces and the inability of social democracy to respond with alternatives. Right-wing populism offers illusionary alternatives to neoliberalism after social democratic illusions about a return to prosperity and class compromise have been smashed in the whirlwinds of financial panics and economic crises. The recourse to a mystical past of national or religious glory, yet untainted by capitalist production and exchange, in which right-wing ideologues couch their message, unintentionally reveals its illusory character. Nostalgia for welfare and developmental states, respectively, maybe even for Soviet communism, could at least draw on living memories. The paradox of right-wing populism is that it is more successful the more it is disconnected from living memories and current experience. It sells short-term escapes from unsatisfying or even miserable lives and creates its own demand because every escape ends in a hung-over encounter with reality.

This is, of course, still the reality of a neoliberal capitalism in which the only hope for the working classes is to hang on to the remnants of their welfare or development states. It is also a reality in which social democrats have been repeatedly elected but each time they turned out to be incapable of reversing the social devastation produced by neoliberalism. At best, social democratic governments have been capable of slowing the neoliberal transformation of welfare or developmental states. This has been the case with the Workers' Party and Labour governments in Brazil and Norway, respectively. At worst, notably if they are elected during a recession with capitalists demanding instant government support and threatening an investment strike in case of non-compliance, social democratic governments slash public spending and social standards more radically than conservative or liberal predecessors.

This demonstration of the limits set by neoliberal capitalism on social democratic reform policies strengthens the right-wing populists. Growing popular support doesn't make their policies any less illusory though. Wrapped into the invocations of chosen religions, nations or races, their pledge to supporters from the working classes is to exclude the allegedly undeserving from access to jobs, public services and social protections. More concretely, they seek to stop immigration and reduce the import of goods made somewhere else by foreign labour. At the risk of provoking gender troubles amongst their supporters, some of them suggest that women should stay home to do the housework instead of going out and competing with men for scarce jobs.

Any of these measures contradicts the neoliberal programme of boosting global labour supplies in order to weaken workers' bargaining power. The neoliberal turn saw a massive commodification of household labour in the capitalist centres that increased female labour supply and led to the creation of new markets for processed foods and care for children and the elderly. In the peripheries and emerging economies, neoliberalism brought about a new wave of destroying subsistence production that turned peasants into farmhands producing cash crops, and forced many to seek jobs in the sweatshops of burgeoning export processing zones or to migrate to the capitalist centres where they would staff the lowest rungs of increasingly fragmented labour markets (Schmidt, 2014b). Free trade agreements made sure that manufacturing workers from all corners of the world would compete with each other. In non-tradable service industries, the same competition was achieved through migration. The appeal of right-wing populism to those drawn into the maelstrom of neoliberal restructuring is the promise to bring back the good old days. Peasants would return to their lands, workers, most of them men, would return to their factories and women to their homes. Yet, there is no going back. Land has become a commodity with ownership heavily controlled by banks to which farmers are indebted, homes are heavily mortgaged, and factories and surrounding working class neighbourhoods have been transformed into production networks constantly contracting jobs to the lowest bidder.

With neoliberalism's appeal among the working classes gone and capitalists unwilling to accommodate social democratic demands, capitalists, needing some kind of consensus to secure their social position, are increasingly drawn into an alliance with right-wing populists. It's a fragile alliance though. The means through which capitalists seek to overcome recurrent recessions, ever-higher doses of neoliberal belt-tightening for the working classes, and the means through which right-wing populists garner support, raising hopes for protection from the outcome of these policies to exclusive social groups, are incompatible. Without populist support, capitalists risk that neo-liberalism's crisis of legitimacy spirals out of control. Repression alone doesn't secure capitalist rule. The beating and jailing of protestors and strikers by police and judiciary relies on the consent of bystanders who either wholeheartedly support state suppression or at least think it is okay. In fact, right-wing populism goes hand in hand with the trans-formation of democratic neoliberalism, supported by at least segments of the working classes, into a legitimacy-deprived authoritarian neo-liberalism (Bruff, 2014). What this means is that capitalists with their dedication to neoliberal policies and right-wing populists thriving on the growing discontent with these very policies and their outcomes can't escape each other. But this also means that the contradiction between the two has to be dealt with one way or the other. Without capitalists making concessions to at least small sections of the working and middle classes, the populist message of protecting the chosen few against the undeserving can't produce the legitimacy capitalists need so badly. On the other hand, full implementation of the protectionist measures right-wing populists are calling for would destroy the free market regime within which capital accumulation unfolds. Capitalism is already caught in stagnation because of a lack of new markets that could be conquered and because it is burdened with private and public debts still awaiting interest payments out of a barely growing mass of surplus value. Further hindering the accumulation process by imposing protectionist measures and thus pushing up transaction costs is the last thing capitalists want.

Swift responses to the Great Recession, fiscal stimulus and a turn to extremely loose monetary policies have shown that leading factions of the world's ruling classes are willing to deviate from the neoliberal orthodoxy of balanced budgets and tight money control in order to save the neoliberal project, but have no taste for protectionist experiments that might completely disrupt the circulation of capital and thus turn stagnation into depression. They preferred to use the Keynesian interlude that helped to prevent a depression as a pretext for adopting another round of austerity measures. These measures, in turn, provoked significant opposition and even reignited social democratic electorates. However, social democracy's post-Great Recession revival was even more short-lived than the one thriving on the 1990s New Economy bubble (Bailey et al., 2014; Evans and Schmidt, 2012). Where social democrats won elections, they had hardly assumed government responsibility when organized capital confronted them with the choice to either comply with the austerity agenda or defend modest social democratic proposals in an all-out class war against capital. Capitalists reckoned that anti-austerity activism protests were too scattered and weak to compel social democratic governments to stick to their campaign promises. Lacking pressure from streets and picket lines, social democrats bowed to capitalist pressures, probably knowing that this would cost them dearly in the next election. Greece's PASOK, confronted with a united front of domestic and international capital and EU institutions, carried out this most dramatic turn from social democratic campaigning to austerity enforcement, but the unfolding drama of the Euro crisis shouldn't obscure the fact that social democrats in other countries also sacrificed their electoral future on the altar of austerity.

This renewed subordination to neoliberalism made it very clear that the claims made by social democratic strategists prior to the Great Recession, about moving away from the Third Way and readopting more welfare state-oriented policies, never made it beyond table-top exercises (Cramme and Diamon, 2012; Meyer and Rutherford, 2012). After the recession, it became abundantly clear that social democratic parties weren't in a position to move alternatives to neoliberalism forward. Disappointment amongst those who had invested their hopes in social democracy as a left-wing alternative led to disengagement or a turn to the right. It thereby strengthened the surge of right-wing populism that was already underway because of the constant source of discontent produced by neoliberalism. As right-wing populism oscillates wildly between protectionist policies totally unacceptable to organized capital and a radicalized neoliberalism that is poorly covered by identity politics, disappointment amongst supporters from the working and middle classes is pre-programmed. This doesn't mean right-wing populists can't win elections, but it does mean that if they do, they too, like social democrats, face the same conflict between complying with capitalist demands and meeting voter expectations. The apparent irreconcilability between these two poles should help socialists, who always suggested building an economy in which power isn't concentrated amongst a minority of the owners of the means of production, to make their case.

To be sure, the defeats and failures that socialism experienced in the twentieth century weigh heavily on a socialist turn today. The certainties that communist revolutionaries, welfare state architects and anti-imperialist guerrilla fighters displayed at one point or another are gone. Their efforts to at least hang onto whatever they had accomplished earlier slowed the rise of neoliberalism but surely couldn't stop it. Yet, at the same time that neoliberalism produced the conditions that led to social democratic revivals in the 1990s and again during the years immediately following the Great Recession, and that also led to the rise of right-wing populism, a series of movements, sometimes even governments, of the left appeared. These ranged from protests against neoliberal globalization, galvanized in the World Social Forum (Leite, 2005), to the pink tide in Latin America (Sandbrook, 2014), new left parties in Europe (Bensaid, 2011) and lately a grassroots movement trying to reconstruct the British Labour Party as a force of the left. Some of these movements captured public imagination way beyond their activist ranks, notably Occupy's 'We're the 99%', but disappeared as quickly as they emerged. Others, like the World Social Forum, inspired experimentation with new forms of organizing originally invented by the 1960s new left and the 1970s new social movements. Latin America even saw left governments from Chile's Third Wayish socialists to Venezuela's Chavismo. None of the above indicates the return of socialism as a political force anywhere near the level of influence had by diverse socialisms, including the social democratic reformist left in the twentieth century. But they all indicate that people, by actively engaging or supporting any of these left projects, are looking for left alternatives. In fact, they may already be in the midst of making them without really knowing it.

LEFT ALTERNATIVES

Before the rise of neoliberal hegemony, most leftists, equipped with the writing of Karl Marx or, if tending to the moderate left, John Maynard Keynes, thought of themselves as executors of the laws of history or at least as masters in social engineering. Temporary setbacks notwithstanding, labour and anti-colonial movements were marching forward. Only sensitive minds would recognize that the readiness with which dissident voices, cautioning their comrades that even the left can be wrong and is in constant need for self-critique and adjustment of its strategies, were ridiculed, sidelined or suppressed by five-year planners and Keynesian demand-managers was actually a sign of the weakness of these same planners and managers. They might have been well aware of the shortcomings of their own political practice, might even have known that Soviet communism, welfarism and developmentalism were on dead-end roads, and just didn't like to be reminded of that. For the same reason, Hayek's (1974) charge that the left suffered from a pretence of knowledge was either ignored or dismissed, like criticisms coming from within the left. But of course, back in those days, nobody on the left or in the political centre could envision that the ideas of Hayek and his then small band of neoliberal dissenters could capture popular imagination and help recharge the forces of capital in their offensive against left projects of any kind.

These days, it is neoliberals who say they know exactly what to do to get any possible roadblock out of the way to complete market liberation. And it is the same neoliberals who can't accept dissidence or opposition because they fear that this would undermine, rather than strengthen, their political project, which is battered by economic and legitimation crises and doesn't need further exposure of its weaknesses. Meanwhile, the left has abandoned any pretence of knowledge once prevailing in its ranks. Large organizations that had been able to dominate the left have been cut down to a size, where they compete with a multitude of highly diverse voices on the left. Not that there aren't any leftists who think they know exactly what's going on and what's to be done, but none of them is able to dominate the left as some of their know-it-all predecessors did in the past. By and large, the left has turned into a carnival of ideas that is refreshing compared to the eternal truths that impeded its advancement in the past, but is also incapable of putting together a new left project. If there is anything holding the left together these days, it is some kind of left populism (March, 2012, Chapter 6: Left-wing Populism: Populist Socialists and Social Populists).

Where right-wing populists see chosen nations, races and creeds under threat from a conspiracy of lesser peoples, left populism distinguishes between corporate elites and the common people. To be sure, right-wing populism also uses the 'we, the people versus corrupt elites' rhetoric, but because this is so close to socialist notions of a propertied class exploiting the working class majority, it has to be loaded with non-economic signifiers. After all, even where right-wing populists can draw on a basis of plebeian activists, their organizations are usually supported by capitalists thinking that the survival of the neoliberal project requires some ideological redressing that distracts from the all too obvious economic divisions this project produces. In other words, right-wing populism itself is an elite project in search of popular support. It follows in the tracks of nineteenth-century nationalism that the ruling classes advanced as a form of mass integration from above in opposition to the then emergent mass organizations of workers (Hobsbawm, 1989, Chapter 6: Waving Flags: Nations and Nationalism). It also follows in the tracks of the racism promoted by the same ruling classes to justify colonial expansion and the rivalries with other imperialist nations (Balibar and Wallerstein, 1991). Finally, it follows in the tracks of fascism that radicalized the nationalisms and racisms of the nineteenth century and added anti-communism to the mix of right-wing ideologies. To be sure, the seeds for this radicalization already existed in the nationalisms and racisms of the late nineteenth century and then flourished due to the escalation of imperialist rivalries during WWI and the dual challenges posed by revolutionary socialism and the Great Depression of the 1930s. Today's economic and political crises are still much less severe than those during the Age of Catastrophe from 1914 to 1945 (Hobsbawm, 1995, Part I), and there isn't much of a socialist challenge either, but there are indications of radicalization within the rising tide of right-wing populism anyhow.

Left-wing populism follows an entirely different trajectory that goes back to the French revolution and was reinvented by the Popular Fronts of the 1930s and the anti-colonial revolutions from the 1950s to the 1970s. What distinguishes these left populisms from the ethnic-religious particularism of right-wing populism are their universalist claims. Though also carried forward by cross-class alliances within which different groups pursued specific goals, these goals were always part of further reaching aspirations that left no room for any kind of particularism, discrimination or exclusion. Some, but certainly not all, of these aspirations were eventually institutionalized in the welfare and developmental states of the post-WWII era. Many of the social protections provided by these states were means tested, and the criteria used to determine eligibility offered privileges to some groups but denied them to others. As the post-WWII class compromise recognized capitalists' right to manage and make investment decisions, capitalists could pursue discriminatory hiring practices that created divisions within working classes almost at will. Many of the social movements of this era fought against such discriminations and for the universalization of the protections provided by the state. This was true for women, ethnic minorities and immigrants struggling for equal access to the labour market and social services, but also for international solidarity movements trying to build a more equitable international economic order (Dubinsky et al., 2009). Neoliberal populism successfully denounced any such demands, along with those coming from unions, as special interests that had to be rejected in the name of individual market participation. This populism helped to defeat the left upsurge of the 1970s, which was followed by the unmaking of the working classes on which welfare and developmental states rested. Ironically, the defensive struggles against the neoliberal rollback of social protections of all kinds turned the movements that had started out with the aim of reinvigorating universalist aspirations into single issue movements. Tragically enough, these movements looked more and more like the special interest groups they had been denounced as by neoliberal propagandists right from their beginnings.

It wasn't until the World Social Forum and the alter-globaliza-tion movement at large that the left tried to create some kind of unity in diversity. By that time, however, a return to the class politics that underpinned welfare and developmental states in earlier decades, and in fact were key to the making of these states, wasn't possible because neoliberal restructuring had successfully undone the class formations of those earlier decades. The unmaking of working classes secured neoliberalism's success in boosting profits at the expense of wages, public services and, in the South, subsistence producers. But the same unmaking also prepared the ground for a complete rethinking of left politics. Activists in the alter-globalization movement, and any other wave of protest from the 1990s onwards, drew their inspiration and imagination from episodes scattered across the entire history of the left. The falling apart of convictions that a small band of leftists, beleaguered by the advance of neoliberalism, upheld during the 1980s, set free a wild mix of radical imagination blended with romanticization of past rebellions and welfare state nostalgia. This was accompanied by carnivalesque forms of activism and experimentation with new forms of organizing, often dubbed horizontalist to distinguish them from the top-down structures that had permeated almost all previously existing organizations of the left. The widespread rejection of representative forms of politics, reminiscent of similar critiques by the 1960s new left, didn't stop activists from the 1990s onwards from also engaging in the formation of new parties of the left.

Arguably, the atmosphere of departure articulated by World Social Forum participants and protestors from Seattle to Genoa brought the discontent with neoliberalism to the fore, discontent that was already brewing at a time when neoliberal globalization still seemed unstoppable. The same atmosphere that did its share in mobilizing voters for social democratic parties by offering a blend of nostalgia and vaguely defined alternatives to neoliberalism, leaving the issue of protests versus ballot boxes aside, wasn't too different from the mixed-bag of ideas offered by social movement activists. And, in fact, electoral politics and grassroots activism, in the 1990s, though advocating alternatives, were clearly shaped by neoliberalism. The indetermination and multitude of ideas presented by both had actually more in common with Hayek's vision of spontaneous orders than neoliberal practitioners who had inherited the state apparatuses from their much hated Keynesian predecessors and had used them quite effectively for their anti-Keynesian policies.

Hayek's notion of markets as the magical institution creating a spontaneous order out of myriads of seemingly isolated sales and purchases is just an ideological cover for capitalist exploitation and class struggle in general and the politics of organized capital in particular. In contrast, the defiant 'People Over Profit' that movement activists shouted loudly, and social democrats more cautiously, against neoliberal market praise sought to stitch various discontents together into a more unified movement. While neoliberal populism mystifies the realities of capitalism and imperialism, left-wing populism served as a rallying cry for diverse movements to join forces. This populism, then, was a political expression of discontent in a transition period, in which the old class politics of the left had become impossible because the working classes that once pursued them didn't exist any longer, and new classes and class politics were only seeing the first steps towards their making. In fact, the movements rallying behind populist banners from 'People Over Profit' to 'We Are the 99%', but also efforts to build new left parties or recommit social democratic parties to an agenda of social reforms, may actually be part of the making of new working classes.

The working classes that were the social force behind the social democratic, communist and developmentalist projects of the twentieth century didn't spring from the writings of socialist intellectuals, but came out of the struggles of swaths of people who were cut off from their previous means of subsistence by capitalist expansion into non-capitalist economies. Most of these struggles against the deterioration of living conditions along with the destruction of long held moral values, brought about by the new god of capital accumulation, were isolated and often started out with people looking back to the past. At times such nostalgia can be disempowering, but at others it can also incite anger and inspire to struggle for change. Not many of these struggles reached their goals, but they provided experiences from which more effective strategies could be derived. One crucial experience in the making of working classes is the impossibility of bringing back the good old days when craft workers were protected by guilds and peasants, even though they were lacking any other rights, had guaranteed access to land. Only once larger numbers of workers without property or protections understood that bringing back pre-capitalist conditions couldn't happen, could they start thinking about post-capitalist alternatives. It would take decades before capitalist dispossession and its discontents would produce any class agency to speak of (Katznelson and Zolberg, 1986; Thompson, 1963 [1991]). As dispossession occurred at different times and under rather different circumstances in capitalist centres and in the colonies conquered by these centres, the process of global class formation was highly uneven. It started at different times in different regions and brought about different left ideologies, unions, cooperatives and cultural and political organizations. Mass parties, more or less clandestine cadre parties and guerrilla armies were the most important political organizations invented by the left. They had a critical impact on establishing welfare capitalism,

Soviet communism and developmental regimes and contributed to the institutionalization of class struggles. This institutionalization locked in certain social reforms during the post-WWII era but stood in the way of an effective fight-back against the neoliberal offensive from the 1980s onwards. The forward march of neoliberalism emptied welfare and developmental states of the class power once institutionalized in them, Soviet communism unceremoniously collapsed under the weight of its inability to reform. This emptying out is why left organizations, be they social democratic, communist or post-communist parties, or even liberation movements turned into ruling parties, lost the social backing that first helped to create them and then turned them into veritable social forces from below. Their erratic and inconsistent flirtations with neoliberalism and left populism are desperate attempts to secure organization survival. At best, they contribute to the making of new working classes in similar ways as grassroots movements do (Cox and Nilsen, 2014; Schmidt, 2014a).

Repeated efforts to diminish the full effect of the neoliberal offensive by embracing a softer version of neoliberalism have convinced many who are looking for alternatives that social democratic parties, or other organizations that turned to Third Way social democracy, won't deliver them. At best, such efforts ended in torturous processes of alienation between party apparatuses and voters; at worst, social democrats, eager to demonstrate their reliability to capitalists, prescribed harsher doses of neoliberalism than conservative or liberal successor governments had ever done. Similarly frustrating were election campaigns that borrowed their slogans from grassroots movements but were never followed by efforts to build mutually beneficial alliances between parties and protest movements. To be sure, protest movements against neoliberal globalization, war and, more recently, austerity measures following the Great Recession haven't done any better than social democratic parties in opposition or government. And neither have left parties, like the Workers' Party in Brazil or Syriza in Greece, which have been established in response to the neoliberalization of social democratic parties. Some of them, for example, the Socialist Left Party in Norway or communist support for the *Concertación* government in Chile, surrendered to the temptation of engaging in coalition governments and ended up attracting more of the disappointment, because of their accommodation to capitalist demands, than their significantly bigger social democratic coalition partners. Others, such as the new anti-capitalist party in France, stuck to their radical agendas but were unable to attract any significant following.

In light of these failures to offer left alternatives to neoliberalism, it is no wonder that right-wing populists, or even fascists, are attracting so many who are discontent with neoliberalism. A prime example is France, where the socialist president François Hollande disappointed his voters, the new anti-capitalist party never took off and the efforts to build a Front de Gauche are stuck in paralysis. This made it easy for the Front National (a right-wing fascist party) to establish itself as a major player in French politics. In Britain, a Labour Party unable to leave its Blairite past behind helped David Cameron to win a second term and contributed to the establishment of right-wing populists, the UK Independence Party (UKIP) as agenda-setters in British politics. But the shock about Labour's defeat in the 2015 elections also triggered the movement to reinvent Labour as a genuine social democratic party under the leadership of Jeremy Corbyn. Disappointment with communist-led governments in West Bengal and Kerala contributed to the rise of the Hindu-nation-alist Bharatiya Janata Party on the federal level, but it is by no means clear whether Indian communism is a spent force or will be able to reinvent itself (Prashad, 2015). And while the Brazilian Workers' Party that developed as a left alternative to social democracy is now struggling with the same problems as long established social democratic parties, a new generation of leftists is building a new left party in post-communist Slovenia. The examples of Britain, India and Slovenia show that a turn to the right is not the only response to social democracy's inability to offer alternatives to neoliberalism.

Reorienting existing or building new parties of the left are other possible responses. So is the turn from party politics to the various kinds of grassroots activism that is blossoming in many countries despite the setbacks that this form of politics suffered since the legendary Battle of Seattle or the Workers' Party-sponsored World Social Forum in Porto Alegre. In South Africa, the neoliberal turn of the African National Congress (ANC) provoked a whole string of militant strikes and shook the alliance between unions and the ANC. Similarly, austerity in Greece, executed by a succession of conservative, PASOK and SYRIZA governments, led to a series of strikes but also to workers taking over workplaces and running them as self-organized enterprises. A mix of strikes, new forms of union organizing and worker-controlled enterprises is often associated with the *piquetero* movement and factory occupations in Argentina following the economic crisis from 1998 to 2001. Yet, the same mix can also be found in many other countries (Ness, 2015). None of these mobilizations or organizing efforts have had a lasting effect, at least not so far. Their sheer number, though, not to speak of their ebb and flow, is mind-boggling. What is particularly perplexing is that the failures and defeats suffered by activists at one place don't stop others in trying the same thing or something else at some other place or time. Each setback implies the loss of activists because they are burnt out or can't get over the experience of being defeated. Starting over often feels like reinventing the wheel and can therefore be frustrating for anyone who's been part of left organizing efforts and mobilizations before. Yet, there are always some who carry on the torch, and new activists ready to take up the fight against all odds.

Over time, though, a treasure of collective experiences, identities and understanding is accumulated that each following generation of activists can draw upon. This treasure exists in formal organizations, media outlets and informal networks through which activists communicate with each other. It provides ideas about how to best act under certain conditions and draws ever more individuals into collective agency, even though not everybody will be active all of the time. The accumulation of collective experiences, identities and understandings, which by no means rules out diverse points of view, is nothing else but the making of new working classes ready to find new and more effective forms of organizing in their struggle against the forces of capital. If the unmaking of the working classes is one of the main reasons why social democracy lost its ability to negotiate class compromises, the making of new classes may also lead to the reinvention and strengthening of existing social democratic parties or encourage new organizations of the left to adopt a social democratic programme. However, if economic prosperity was the other main reason why social democrats could negotiate such compromises during the post-WWII boom, there is little prospect of doing it again in the future. One should never underestimate capitalism's abilities to find new markets and cost-saving technologies, but for the foreseeable future its innovative powers seem to be running low. One might even argue that the present absence of equally combative and strong left movements, unions and parties gives capitalists little incentive to seek further developments of the forces of production and sales opportunities. As long as this is the case, the easiest way to sustain capitalism is to constantly roll back wages, social protections and public services and thereby contribute to the discontents and subsequent protests, strikes and organizing efforts that help to create capitalism's potential gravediggers. Understanding the limits of capital and of social democracy, of course, is just one step, possibly the smallest, towards building socialist alternatives. Finding ways to organize and mobilize that overcome the resistance that capitalists will surely put up against any such challenge requires much bigger steps.

BIBLIOGRAPHY

Ahmad, A. (2015). 'India: Liberal Democracy and the Extreme Right'. *Socialist Register 2015*: 170–92.

Amin, S. (1989). *Eurocentrism*. New York: Monthly Review Press.

——(2014). *The Return of Fascism in Contemporary Capitalism. Monthly Review*, 66 (4): 1–12.

Andor, L. and Summers, M. (1998). *Market Failure – Eastern Europe's 'Economic Miracle'*. London and Chicago: Pluto Press.

Ayyangar, S. (2007). 'Cleaning the Augean Stables: Populism in Latin America and India'. *SAIS Review*, 27 (1): 93–101.

Bailey, D., De Waelle, J.-M., Escalona, F. and Vieira, M. (eds) (2014). *European Social Democracy During the Global Economic Crisis: Renovation of Resignation?* Manchester: Manchester University Press.

Balibar, E. and Wallerstein, I. (1991). *Race, Nation, Class: Ambiguous Identities*. London and New York: Verso.

Bensaid, D., Sousa, A. and Thornett, A. (2011). *New Parties of the Left: Experiences from Europe*. London: IMG Publications.

Bray, M. (2015). 'Rearticulating Contemporary Populism: Class, State, and Neoliberal Society'. *Historical Materialism*, 23 (3): 3–26.

Bruff, I. (2014). 'The Rise of Authoritarian Neoliberalism'. *Rethinking Marxism*, 26 (1): 113–29.

Cox, L. and Nilsen, A.G. (2014). *We Make Our Own History: Marxism and Social Movements in the Twilight of Neoliberalism*. London: Pluto Press.

Cramme, O. and Diamond, P. (eds) (2012). *After the Third Way: The Future of Social Democracy in Europe*. London and New York: I.B. Tauris.

Dubinsky, K., Krull, C., Lord, S., Mills, S. and Rutherford, S. (2009). *New World Coming: The Sixties and the Shaping of Global Consciousness*. Toronto: Between the Lines.

Evans, B. and Schmidt, I. (eds) (2012). *Social Democracy After the Cold War*. Athabasca: Athabasca University Press.

Fraser, N. (2009). 'Feminism, Capitalism and the Cunning of History'. *New Left Review*, 56 (March/April): 97–117.

Harvey, D. (2005). *A Brief History of Neoliberalism*. Oxford: Oxford University Press.

Hayek, F.A. (1974). *The Pretence of Knowledge*. Lecture to the Memory of Alfred Nobel, Stockholm.

Hobsbawm, E. (1989). *The Age of Empire, 1875–1914*. London: Abacus.

——(1995). *The Age of Extremes, 1914–1991*. London: Abacus.

Huntington, S.P. (1993). 'The Clash of Civilizations?'. *Foreign Affairs*, 72 (3): 22–49.

International Labour Organization (2014). *Global Wage Report 2014/15: Wages and Income Inequality*. Geneva.

Katznelson, I. and Zolberg, A.R. (eds) (1986). *Working Class Formation: Nineteenth-century Patterns in Western Europe and the United States*. Princeton: Princeton University Press.

Kitschelt, H. (1994). *The Transformation of European Social Democracy*. Cambridge: Cambridge University Press.

Kriesi, H. (2014). 'The Populist Challenge'. *West European Politics*, 37 (2): 361–78.

Langenbacher, N. and Schellenberg, B. (eds) (2011). *Is Europe on the 'Right' Path? Rightwing Extremism and Rightwing Populism in Europe*. Berlin: Friedrich Ebert Stiftung.

Leite, J.C. (2005). *The World Social Forum: Strategies of Resistance*. Chicago: Haymarket.

Li, M. (2008). *The Rise of China and the Demise of the Capitalist World System*. New York: Monthly Review Press.

—— (2016). *China and the 21st Century Crisis*. London: Pluto Press.

March, L. (2012). *Radical Left Parties in Europe*. London and New York: Routledge.

Marcuse, H. (1964). *One-dimensional Man: Studies in the Ideology of Advanced Industrial Society*. Boston: Beacon Press.

Meyer, H. and Rutherford, J. (eds) (2012). *The Future of European Social Democracy: Building the Good Society*. Houndmills, Basingstoke: Palgrave Macmillan.

Meyer, T. (2008). *The Theory of Social Democracy*. Malden: Polity.

Ness, I. (2015). *Southern Insurgency: The Coming of the Global Working Class*. London: Pluto Press.

Prashad, V. (2007). *The Darker Nations*. New York: The New Press.

—— (2015). *No Free Left: The Futures of Indian Communism*. New Delhi: Left Word Books.

Priester, K. (2012). *Rechter und Linker Populismus*. Frankfurt and New York: Campus.

Rennwald, L. and Evans, G. (2014). 'When Supply Creates Demand: Social Democratic Party Strategies and the Evolution of Class Voting'. *West European Politics*, 37 (5): 1108–35.

Saad-Filho, A. and Boito, A. (2015). 'Brazil: The Failure of the PT and the Rise of the New Right'. *Socialist Register 2015*: 213–30.

Sandbrook, R. (2014). *Reinventing the Left in the Global South: The Politics of the Possible*. Cambridge: Cambridge University Press.

Schmidt, I. (ed.) (2008). *Spielarten des Neoliberalismus*. Hamburg: VSA Verlag.

—— (2011). 'There Were Alternatives: Lessons From Efforts to Advance Beyond Keynesian and Neoliberal Economic Policies in the 1970s'. *WorkingUSA*, 14 (4): 473–98.

—— (2012). 'It's the Economy, Stupid! Theoretical Reflections on Third Way Social Democracy'. In B. Evans and I. Schmidt (eds), *Social Democracy After the Cold War*. Athabasca: Athabasca University Press: 13–44.

—— (2014a). 'The Downward March of Labor Halted? The Crisis of Neoliberal Capitalism and the Remaking of Working Classes'. *WorkingUSA*, 17 (1): 5–22.

—— (2014b). 'Capital Accumulation and Class Struggle from the "Long 19th Century" to the Present – A Luxemburgist Interpretation'. *International Critical Thought*, 4 (4): 457–73.

Silver, B. (2003). *Forces of Labor: Workers' Movements and Globalization Since 1870*. Cambridge: Cambridge University Press.

Subramanian, N. (2007). 'Populism in India'. *SAIS Review*, 27 (1): 81–91.

Tamás, G.M. (2015). 'Ethnicism and After Nationalism: The Roots of the New European Right'. *Socialist Register 2015*: 118–35.

Teulings, C. and Baldwin, R. (eds) (2014). *Secular Stagnation: Facts, Causes and Cures*. London: Centre for Economic Policy Research.

Thompson, E.P. (1963). *The Making of the English Working Class*. London: Penguin 1991.

Weyland, K. (1999). 'Neoliberal Populism in Latin America and Eastern Europe'. *Comparative Politics*, 31 (4) 379–401.

Williamson, J.B. and Sano, J. (2008). 'Factors Affecting Union Decline in 18 OECD Countries and their Implications for Labor Movement Reform'. *International Journal of Comparative Sociology*, 49 (6): 479–500.

Wolf, F.O. (2007). 'Party-building for Eco-socialists: Lessons from the Failed Project of the German Greens'. *Socialist Register 2007*: 310–36.

Wright, E.O. (2012). 'Class Struggle and Class Compromise in the Era of Stagnation and Crisis'. Unpublished manuscript based on a presentation at the Nicos Poulantzas Institute, Athens, in December 2011.

Yates, J.J. (2007). 'The Resurgence of Jihad and the Specter of Religious Populism'. *SAIS Review*, 27 (1): 127–4.

Contributors

Ximena de la Barra Mac Donald is an independent consultant and former UNICEF Policy Advisor for Latin America now living in Spain.

Patrick Bond is Professor of Political Economy at the University of the Witwatersrand in Johannesburg, South Africa.

Max Crook is an adjunct instructor at Seton Hall University and State University of New York at New Paltz, USA.

Fabien Escalona is a researcher at the Laboratoire de Recherche en Sciences Sociales, Sciences Po Grenoble and associate researcher at the Centre D'étude de la Vie Politique, Université Libre de Bruxelles, France and Belgium.

Mariano Féliz is an economist at the Instituto de Investigaciones en Humanidades y Ciencias Sociales and the Consejo Nacional de Investigaciones Científicas y Técnicas, Universidad Nacional de La Plata, Argentina.

Idar Helle is a labour historian at De Facto Centre for Trade Unionists and the University of Oslo, Norway.

Knut Kjeldstadli is a historian at the University of Oslo, Norway.

Anej Korsika is a freelance writer in Ljubljana, Slovenia.

Ioannis (John) Milios is a political economist in the Department of Humanities, Social Sciences and Law, National Technical University of Athens, Greece.

Jörg Nowak is a political scientist at Kassel University, Germany.

Ingo Schmidt is the coordinator of the Labour Studies Programme at Athabasca University, Canada.

Arup Kumar Sen is an economist in the Department of Commerce, Serampore College, West Bengal, India.

Lucian Vesalon is a lecturer at West University of Timisoara, Romania.

Index

Movimento de Trabalhadores Sem
Terra (MST), (Brazilian Landless
Movement), 185

nationalism, 21, 42, 80–1, 157–8, 202,
260–1, 267
nationalization, 31, 84, 95, 100, 119
Naxalite movement, 205
Nehru, Jawaharlal, 202
neocolonialism, 14
neodevelopmentalism, 91, 97, 159,
197
neoliberalism: and discontent, 5; and
European integration, 36, 63, 130;
and globalization, 1, 16, 18, 269;
and rollback of social reform, 16,
18, 34, 58; and social democracy,
74, 108, 154, 158, 161–2, 223
New Economy, 20, 255
New International Economic Order
(NIEO), 14
New Labour, 71–3
new social movements, 253
North Atlantic Treaty Organization
(NATO), 53
Norwegian Arbeiderpartiet (AP),
(labour party), 46–7, 49–52, 56–8
Nueva Mayoría (New Majority), 113

Organized Capitalism, 9–11, 48

Parti Communiste Français (PCF), 29,
32, 41–2
Partida da Social Democracia
Brasileira (PSDB), 184, 194
periphery, 3–5, 14, 19–20, 29, 53,
92–3, 97, 130, 197, 254, 256–8
Peronism, 94–6, 98
piqueteros, 93–6, 272
Ponta, Victor, 151
Popular Front, 6, 10, 30, 118, 268
populism: in Argentina, 95, 102, 258;
in Brazil, 258, in India, 258; on the
left, 254, 267–8, 270; and
nationalism, 80; and neoliberalism,

252, 254, 258–9; on the right, 254,
260–5; in Romania, 159
poverty, 21, 34, 74–7, 97, 153, 161–2,
183, 198
privatization, 58–9, 95, 152–3, 158,
160–1, 168, 170, 193, 237
prosperity, 4, 10, 15, 20–2, 73, 97, 130,
170, 183, 254–7, 273
public spending, 39, 42, 75–6, 78, 100,
238–9

Romanian Communist Party (PCR),
149
Romanian Democratic Party (PD),
148–50
Romanian National Salvation Front
(FSN), 148–50, 154
Romanian Social Democratic Party
(PSD), 148–50, 154, 157
Rousseff, Dilma, 184, 191, 193–6
rural areas, 49–50, 60, 153, 206, 213,
256

Scottish National Party (SNP), 80
Second International, 5–6, 20, 201
service proletariat, 58
shock therapy, 93, 127, 159, 162,
168–9
Silva, Marina, 194
Slovenian Coalition of the United Left
(ULC), 165, 172, 174, 178
Slovenian Initiative for Democratic
Socialism, 174, 176, 178
Slovenian United List of Social
Democracy (SD), 165, 169–70
social democracy: and corporatism, 8,
10, 12, 34, 52, 69, 231, 233; in
Eastern Europe, 2–3, 9, 18, 20–1,
146; globalization of, 18; and
modernization, 196; in the South,
18; and welfare state retrenchment,
40, 56, 73, 132–3, 223; in Western
Europe, 5–8, 11–13, 18
Socialist International, 54, 108, 148,
157